EUSTACE MULLINS

NEW HISTORY

OF THE JEWS

&

The Biological Jew

ℴMNIA VERITAS

EUSTACE CLARENCE MULLINS
(1923-2010)

NEW HISTORY OF THE JEWS
& *The Biological Jew*

1968 & 1992

Published by
OMNIA VERITAS LTD

www.omnia-veritas.com

ABOUT THE AUTHOR	11
NEW HISTORY OF THE JEWS	13
CHAPTER ONE	15
Jews and civilization	15
CHAPTER TWO	22
The Biological Jew	22
CHAPTER THREE	32
The origin of the Jews	32
CHAPTER FOUR	43
Jews in ancient history	43
CHAPTER 5	61
The Jews and the passion of Jesus Christ	61
CHAPTER 6	69
Jews and ritual murder	69
CHAPTER 7	90
Jews in Europe	90
CHAPTER 8	126
Jews and Communism	126
CHAPTER NINE	152
Jews and the United States	152

CHAPTER TEN 177

Jews and our future 177

THE BIOLOGICAL JEW 191
FOREWORD 193
CHAPTER ONE 196

The parasite 196

The ability to modify 199
Known as the Jews 200
Other biological aspects 200
The Scientific Approach 202
Not commensalism 203
Modification of the organism 204
Violates nature 205
Temporary parasites 205
Evolution and parasites 206
Specialization among parasites 207
Adult phases of the parasite 209
Pronounced changes on skeletal structure 211
Cultural artifacts 212
Hatred 213
Adaptive modifications 214
Reproductive phases 215
Defense reactions 216
Parasitic damage 216
Other parasites 217
Reactions against the parasite 218
Knowledge of the parasite 219
Always an enemy 220

CHAPTER TWO 222

The biological Jew 222

A late theory 223
Importance of biology 225
Pattern of the parasite 226

The inextricable hold 227
Foreign bodies 228
Parasite's attitude 229
The anal complex.. 230
Parasites in many aspects of life 231
The Dreyfus case.. 232
Our own Dreyfus cases 232
Gentile opportunists 233
Necessity of control 234
Aggression 235
Parasite's budget 236
Trend to degeneracy 236
Symbol of victory 237
The biological pattern.. 238

CHAPTER THREE 240

THE SHABEZ GOI 240

The advanced civilizations 240
A definition 241
Conviction and expulsion 242
Weakness of the host 243
Bound by no codes 244
Paradox of the parasite 244
Hard work 245
The theory of biological parasitism 246
The function of government 247
What justice?.. 248
Direct influence.. 249
The greatest peril... 250
What is shabez goi?.. 251
Sexual degeneracy 252
Soft and treacherous 253
A hopeless life 254
The joy of a healthy life 255
Deep alienation.. 257
Intense suffering 257
The task before us.. 258
No heroes... 258

The Mullins report	259
Prescience	264
Paralyzed by parasites	265
A hamstrung economy	265
Supreme court	266
The scum of the earth	267
The end of the road?	267
Will communists stop themselves?	268
The ruinous effect	270
Planning of the riots	270
Communist influence	271
Mass destruction	272
Guarantee of safety	273
Looting according to plan	274
Petitions the united states	275
Mongrelization program	276
An advertisement backfires	277
Slow paralysis	278
The role of the churches	279
Church administration exposed	280
Disoriented fools	280
Students are uninformed	281
Students are cheated	281
The MacLeish syndrome	282
Gullibility	283
A student awakening?	284
Mental bondage	284
Disasters in publishing	286
Does Buckley exist?	287
Shabez goi antics	287
Why not?	288
Tested techniques	289
The silent treatment	290
Children of the shabez goi	290
A correct reaction	291
They live in darkness	292
Applaud treachery	292
No freedom	293
He owns it all	294
A law of nature	295

BIBLIOGRAPHY 297
OTHER TITLES 299

ABOUT THE AUTHOR

In forty years of dedicated investigative research, **Eustace Mullins** has drawn considerable return fire. He was kept under daily surveillance by agents of the FBI for thirty-two years; no charges were ever placed against him. He is the only person ever fired from the staff of the Library of Congress for political reasons. He is the only writer who has had a book burned in Europe since 1945.

After serving thirty-eight months in the U. S. Army Air Force during World War II, **Eustace Mullins** was educated at Washington and Lee University, Ohio State University, University of North Dakota, and New York University. He later studied art at the Escuela des Bellas Artes, San Miguel de Allende, Mexico, and the Institute of Contemporary Arts, Washington, D.C.

While studying in Washington, he was asked to go to St. Elizabeth's Hospital to talk to the nation's most famous political prisoner, Ezra Pound. The outstanding literary figure of the twentieth century, Pound had seen three of his pupils awarded the Nobel Prize, while it was denied to him because of his pronouncements as a native American patriot. Not only did **Eustace Mullins** become his most active protege, he is the only person who keeps Ezra Pound's name alive today, through the work of the Ezra Pound Institute of Civilization, which was founded shortly after the poet's death in Venice.

Eustace Mullins (1923-2010) is considered one of the greatest political historians of the 20th Century.

NEW HISTORY OF THE JEWS

Chapter One

Jews and Civilization

Throughout the history of civilization, one particular problem of mankind has remained constant. In all of the vast records of peace and wars and rumors of wars, one great empire after another has had to come to grips with the same dilemma... the Jews.

Despite the persistence of this problem, and despite the enormous amount of literature on this subject, not one writer, either pro or con, has ever faced the dilemma at its source namely, who are the Jews and why are they here?

This question can be answered only if man brings to bear upon it his full intelligence. This question must also be approached on the highest spiritual level, with the deepest motives of Christian charity, and above all, with the greatest respect for man himself, what he is, what his roots are, and what he is becoming.

The history of man is the history of conflict, of wars between the haves and the have-nots, of exploitation of man by man, and of terrible massacres. In this blood-stained record, however, the scholar finds only one people who have aroused the most violent antagonisms, no matter where they have settled. Only one people has irritated its host nations in every part of the civilized world to the point that the host has turned against them and killed them or driven them out. This people is called the Jews.

The problem has been misunderstood because group antagonisms are encountered in many countries. Massacres of the Greeks by the Turks occurred sporadically over thousands of years, with the last such incident taking place only a generation ago and affecting the lives of many of those living today. The massacres of the Huguenots in France several hundred years ago proved that people of the same blood, set against each other by religious differences, could be as terrible as the conflicts between differing racial groups. After these massacres, however, the group always settled down once more to the business of living. Either the differences were reconciled, or the remainder of the victims went elsewhere to live. In the case of the Huguenots, the refugees provided the stock from which came most of the leading thinkers of the American Revolution.

In only one instance can we find no evidence of a reconciliation or of the victims emigrating permanently to other countries. The history of the Jews demonstrates two things; first, that there has never been a reconciliation between them, and their hosts; second, that no nation has ever succeeded in barring them permanently. Even more surprising is the fact that in every case where the Jews were expelled from a nation, often under conditions of great suffering, within a few years, the Jews have returned! Again one can find no parallel in the historical records of other groups, this strange compulsion, this incredible persistence in putting their heads into the lion's mouth again and again. It has been suggested that the explanation lies in an odd and perverse characteristic of the Jews, their willingness to endure suffering, but the idea of group masochism fails to explain many other facets of the Jewish problem.

In truth, like the answers to many of man's problems, the solution to the Jewish problem have been before us for more than two thousand years. It is we who have been unable to see it because we have refused to face this problem honestly.

The Jewish problem is an essential aspect of Christianity, and we can solve it merely by accepting the solution which Christ offered us, and in so doing, gave up His human life, some two thousand years ago. The story of Christ is the story of mankind, the thrilling experience of finding redemption, the salvation of the soul. The Jew represents all of the temptations of animal existence which it is intended that we shall transcend during our stay on earth. Because of the Jew, salvation becomes a conscious choice, instead of an involuntary or accidental decision. Without the Jew and the evils which he embodies, man might not have the choice placed before him in black and white. He would have the excuse that he did not understand the choice he was asked to make. With the presence of the Jew, no such excuse can be made. In the civilized world, at some point in his life, every man is faced with the supreme temptation, he is taken to the top of the mountain by Satan, the pleasures and delights of physical existence are spread out before him, and Satan says, 'All this, and more, will be yours if you will obey me.'

A majority of those who command wealth and power in the civilized world of today are those who have accepted Satan's offer, who have renounced the possibility of the salvation of their souls through Jesus Christ. These men are working for the Jew. Winston Churchill as the helpless tool of Bernard Baruch, Franklin D. Roosevelt as the misshapen vassal of Bella Mosckowitz, Stalin as the demonic instrument of Kaganovich, all these were men who had been taken up to the top of the mountain, shown the fabulous splendors and riches of earthly success, and asked to obey Satan. These men agreed, and because of their agreement, millions of people died violently, great wars spread across the world like a virulent plague, and a Jewish bomb was exploded which threatened the life of every human being on earth.

Churchill and Roosevelt and Stalin are dead, but their heritage of Jewish terror is with us today. *All power to the Jews!*

This was the Satanic pact which Roosevelt and Churchill signed, and because of it, each of these men died cursing the Jews, facing eternal damnation. All was ashes in their mouths, and they faced eternity with the terrible realization that for a few young girls and some bottles of whiskey, they had sold their peoples into slavery to the Jews.

To those who know the history of mankind, there is nothing new or shocking in this. For five thousand years, political leaders have been listening to the blandishments of the Jews, and they have each and every one wrecked their nations on this same reef. In the publications of the Jews themselves, we discover such little known facts as the startling revelation that Julius Caesar, the master of the civilized world, was murdered by his own Senators because he had sold out the Roman people to the Jews. For weeks afterward, Jews gathered to weep at the spot where he had been slain, just as they gathered to weep for Roosevelt, for Churchill, for John F. Kennedy. Throughout history, this sordid tale is repeated again and again, and throughout history, for the leaders and for the led, the message of Jesus Christ remains the same, "Turn away from Satan and follow Me."

Despite the simplicity of this message, these magical seven words which offer mankind everything, millions of people have been unable to understand it and have died without salvation. Why is this? First of all the Jews have survived because they are masters at confusing the issues. After the crucifixion of Christ, when His message of salvation began to attract thousands of followers, the Jews made a typical move. Rather than oppose Him, they tried to take Him over. They proclaimed to the world that Christ was a Jew, Therefore, one could become a Christian merely by doing whatever the Jews ordered you to do.

In doing this, the Jews ignored Isaiah, 5;20, "Woe unto them that call evil good, and good evil; that put darkness for light, and light for darkness; that put bitter for sweet, and sweet for bitter!" Incredibly enough, millions of people were tricked by this stratagem of the Jews. Despite all records which proved that Jesus Christ in His physical form was a blue-eyed, flaxen-haired gentile from Galilee, thousands of Christian ministers tell their congregations, "Let us worship Christ the Jew." Not only is this the ultimate blasphemy against Our Savior, but it also violates every canon of common sense. If Christ was such a good Jew, why did the Jews demand that He be crucified? Why did the Elders of Zion, meeting in secret in the Synagogue of Satan, plan to bring about His physical death? Amazingly enough, there is not a single, so-called Christian minister in the United States who is willing to stand before his congregation and raise this question.

Instead, some Christian ministers today are leading the program to Judaize the people.

Some religious leaders meet in solemn conclave to absolve the Jews of all complicity in the crucifixion of Jesus Christ. The Jews are advancing millions of dollars to accomplish this end. In effect, this convocation of religious leaders would proclaim to the world that the Holy Book, God's own record, is a lie! What is the meaning of this? The meaning is plain. Priests too are human beings. They too can be led to the top of the mountain by Satan. In the final analysis, no intermediary can face the reckoning of the individual, who must meet God face to face. The real function of the priests is to emphasize for us the message of Christ, the offer of redemption of our souls.

Records can be altered or destroyed, men can be persuaded to follow false gods, but in only one place can the truth never be falsified, and that is in the soul Consequently, those who listen to the inarticulate heart's tone, those who follow the precept of not lying to oneself, can make the correct choice, the choice that the presence of the Jew on earth has simplified for us. We can live life as a Jewish lie, and die without salvation, or we can embrace the truth of Jesus Christ and rise to glory in His arms.

It is this knowledge of redemption which has inspired the great artists and musicians and philosophers of our civilization. In the soaring passages of the music of Johann Sebastian Bach, in the paintings of hundreds of Renaissance artists, in the writings of many Christian philosophers, the splendor of the Christian way of life has been made plain for us. But here too, the Jew has not failed to meet the competition. He has flooded the art world with meaningless daubs, in some cases made by dogs and monkeys, as the ultimate expression of the Jewish contempt for the gullibility of the goy, or gentile; he has turned the world of music into the cacophonous screechings of automobile horns and mindless poundings of drums; he has turned the world of writing into repetitious tales of human debauchery.

We well may ask… how can the Jew do this, how can he commit such outrages of human sensibility? The answer is that the Jewish life can only be one of hatred and revenge, because, by his very nature, be cannot accept Christ's offer of redemption of the soul. He is a snarling animal, forever condemned to the earthly sphere. Heaven is denied him. This is the real tragedy of the Jew.

Young people today, their heads turned by this flood-tide of Jewish filth, find it difficult to hear the message of Jesus Christ.

But, as the great poet, Lord Byron, said, lying adversity is the road to truth." For those young people who can hold their heads up in this time of universal degradation, who can still hear the message of Jesus Christ, the rewards are great. And for those whose hearts are not yet opened to Jesus Christ, this book has been written. It is the factual history of the Jews, and if, after reading it, one can still deny Christ, then one is lost indeed.

Chapter Two

The Biological Jew

We have already referred to the role of the Jew in civilization, and the presence of the Synagogue of Satan. But man, as a philosophical being, as a creature of God, if you will, occupies on earth a biological body. What is the biological relationship of the gentile and the Jew? We stated, without fear of contradiction, that no writer has ever faced this Jewish problem at its source. Why is this? The answer is clear. No writer has ever been able to face the Jewish problem honestly because of an emotional or biological reaction either for or against the Jews. Logically, there must be an explanation of the conflict between Jews and gentiles over thousands of years, and logically, a writer should be able to write about it. Nevertheless, no gentile writer has ever been able to deal with this problem. No Jewish writer has ever been able to write logically about the Jews, but this has not prevented them from writing hundreds of books on the subject.

Interestingly enough, every book written by a Jew to explain anti-Semitism comes up with the same answer – "The gentiles don't like us because of our religion." From the beginnings of time, this is the only answer that the Jews have ever been able to offer to the problem of anti-Semitism. Is it not strange that so clever and resourceful a people, who have managed to survive for thousands of years in hostile environments, can offer so illogical an answer?

Let us suppose that we could assemble one thousand gentiles who did not like Jews and who would be willing to state publicly that they did not like Jews. We would ask each one of them - What do you know about the Jewish religion? And each one of them would have to answer, I do not know anything about the Jewish religion.

The only thing that gentiles know about the Jewish practice of religion is that they meet in synagogues. In view of this lack of knowledge, how could any gentile hate the Jews because of their religion? If gentiles could read the Jewish holy book, their Talmud, and find out something about the Jewish religion, they would really become anti-Semitic, because this book is filled with vile names for Jesus Christ, descriptions of weird sexual rites, and formulas for cursing the gentiles. Consequently, the Jews for centuries have had a rule that any gentile who found out the contents of the Talmud, or who possessed a copy of it, must be instantly killed.

The real reason for anti-Jewism among the gentiles is explained in the Bible, in numerous references to the Jews. Thus, Ezekiel, 36, verses 31-32:

"Then shall you remember your own evil ways, and your doings that *were* not good, and shall loathe yourselves in your own sight for your iniquities, and for your abominations." "Not for your sakes do I do *this*, said the Lord God, be it known unto you: be ashamed and confounded for your own ways, O House of Israel."

Anti-Semitism, then, throughout history has been the reaction of the gentiles to the deeds of the Jews in their midst. Who are the Jews and what are they doing living in the midst of the gentiles? For this knowledge, we again must revert to the biological facts. The Jews are a parasitic people whose members roam the civilized world, seeking any spot where they can settle down in the midst of an established community, and where they can remain and prosper at the expense of others.

As a parasitic people, the Jews can only survive by living on the work of others... They bring nothing with them, and they exist by appropriating the property of their hosts. Perhaps the memories of our readers are not too short. They may remember 1948, when, so we are told, brave Jewish pioneers went out into the wilderness and founded the State of Israel. At least, that is the way they tell it. But, in fact, didn't the Jews invade a peaceful Arab country and, with the aid of millions of dollars worth of arms from Jewish bankers in many countries, seize the towns and farms and businesses of a hard-working Arab nation? The very origin of the only Jewish nation in the history of the world identifies this people as a tribe of bandits.

Since the Jews bring nothing with them, how is it that the host nations allow them to remain? Why do they let the Jews appropriate their goods, and even their lives? In reality, the Jew does bring something with him. He brings his wits, and he brings his determination to remain in the host country, in spite of all efforts to dislodge him. Using his wits, the Jew pretends to offer something that the host people want or need. The Jew offers trade connections with foreign lands, information about enemies or potential enemies; or he appears as a comedian or a magician offering entertainment; or he appears as an occult being, offering new roads to heaven and guaranteed passports to paradise. If the host people needs money, he offers that, or the promise of money. In any case, if the Jew is allowed to remain, even for a short while, he sinks his tentacles into the host people, and it is soon impossible to dislodge him.

When the host people comes to its senses, and realizes that it has allowed a dangerous parasite to enter its being, and to threaten its continued health and prosperity, does the host people pause to calmly analyze the problem? Of course not. The host people reacts biologically. Throughout nature, one can see animals and fish darting about erratically, flinging themselves into the air, and making wild gyrations. In many cases, these are hosts who are attempting to dislodge parasites.

Among humans, the host acts no less desperately and unthinkingly. The first reaction of the gentile community to the Jew is panic. Then comes anger, and finally, violence. The panic ensues when the community discovers that it harbors a dangerous and unknown quantity, one which obviously means it no good. Anger follows - the community will attack this parasite and drive it out. Then the violence takes place, the traditional pogrom against the Jew. As the Jew says, "Oy, gewalt!" This is one of the oldest Yiddish phrases, which translates, "Oh, violence."

The Jew knows when he enters the gentile community that sooner or later, his presence there will provoke violence. Consequently, he is prepared for it. The gentile community attacks the Jews, but does little real damage. A few Jews are tarred and feathered, some of their buildings are burned. The Jews do not care. They know that the gentiles will have to pay for this.

Now the gentile leaders tell their community that the Jews have learned their lesson. They will behave themselves. The gentiles settle down once more to a quiet existence. But the pogrom has been valuable to the Jews. It has revealed to them just who they must fear among the gentiles, the natural leaders who can respond to a threat of this kind. The Jews have not been shaken at all by the uprising against them. Now they can take over the community. The parasite has extended its tentacles too deeply into the community to be removed by an angry mob, a few burnt buildings, or a scorched behind.

The parasite begins to stealthily undermine and destroy the natural leaders of the gentile community, those who led the pogrom. These leaders suddenly find that their fortunes are disappearing. Papers are discovered which prove that their property belongs to someone else. Their daughters are debauched and wander off to other cities. Their reputations are ruined, and the gentile community turns against them. Now some new leaders emerge among the gentiles. Without exception, these are men suddenly come into good fortune, and without exception, their good fortune can be traced to the Jews.

Anyone who dares to oppose the new leaders shares the fate of the ruined ones. Their property is confiscated, their families are broken up, the community is persuaded that they are evil and dangerous men, and they are driven out. Thus the host people, deprived of its loyal native leaders, now finds itself under the iron control of men who in turn must answer to the Jews. So it has happened in nation after nation, throughout the centuries, and when it happened in Russia, the Jewish disease was given a new name, Communism.

Should the new leaders at any time undergo a change of heart, their hearts soon stop altogether, for the Jews are always prepared against a possible defection. This seldom happens, for the Jews never allow anyone to rise to a position of leadership among the gentiles who does not have a Panama. Now, a Panama does not refer to a hat, but to a canal. Although the Panama Canal is not generally thought of as a turning point in American history, in reality it is, for the Panama Canal marks the final success of the Jews in obtaining mastery over the political leaders of the United States. Through the medium of bribes, to the tune of forty millions of dollars, paid from the United States Treasury, of course, and passed out to politicians in Washington, the Jews had these men, and through them, the American people, at their mercy.

The Jews kept records of these bribes, and since that time, the politicians have been able to refuse them nothing. Consequently, every prominent American politician for the past fifty years is said to have his Panama. That is to say, no American is allowed to rise to a position of political leadership unless he has some financial scandal, some Panama, in his background which the Jews can use to bring him to heel at any time. For this reason, most American politicians in the last five decades have been classic examples of the Rags to Riches theme. Far from illustrating the Horatio Alger legend of hard work and integrity, however, each of these careers of sudden wealth stems from the looting of the public till with the connivance of the Jews.

We have already pointed out that the host people, in some five thousand years, has never been able to dislodge the Jewish parasites through the common biological reactions of panic, anger and violence. Because of their inability to dislodge the parasites, in every case, the gentile community had gone down a dark road to oblivion. The records are there for anyone to see. Despite the falsification of history on an enormous scale, despite the burning of libraries for thousands of years, the Jews have not been able to eradicate the records of their misdeeds. Most of the records that have survived are now classified as "rare books", and they are hidden away from the public in special archives. These records are made available only to Jewish-approved scholars who can be depended on not to reveal what they find out. Even so, we know the history of the Jews.

We know that Babylon was a great civilization, that Babylon became host to a sizeable Jewish community, and that Babylon was destroyed. We know that Egypt was a great civilization, that Egypt became host to a sizeable Jewish community, and that Egypt was destroyed. We know that Rome was a great civilization, that Rome became host to a sizeable Jewish community, and that Rome was destroyed.

We know that England had a great Empire, that England became host to a sizeable Jewish community, and the British Empire vanished in a few decades. Whether or not this is a simple coincidence which reappears throughout the history of mankind, we should remember that the United States has a sizeable Jewish community.

Why is it that the Jews destroy a gentile nation once they gain control of it? This too is a natural process. One cannot expect that the parasite can successfully administer the affairs of the host, even if it wishes to do so. The Jew does not wish to do so because his first concern is his own security. He must remain attached to the host, and everything else, including the future of the host, is sacrificed to this goal. Even though he exercises complete mastery over the host, the Jewish parasite can never feel secure.

His own health depends entirely upon the gentile host, and for this reason, the Jew develops a terrible, irrational hatred of the host. The Jewish Holy Book, the Talmud, is filled with wild imprecations against the gentiles and against the Christ who offered to lead them to salvation, and to save them from the Jew. So vile are these expressions that when the gentile community learns of them, they rise against the Jews.

These expressions of hatred, however, are biological manifestations, rather than genuine hatred. The Jew hates the gentile because the host is all that the parasite can never be; self-sustaining, able to defend itself against physical enemies through strength rather than through cunning, and able to accept salvation of the soul. The Jew can be none of these things. Therefore, every Jewish gathering expresses contempt for the gentile cattle, the *goyim*. The Jew regards the gentile people as cattle in the field, to be slaughtered for harvest. And if they are beasts in the field, what is the Jew but a manure-eating fly which perches on the backs of the cattle? This too, the Jew knows, and if he bas contempt and hatred for the gentile cattle, he has even greater contempt and hatred for his own kind. No gentile can understand what rudeness is until he hears Jews addressing one another. When a rabbi was shot down recently while holding services in a Detroit temple, it was no anti-Semitic gentile who did the deed, but another Jew unable to stand the sight of his own kind.

The Jew, then, regards his gentile host with terrible mixed feelings of hatred, envy and contempt. He feels this way, and yet he knows that his own well being depends upon the host. This sets up a strange dichotomy in the Jewish mind which often results in violent schizophrenia, that is, a split personality and hopeless insanity. On the one hand, the Jew wants to destroy the hateful gentile body on which he depends; on the other band, he knows that it is suicidal for him to do so. Because of this schizophrenia in the Jew who has become master of the gentile destiny, he leads the gentile community into wild ventures. Often he brings great prosperity, but only for a short time, and through reckless waste, such as the willful destruction of natural resources, suicidal ventures into foreign wars, and debauching the young people so that they are unable to raise healthy families.

And always the Jews are dickering abroad with the enemies of the gentile host, never deviating from their pattern of subversion and betrayal. When Cyrus and his armies arrived at the gates of Babylon, it was the Jews who opened the gates for him. In a single day, he became Cyrus the Great, and Persia became the master of the world. Of course Cyrus was grateful. He extended every privilege to the Jews. Alas, it was not long before the spider was spinning his web in the dusty ruins of Cyrus' palace.

The Jews had a thriving and prosperous community in Babylon, and they lived there for hundreds of years. Yet they eagerly destroyed Babylon because of a chance to make a deal with the Persians. Not only that, but in their anxiety to conceal the record of their treachery, they destroyed every library in Babylon, and ever since, they have fulminated against the Babylonians with all the hatred of which they are capable. The Whore of Babylon Who has not heard that phrase? Yet classical scholars tell us that the Babylonians were a sober and decent people, devoted to the arts and to gracious living. Nevertheless, the Jews have been able to impress upon the world their distorted version of a nation living only for depravity.

In all of recorded history, there was only one civilization which the Jews could not destroy. Because of this, they have given it the silent treatment. Few American college graduates with a Ph.D. degree could tell you what the Byzantine Empire was. It was the Empire of East Rome, set up by Roman leaders after the Jews had destroyed Rome. This empire functioned in Constantinople for twelve hundred years, the longest duration of any empire in the history of the world. Throughout the history of Byzantium, as it was known, by imperial edict, no Jew was allowed to hold any post in the Empire, nor was he allowed to educate the young. The Byzantine Empire finally fell to the Turks after twelve centuries of prosperity, and the Jews have attempted to wipe out all traces of its history.

Yet its edicts against the Jews were not cruel; in fact, the Jews lived unmolested and prosperously in the empire throughout its history, but here alone the vicious cycle of host and parasite did not take place. It was a Christian civilization, and the Jews were not able to exercise any influence. Nor did the Orthodox priests bewilder their congregations with any vicious lies about Christ being a Jew. No wonder the Jews want to eradicate the memory of such a culture. It was Ezra Pound who launched upon a study of Byzantine civilization, and who reminded the world of this happily non-Jewish land. From the Byzantines, Pound derived his non-violent formula for controlling the Jews. "The answer to the Jewish problem is simple," he said. "Keep them out of banking, out of education, out of government."

And this is how simple it is. There is no need to kill the Jews. In fact, every pogrom in history has played into their hands, and has in many instances been cleverly instigated by them. Get the Jews out of banking and they cannot control the economic life of the community. Get the Jews out of education and they cannot pervert the minds of the young to their subversive doctrines. Get the Jews out of government and they cannot betray the nation.

Chapter Three

THE ORIGIN OF THE JEWS

Despite the thousands of scholarly works written about the Bible and about ancient history, the origin of the Jews remains shrouded in mystery. As we shall see, this is not an accident. Reverend A. H. Sayce, a leading Biblical scholar, wrote in 1897, "The historian of the Hebrews is met at the very outset by a strange difficulty. Who were the Hebrews whose history he proposes to write?"

The Jews have never bothered about the obscurity surrounding the mystery of their origins. They have simply informed us that they are the Chosen People of God, a very special people, indeed. They also claim the longest historical record of any people on earth. Some historians, such as Dubnow, make sweeping statements, such as "All of history is Jewish history." These modern historians ask us to ignore the great civilizations of China, Egypt, India, Greece and Rome, because these civilizations were not important. Only the great civilization of the Jews is important, say these historians.

It would be easier for us to accept this claim if there had ever been a Jewish civilization. We got the art of printing from China, fine art and philosophy from Greece, law from Rome. What did we get from the Jews? They have done everything possible to prevent us from finding out, but once we know the true origin of the Jews, we know what they have brought to us, and this is no longer a secret.

Although the Jews appear and reappear in the histories of other nations for five thousand years, they were never able or willing to establish a nation of their own. This is a sorry record for such a distinguished race, and incredible when one considers that they were the favorite people of God. Indeed, no other people has such a pathetic record of civilization. Even the African pygmies developed a civilization of their own.

Most records of the Jews are such a mixture of fact and fiction that it becomes a matter of detective work to track down the truth. Josef Kastein's *History of the Jews* is accepted as the most reliable history of this people which was written by one of their own. A German Jew, Kastein shortened his name from Katzenstein and spent much of his life as a Biblical scholar. Yet he writes in his History of the Jews, page 130,

"The ten tribes, the first large body of Jews to be carried into captivity, vanished without leaving a trace."

Historians do not usually write so matter-of-factly about a people who vanished without a trace. Most historians work from source material, yet Kastein flings at us one of many oral traditions of the Jews, which can only be accepted without evidence of any kind.

The origin of the Jews is revealed by the origin of their tribal name. The word "Jew" was unknown in ancient history. The Jews were then known as Hebrews, and the word Hebrew tells us all about this people that we need to know. The Encyclopedia Britannica defines Hebrew as originating in the Aramaic word, *Ibhray,* but strangely enough, offers no indication as to what the word means. Most references, such as Webster's International Dictionary, 1952, give the accepted definition of Hebrew. Webster says Hebrew derives from the Aramaic *Ebri,* which in turn derives from the Hebrew word, *Ibhri,* lit. "one who is from across the river. 1. A Member of one of a group of tribes in the northern branch of the Semites, including Israelites."

That is plain enough. Hebrew means "one who is from across the river." Rivers were often the boundaries of ancient nations, and one from across the river meant, simply, an alien. In every country of the ancient world, the Hebrews were known as aliens. The word also, in popular usage, meant "one who should not be trusted until he has identified himself." Hebrew in all ancient literature was written as "Habiru". This word appears frequently in the Bible and in Egyptian literature. In the Bible, Habiru is used interchangeably with "sagaz", meaning "cutthroat". In all of Egyptian literature, wherever the word Habiru appears, it is written with the word "sagaz" written beside it. Thus the Egyptians always wrote of the Jews as "the cutthroat bandits from across the river". For five thousand years, the Egyptian scribes identified the Jews in this manner. Significantly, they are not referred to *except* by these two characters. The great Egyptian scholar, C. J. Gadd, noted in his book, The Fall of Nineveh, London, 1923,

"Habiru is written with an ideogram... sa-gaz ... signifying 'cutthroats'."

In the Bible, wherever the word Habiru, meaning the Hebrews, appears, it is used to mean bandit or cutthroat. Thus, in Isaiah I:23, "Thy princes are rebellious, and companions of thieves," the word for thieves here is Habiru. Proverbs XXVIII: 24, "Whoso robbeth his father or his mother, and saith, 'It *is* no transgression; the same is the companion of a destroyer," sa-gaz is used here for destroyer, but the word destroyer also appears sometimes in the Bible as Habiru. Hosea VI: 9, "And as troops of robbers wait for a man, so the company of priests murder in the way by consent; for they commit lewdness." The word for robbers in this verse is Habiru.

In his *History of the Jews*, Kastein identifies many of the great names in Jewish history as bandits. He mentions Jepthah as one of the saviours of the Jewish people, and on page 21, says, "Jepthah was a robber chief of Gilead, whose fellow-tribesmen drove him out."

Again, Kastein, page 31: "At the time of Saul's death, we find David the leader of a band of free-booters, living in Ziklag. On hearing that the throne was vacant, David immediately hastened to Hebron in Judah. Nobody had summoned him, but he put forward his claim to the kingship, declaring that Samuel had secretly appointed him." So much for one of the great names of Jewish history, a usurper who split the Jewish tribe in two and paved the way for its downfall. Kastein also tells us, page 34, that "Shelmo, Solomon the Peaceable, inaugurated his rule by committing three murders which cleared his path and got rid of his only brother, and he did so without the slightest qualms of conscience."

The fact is that both Solomon and David, who were bloodthirsty bandits, were typical Jewish leaders. The Jews have been a part of history since the dawn of civilization, simply because crime has been a part of history since the dawn of civilization. It is no accident that the Jews were first heard of in Palestine, for this was the crossroads of all the trade routes, both sea and land, of the ancient world. Inevitably, the rich caravans were plagued by pirates and bandits, who could make their getaway into one of the many coves on the sea, or into the impenetrable mountains, taking advantage of natural hideaways in the area which has been termed "the physical center of the movements of history from which the world has grown."

The record of the Hebrews is at great variance with the Jewish claims to "a great culture". But all Jewish claims of culture are entirely without foundation. The Horizon Book of Christianity, a standard reference work, says, page 10,

"The Jews began as an agglomeration of small tribes who later attained independence only in the interlude between the rise and fall of great empires. They have bequeathed no monuments testifying to magnificence. There are no tombs of Hebrew kings with chaplets of gold and chariots studded with jewels. Palestine archeology has unearthed no statues of David or Solomon, but only water pots like the one from which Rebecca watered the camels of Abraham's servants.

The Oriental Institute of Chicago contains one of the world's definitive collections of the fine arts, specializing in Egyptian, Syrian and other cultures of the Near East, in the area which the Jews claim as their origin. One would expect to find the Jewish contribution to civilization well represented here. After walking through vast halls filled with great works of art, splendid statues, exquisite jewels and other artifacts from the tombs of Egyptian and Assyrian conquerors, we come to the Jewish exhibit. Here is a glass case filled with broken bits of clay pots, crude, undecorated, and unglazed utensils which might have come down to us from the Stone Age. This is the great Jewish culture about which we have heard so much. It is all that they have to offer.

The fact is that the Jews were known only as destroyers in the ancient world. They produced no art, founded no dynasties, built no great cities, and, alone of ancient peoples, had no talent for the finer things of civilized life. Is this not at variance with the Jewish claim that they, and they alone, are the sole torchbearers of civilization?

It is also a fact that the Jews, who were not always successful bandits, eked out a precarious living in Palestine, and they were often on the verge of starvation. Their diet consisted chiefly of coarse barley cakes, and the story of Esau, who sold his birthright for a mess of pottage, is typical of their poverty. The pottage was simply a bowl of lentil soup, yet Esau was glad to sell his birthright for it.

The historian, Arnold Toynbee, defined the Jews for all time a few years ago, when he described them as a "fossil" people. He meant that they were a people who had failed to develop since the Stone Age, as their primitive clay pots prove to us. They were unable to master agriculture, animal husbandry, architecture, or any of the civilized arts.

Kastein says of his people, page 7,

> "They (the Jews) first made their appearance on the lower reaches of the Euphrates, then traveled northward into Mesopotamia, and followed the route used by all groups of people at that time and in that part of the world... the road via Syria to Canaan and the wilderness beyond; when hunger drove, they even penetrated into Egypt. The nations they encountered called them the people 'from the other side' of the river. The Hebrew for 'the other side' is *'eber'*. Those who hailed from the other side were 'Ibrim', or, in English, Hebrews.

> "Some (of the Jews) remained within the confines of Canaan, others settled down along the great military highway of the East, and in the neighboring deserts and wildernesses, where they led a nomadic existence, while a smaller section, driven by hunger, finally succeeded in reaching Egypt, where the Pharaohs took them under their protection."

It may strike some readers as odd that the Jews should remain in the deserts and wildernesses, or that they should prefer to do so, but such areas are the natural habitats of bandits. We have only to remember that the outlaws of the American West always fled to the desert or to the unexplored reaches of the mountains. To continue with Kastein, "Everything was calculated to make these bands of emigrants to Egypt become disintegrated in that country, or to be swallowed up in other branches of the Semitic race who had also emigrated thither... Yet no disintegration took place."

Although racial distinctions were not maintained in Egypt, the Jews alone held themselves apart. They soon rose to high positions in the land of the Pharaohs, and simultaneously, as was to happen in so many other countries, the empire began to disintegrate. Gangs of bandits in the outposts of the empire grew bolder; they seemed to know just when to strike, and which of the towns were poorly guarded. At the same time, the empire began to decay from within. Its leadership became apathetic, and the morale of the people was undermined.

One of the great sources of the history of this period is the Tell El Amarna Letters, written by the governor of an outlying province. The discovery and translation of these letters opened an entire new era of Egyptology. It also revealed the destructive effect of the Jews. These letters are filled with pleas for help and addressed to a seemingly deaf Pharaoh. They describe the raids of the Habiru and the impossibility of defending the border towns any longer. Perhaps the Pharaoh never received the letters; perhaps he was too busy listening to his Jewish Prime Minister, who was interpreting his dreams for him. We do not know exactly what happened, but we do know that the empire fell. This, in Letter No. 76, the governor says, "Behold, he (Abdi-Ashirta, a Habiru bandit chieftain), has now mustered all *amelut gaz* against Sigata and Ambi."

The governor meant that a great alliance of bandits and cutthroats was menacing the empire. Amelut gaz was synonymous in ancient Egyptian with amu and sa-gaz, and amu was the word by which the Egyptians often referred to the Hebrews. Amelut gaz meant, 'the Jewish bandits'. Sayce tells us that "the Egyptian equivalent of Hebrew is amu."

A considerable portion of Egyptian literature deals with the social distress of this period, when the Jews were undermining the greatest civilization known to man until that time. Thus, we have "Admonitions of an Egyptian Sage from a Hieratic Papyrus in Leiden," translated and published by Alan H. Gardiner in 1909. Gardiner translates:

"Egypt was in distress; the social system had become disorganized; violence filled the land. Invaders preyed upon the defenseless population; the rich were stripped of everything and slept in the open, and the poor took their possessions. It is no merely local disturbance that is here described, but a great and overwhelming national disaster. The Pharaoh was strangely inactive."

Another source, the famous Ipuwer Papyrus, says, "The towns are destroyed... years of noise. There is no end to noise. The fish in the lakes and rivers die, and worms, insects and reptiles breed prolifically."

What a strange occurrence! No battles are described; the empire was not attacked from without. The description is oddly like the French and Russian Communist Revolutions... the rich were stripped of everything and slept in the open. There are also parallels to modern America... the fish in the lakes and rivers die... there is no end to noise.

One of the great sources of Egyptology is Manetho's History of Egypt. He describes the downfall of the empire as follows:

"A people of ignoble origin from the East, who had the audacity to invade the country, which they mastered by main force, without difficulty or even a battle."

Although incredible, this happened again and again in the ancient world. How did it happen to the most powerful empire ever known? It has already happened in Babylon. The Jews paved the way for the conquerors. These conquerors of Egypt were the Hyksos, or Shepherd Kings, who won Egypt without a battle and maintained an iron dictatorship over the people for 511 years. Some scholars believe that the Hyksos were the Jews, because the Egyptian word amu is occasionally used to refer to the Hyksos, although in most papyri it refers to the Jews. This confusion existed even among some of the later Egyptian historians of the Hyksos period, and it came about because the Jews, who had opened the gates of the land to the conquerors, became a favored minority during their rule. Manetho says, "The Hyksos were known as the protectors of the Jews."

During this 511 year period, the Jews were princes in Egypt, taking what they wanted from the enslaved Egyptians, and incurring their enmity by their vicious arrogance over the betrayed population. At last, the native leaders of the Egyptians led a successful revolt, and expelled the Hyksos forever. Manetho writes that after the Hyksos were driven out, the Egyptians punished the Jews for their treachery, and enslaved them for life at hard labor.

This brings us to the period of Moses, when the Jews were complaining about their hard lot in Egypt. Before they betrayed the nation to the Hyksos, they had enjoyed every freedom in Egypt, and it was only natural that they should be punished for their treason. Rather than endure this slavery, they petitioned the Pharaon to let them return to Palestine, and resume their life of nomadic banditry. But the outraged Egyptian people demanded that they serve out their punishment, and the Pharaoh was forced to agree. Now the Jews used every device to obtain their freedom, bringing plagues upon the Egyptian people through the use of poisons and contaminating the water. They were finally allowed to depart from Egypt.

Although these are the facts of the Jewish sojourn in Egypt, a sordid record of treachery and destruction, these facts are related here for the first time in English, although these sources have been known for centuries. The true origin of the Jews, and the definition of Habiru and sa-gaz as it describes the nature of this people, have long been known to Biblical scholars. Why did they deliberately withhold all mention of the fact that throughout the ancient world, the Jews were known and feared as cutthroats and bandits? First of all, they believed the Jewish lie that Christ was a Jew. If they published their findings, about the origin of the Jews, they would be identifying Christ as a descendant of bloodthirsty outlaws. Obviously, this could not be true. Consequently, they omitted all references to Habiru and sa-gaz from their works. Literally thousands of scholars have withheld this vital information in the thousands of books published about ancient history during past centuries. Now we must re-evaluate the entire history of the early civilizations in the light of what we know about the Jews.

Another area in which the scholars and the universities have been greatly remiss is their incredible glorification of the Hebrew language. We have been told that Hebrew is one of the great languages of all time; that much of the world's great literature was written in it, and that it is a language formulated to express the most noble sentiments. Yet we have only to open the Encyclopaedia Britannica to find that Hebrew is a very limited language with only 500 or so basic words, much like the Basic English publicized during the Second World War. Furthermore, according to the Britannica, Hebrew is not really a language at all, but a composite of other Near Eastern tongues. The Britannica says,

> "A composite language of the Semitic peoples; consisting of Aramaic, Canaanite, Arcadian and Assyro-Babylon."

In plain words, Hebrew was simply the Yiddish of the ancient world, a polyglot jargon which the Jews used in their underworld activities. Thus another Jewish lie is exploded. And the great literature supposedly written in this language is another myth, with no basis in fact. The Gospels of the new Testament, so most Biblical scholars tell us, were written in Greek, rather than in Hebrew. Jewish writers admit that most of the "Hebrew" writings were merely taken freely from Babylonian and Egyptian sources. The Psalms, supposedly a series of great Hebrew poems, were taken word for word from Akhenaton's Hymns to the Sun, written 600 years earlier in Egypt. Horace Meyer Kallen, a professor at the Jewish New School of Social Research, says that the Book of Job was lifted bodily from an early and obscure Greek play. Velikovsky admits that there are "many parallels" between the Vedic Hymns and the Books of Joel and Isaiah. The Decalogue was taken wholly from the Egyptian Book of the Dead. And so on, throughout the entire list of "great Jewish writings." Yet the students of our universities know nothing about all this. They accept without question the statements of their professors (who are mostly Jews, nowadays), the myth of the great Hebrew language and the great Hebrew literature. The fact is that the Jews, entirely lacking in creative talent of any kind, stole literature just as they stole everything else from the peoples who tolerated them.

Chapter Four

Jews in Ancient History

We have already seen how the Jews weakened and destroyed the civilization of Egypt, but what was the process? It was the biological consequence of an encysted parasitic, growth, the Jewish alien, which had fastened itself onto the Egyptian nation and which proceeded to do everything it could to destroy its host, even though it was deriving all of its sustenance from its host. This process was repeated by the Jews in each of the ancient civilizations.

In the Old Testament, the Jews try to justify their homeless state by pointing out that God was displeased with them, and then He sent them out to wander across the earth because of their own wickedness. This theme is repeated many times in the Bible. (Greek biblos, or book). The verses of Ezekiel XXXVI: 17-20 are typical:

"Son of Man, when the House of Israel dwelt in their own land, they defiled it by their own way and by their doings: their way was before me as the uncleanness of a removed woman. Wherefore, I poured my fury upon them for the blood that they had shed upon the land, and for their idols wherewith they had polluted it. And I scattered them among the heathen, and they were dispersed through the countries; according to their way and according to their doings I judged them. And when they entered unto the heathen whither they went they profaned my holy name, when they said to them, These *are* the people of the Lord, and are gone forth out of his land."

Thus God states that it is blasphemy for the Jews to claim to be "the people of the Lord," and considering their record, it is a fantastic claim. He also states that they were expelled because of the blood accusation, of spilling blood before the polluted idols, the age-old custom known as "ritual murder." Although God's anger is given here as the reason for the Jewish Dispersion, it is notable that the blood accusation, which always was made when they were expelled from a nation, is also used. In this regard, we should not ignore the Jewish predilection for following their innermost compulsion to spread over the civilized world, and it is even more strange that no historian or philosopher of modern times has seen fit to comment upon this worldwide phenomenon, which has had a devastating effect upon every culture which has been poisoned by them. A leading businessman, J. J. Cavanagh, has compared the dispersion of the Jews to the physiological effects of cancer.

"The Jews," he stated in a speech to a Chicago business group, "can be best understood as a disease of civilization. They can be likened to the spread of cancer throughout the human system. Just as the Jews spread out through the civilized world, following the trade routes, so cancer cells spread through the body, travelling along the arteries and veins to every part of the system. And just as the Jews gather in critical areas of the world and begin to multiply, and strangle and poison whole communities and nations, so cancer cells gather and multiply and destroy the organs of the body, and finally, the body itself." Many historians of the ancient world noted the Jewish phenomenon, and commented upon it, but most of these works have since been destroyed. Among the few comments on the Jews which have survived the Jewish destruction of libraries are those of Philo and Strabo. Philo, an important historian, wrote that "Jewish communities have spread out over all the continents and islands."

Strabo's comments upon the Jews, written in the time of the Emperor Augustus of Rome, is even more revealing. He wrote, "There were four classes in the state of Cyrene. The first consisted of citizens, the second of farmers, the third of resident aliens, and the fourth of Jews. This people has already made its way into every city, and it is not easy to find any place in the habitable world which has not received this nation and in which it has not made its power felt."

Strabo's observation is probably the most illuminating comment on the Jewish problem in the ancient world. He takes care to point out that the Jews occupied a lower status than that of resident aliens - in other words, they were a group of resident aliens who were considered so dangerous that they were regarded as a group in themselves. The Jews had already become known as the destroyers of nations, and they were allowed to exercise little or no political power, but they still managed to make their power felt, as Strabo points out. They did this through their trade in precious stones and gold, and through their international connections as bankers, and as fences for stolen goods. The lending of money was a basic enterprise of this people, because it gave them power over spendthrift aristocrats, who could then be used to enslave the people for Jewish purposes.

Although the Jews tended to settle in the larger cities, they were found in the most remote outposts of the empire. The Rev. Chas. H. H. Wright, in his book "Light from Egyptian Papyri," London 1908, page 3, says,

"Not many years after the destruction of Jerusalem by Nebuchadnezzar, a colony of Jews found their way to Assuan, the southern frontiers of Egypt. There they acquired for themselves houses and fields. Some of them carried on traffic as moneylenders, and one might say, even as bankers. This is proven from the papyrus marked L, in which a regular bargain for a loan of money is duly recorded. Careful stipulations were made for interest to be paid monthly for the money so lent. Five witnesses affixed their signatures to the document. In those papyri there is mention of the House of Yahu (Jehovah), and of an altar upon which sacrifices were daily offered."

Thus the Jews, thousands of years ago, were carrying on money-lending activities in the remote province of Aesuan, and these activities were an integral part of the economic and religious life of the Jewish community. In those days, the Jews openly worshiped Baal, their God of Gold, but so vile and obscene were the orgies which they practiced before his altar that the Jewish religion was forced to go underground because of popular resentment. The idols of Baal were melted down, and the Jews renamed him Yahu, or Jehovah, and they concealed many of their religious observations in his honor.

Despite the Jews' claims to having 'been the most important civilization of the ancient world, in fact the Jewish tribe in Palestine was given scant notice in ancient records. On page 54, Kastein says, in The History of Jews:

> "The insignificant little state of Palestine was a vassal of Assyria and on account of its very minuteness, was left to its own resources. All about it colossal powers had sprung up who desired empire."

How does one reconcile the historian of the Jews, Kastein, with his definition of Palestine as "an insignificant little state," with the scholars and professors in our modern universities who tell their students that the Jews had the greatest civilization ever known to man? The fact is that there has never been a Jewish civilization. There have been only infections of healthy civilizations by Jewish parasitic growths, which infections have always proved fatal to their hosts.

Typical was the fate of Babylon. Nebuchadnezzar, the mightiest ruler of the ancient world, had received many complaints about the Jewish bandits operating in Palestine that he marched against them. The Babylonian armies pursued the Jews relentlessly into the deserts and wildernesses until they had killed or captured all of them. This took place in the year 586 B.C. As was customary at that time, Nebuchadnezzar took the survivors home with him as slaves. These 30,000 Jewish captives were settled in the Babylonian Empire and they were allowed to form their own settlements. The Jewish historian Gerson Cohen, writes that "Many a locality in Babylon had an exclusively Jewish population."

Within less than five decades, Babylon was no more. Despite the freedom they enjoyed, the Jews began to plot the overthrow of the empire. At that time, Cyrus, leader of the Persians, wished to attack Babylon and seize its riches, but he knew that his army was not strong enough. Jewish emissaries came to him and declared that they were willing to open the gates for him. At first, Cyrus suspected a trap, and he is said to have put the first such Jewish messenger to death, but the Jews later convinced him that they were sincere. They asked in return that he restore to them their land in Palestine.

In the year 539 B.C., the army of Cyrus appeared before Babylon. On page 65, *The History of the Jews*, Kastein says, "The conquest of Babylon was achieved without difficulty; the city fell without a fight." What a coincidence! That is exactly what Manetho wrote about the fall of Egypt to the Hyksos invaders. There was no battle. Although ancient history is filled with accounts of long and desperate battles between nations and sieges of cities which lasted for many years, when a city had a significant Jewish community, these battles did not seem to take place. No doubt the Jews did not wish to see their homes and businesses damaged by an attack.

Kastein continues on page 65, *The History of the Jews*, "The Jews welcomed Cyrus with open arms." Here is another theme which is repeated throughout the history of the Jews. In every nation which falls without a struggle, the Jews rush out to welcome the invaders. Kastein tells us that Cyrus allowed the Jews to return to their own country, but many of them preferred to remain in Babylon. Under the protection of Cyrus, the Jews were allowed to despoil the natives of Babylon, and what riches Cyrus did not carry off to Persia became the property of the Jews. Consequently, the Jews formed a wealthy and powerful ruling class in Babylon, and they devoted their time and money to formulating a Jewish ethic, which was written down as the Babylonian Talmud. In the English edition, published in London in 1935 as the Soncino Talmud, Rabbi Hertz says, page XXI,

> "When we come to the Babylonian Gemara, we are dealing with what most people understand when they speak or write of the Talmud. Its birthplace, Babylonia, was an autonomous Jewish centre for a longer period than any other land; namely, from soon after 586 before the Christian era to the year 1040 after the Christian era - 1626 years."

Note that Rabbi Hertz proudly states that after being conquered by Cyrus, Babylonia became an autonomous, or self-governing Jewish centre! No statement could be more revealing of the role played by the Jews in betraying the nation to Cyrus.

Not only did the Jews take over the Babylonian Empire, they also went home with Cyrus and formed large colonies in Persia. Max Radin, in *"The Jews among the Greeks and Romans,"* says page 61,

"The virtual autonomy of the Persian period allowed the development of a well-organized ruling class of priests, the Soferim or Scribes, men learned in the law, who had no definite priestly functions."

What Radin does not tell us is that these scribes were not priests, they were the rulers of the autonomous Jewish community. It was Scribes of this type who met to condemn Jesus Christ to be crucified.

The influence of the Jews in the Persian Empire soon caused it to go the way of earlier civilizations. One of the shortest books of the Bible is the Book of Esther, the most Jewish of the books, and the only one in which God is not mentioned. The story of Esther gave rise to the Jews' most important religious ceremony, the Purim festival which celebrates the victory of the Jews over the gentiles, when Esther succeeded in having Haman executed. At this time, Ahasuerus was King of Persia, and his prime minister was a conscientious, hard-working gentile named Haman. Haman had been troubled about the growing power and insolence of the Persian Jews. Thus Esther III; 8-9:

"Haman said unto King Ahasuerus: There is a certain people scattered abroad and dispersed among the people in all the provinces of thy kingdom; and their laws are diverse from those of every people; neither keep they the king's laws; therefore it is not fit for the King's profit to suffer them. If it please the King, let it be written that they be destroyed."

This request seemed reasonable enough to King Ahasuerus, and he authorized Haman to prepare for a day in the near future when the Jewish problem could be solved. Unbeknownst to them, the king's favorite wife, Esther, was a secret Jew named Hadassah. She was the niece of a Jewish leader named Mordecai, and he had had her smuggled into the palace to give her charms to the King, and so the Jewish harlot became Queen.

The Jews soon learned of King Ahasuerus' plan, and Mordecai hurried to the palace, where he informed Esther of the peril of the Jews. Esther boldly went to the King, said that she was a Jewess, and dared him to carry out Haman's request. The King was unable to resist her charms, and he agreed to do anything she asked. Esther asked only that the gallows which Haman was building to hang Mordecai and the other Jewish conspirators should be completed, and then that the King should have Haman hung there instead.

The King agreed, and when Haman had been hung, Esther forced the King to inaugurate a reign of terror against his gentile subjects. Esther VIII:7, "Then the King Ahasuerus said unto Esther the Queen and to Mordecai, the Jew, Behold, I have given Esther the house of Haman, and him they have hanged on the gallows, because he laid his hands upon the Jews."

The Jews made further demands, and again the King agreed, because he was unable to deny Esther anything. Esther VIII; 11: "Wherein the King granted the Jews which *were* in every city to gather themselves together, and to stand for their life, to destroy, to slay, and to cause to perish, all the power of the people and province that would assault them, *both* little ones and women, and to *take* the spoil of them for a prey."

This verse reveals the innate bloodthirstiness of the Jews, in their demand to be allowed to massacre women and children who had done them no harm. Haman's action against them had been planned as a governmental program, but the Jewish counterattack became a wild slaughter of the innocents. The massacre begins, as described in Esther VIII: 17. "And in every province, and in every city, whithersoever the King's commandment and his decree came, the Jews had joy and gladness, a feast and *a* good day. And many of the people of the land became Jews; for the fear of the Jews fell upon them."

At Esther's request, King Ahasuerus now hung all of Haman's ten sons, their only crime having been that Haman had been their father, and his house and goods were given to Esther's relatives. The massacres of the gentiles were carried out throughout the Persian Empire, and the bloodletting of the native leaders so weakened the nation that soon afterwards the empire was easily conquered by Alexander the Great. Because Haman had cast the lot, or Pur, to attack the Jews, the victorious Jews took the name of Purim, or Day of the Lot, to celebrate their victory over the gentiles. The last verse of Esther describes their happy Jewish community; Esther X: 3, "For Mordecai the Jew *was* next to King Ahasuerus, and great among the Jews, and accepted of the multitude of his brethren, seeking the wealth of his people, and speaking peace to all his seed."

The civilizations of Egypt, Babylon and Persia had now fallen because of Jewish subversion. Next to bear the brunt of Jewish parasitism was Greece. In all history, no two peoples have been more diametrically opposed than the Jews and the Greeks, and the Jews have always borne great hatred for Greek culture. The Greeks represented the refinement of the civilized gentleman and individual, while the Jew continued to be a brutalized, earthbound, noncreative, unartistic and nameless member of a bandit tribe.

Ralph Marcus writes, in *Great Ideas of the Jewish People*, page 103,

> "We know from recent architectural discoveries that the Hellenistic cities on the borders of Judea were rich in Greek architecture and art."

Greek culture extended to the edge of the wilderness, and it stopped where the Jewish bandits began.

In his *History of the Jews*, Kastein says, page 92,

"The Greeks had had vast experience in this world, their imagination had been fertile and they had created much... that, in these circumstances, they should fall in with a people imbued with a calm and sometimes stolid and bucolic certainty where its spiritual possessions were concerned, barbarians with no sculpture or breeding, necessarily tinged their contempt with impotent wrath. The inevitably logical result of this attitude on the part of the Greeks was the growth of anti-Semitism, of hatred of the Jews."

Thus Kastein attributes anti-Semitism to the Jews, but says nothing of the Jewish hatred for Greek culture. On page 88 of his *History of the Jews*, he gives a more plausible reason for anti-Semitism:

"Judea paralyzed the Greek attack while the Alexandrian Jews brought about the disintegration of Hellenic civilization."

This is the most startling admission which a Jewish historian has ever made about the destructive impact of the Jews. Alexandria was the intellectual center of the late Greek Empire, and its library was the greatest in the world. It was here, as Kastein says, that the Jews brought about the disintegration of Hellenic civilization. They later burned the great library, because it contained hundreds of historical references of the destructive activities of the Jews.

With Greek civilization on the decline, the Jews now began to infect Rome. From the very onset of Jewish influence in the empire, the Romans were aware of the danger, but they seemed powerless to counteract the insidious effect of the Jews. The Roman historian Diodorus wrote, "The Jews, alone of all peoples, utterly refuse to have dealings with any other people, and regard all men as enemies."

This was not entirely accurate. The Jews regarded all other men as a species apart from themselves, in which they seem to be correct. They also regarded other men as ignorant beasts who could be used like cattle and slaughtered for the profit of the Jews. The Roman scholar Williamson comments in this regard, "The separation was not between races; it was between those who gave their allegiance to the Law of Moses and those who rejected it... a man of any race might be accepted (by the Jews). The one essential was the acceptance of circumcision, for which they were held in contempt by the Romans."

Thus one finds that the Jews did not exclude anyone from their gang who could accept the barbarous Law of Moses, an eye for an eye and a tooth for a tooth. As an international underworld, the Jew needed one irrefutable sign of recognition, a physical password which would identify at once those who were with them. This identification, one on which the Jews have always insisted for this very reason, was that of circumcision. Not only did it identify those who were active Jews, but it also identified those gentiles whom the Jews had enslaved; it was the badge of Jewry.

Consequently, as the Jews rose to power in the Roman Empire, and began to possess many slaves, the first thing they did was to circumcise their gentile slaves as the badge of possession. This circumcision of the gentiles roused the Romans against them. In the year 315 A.D., Emperor Constantine issued the first edict against the Jews, whom he described as "that disgraceful sect". This edict forbade the Jews to circumcise their gentile slaves, and it also limited Jewish self-rule by forbidding them to punish members of their own race. Up to this tune, the Jews had considered themselves above the Roman law, and held their own courts.

Jews who rebelled against the rule of the Elders were severely punished. At this intrusion into their government, the Jews turned against Constantine, and forced him to leave Rome. He went to Constantinople, where he set up the Byzantine Empire.

One of the greatest historians of ancient Rome was Tacitus.

He wrote of the Jews,

"The customs of the Jews are base and abominable and owe their persistence to their depravity. Jews are extremely loyal to one another, always ready to show compassion, but towards every other people they feel only hate and enmity. As a race, they are prone to lust; among themselves nothing is unlawful."

As Tacitus' comments show, the Romans were well aware of the nature of the Jews as a criminal and immoral group. Why then were the Romans, a proud and ambitious people, unable to withstand the insidious effect of the Jews? The answer, oddly enough, lies in the Roman nature. A strong race, the Romans had conquered the world, including the desert of Palestine. But Rome had no defense against the Jews, who had formed their usual parasitic community in the heart of Rome. The Romans tried again and again to get rid of them. Each time, the Jews came back. Rome was the center of wealth of the world. It was impossible to keep the Jews away from such wealth. Historians refer to the expulsion of the Jews by Emperor Tiberius as the "first known example of religious intolerance in international affairs". This is also the first known example of the Jewish adaptation of their favorite excuse for themselves, "religious intolerance".

The Roman historian, Valerius Maximus, wrote in 139 B.C. that the Praetor of Rome forced the Jews to go back to their homeland because they had tried to corrupt Roman morals. The Roman historian Marcus says that Emperorrajan greeted a Jewish delegation in Rome most cordially, "having already been won over to their side by the Empress Poltina". Is not this the story of Esther once again? Like most stories about Jews, the same themes recur over and over again throughout five thousand years of recorded history.

In a papyrus found in Oxyhynchus, Egypt, a Roman named Hermaiscus is tried for treason, apparently because, like Haman in the Persian Empire, he protested against the growing power of the Jews. The papyrus states that in his defense, Hermaiscus said to the Emperor Trajan, "It distresses me to see your cabinet and your privy council filled with Jews." Of course he was executed, having pronounced his own death sentence with this daring statement. How many other gentiles have died for like offenses during the past centuries?·

Scholars and historians have offered many reasons for the downfall of the Roman Empire. One leading theory is that "the Fall of Rome stemmed from a gradual dissolution of old values". This theory fails to state just who dissolved these values, but the record speaks for itself. Another theory is that the barbarians swept over Rome. True, this happened, but why? Why did the finest army in the world lose its will to fight, and allow naked tribesmen to take Rome without a fight? It is the same story that we find in the fall of Egypt, in the fall of Babylon, in the fall of Persia.

And here too, as in the case of the previous civilizations, we find that the parasitic community of Jews had developed a terrible pathological hatred of their gentile host. In his *"History of the Jews,"* Kastein says, page 192;

> "To the Jews, Rome constituted the quintessence of all that was odious and should be swept away from off the

face of the earth. They hated Rome and her device, arms et leges, with an inhuman hatred. True, Rome had leges, laws, like the Jews. But in their very resemblance lay their difference; for the Roman laws were merely the practical application of the arms, the arms but without the arms, the leges were empty formulae."

In this extraordinary paragraph, Kastein admits the feeling which the Jewish parasite always feels for the gentile host, "an inhuman hatred". So terrible is this hatred that the most important thing for the Jew is to mask his feelings. Consequently, he always appears bearing an olive branch. His first word is "Shalom *or* Peace". It is this necessity to conceal his true feelings which leads the Jew to conduct his affairs and his meetings in secret.

We have already seen how the Jew continues to hate the people he has destroyed. Centuries after Babylon is no more, the Jew fulminates again "the whore of Babylon". But of all nations, the Jew hated Rome the most, and even today, the favorite epithet of the Jew for his opponent is "fascist". What does the word "fascist" mean? It refers to the fasces, or rods bound together, which the Roman jurist carried to implement his punishment of the wrong-doer. It means simply the rule of law, that is, gentile law, as opposed to the bloodthirsty Jewish Law of Moses. Yet there is not a university in the world today where the student can learn this simple and accurate definition of Fascism. The Jewish professors tell the students that a "Facist beast" is the most terrible and evil thing that anyone can be, but they never explain it any further.

Few historians make any reference to the part played by the Jews in the fall of Rome, and even fewer give any indication of the power which the Jews achieved in the empire. It is only in books published by the Jews themselves that one discovers these little known-facts. And here too, one finds the facts about the assassination of Julius Caesar. How did this come about? First of all, the Romans had made attempt after attempt to get the Jews out of Rome, but they always came back. In his book, "Jews of Ancient Rome," Harry J. Leon ,of the University of Texas says, page 3,

> "The praetor Hispanus compelled the Jews, who attempted to contaminate the Romans, to go back to their own homes." This book; published by the Jewish Publication Society, continues, page 5,

> "According to Philo (Legatio 23.155), the nucleus of the Jewish community of Rome was made up chiefly of enslaved prisoners of war. Ransomed by fellow-Jews or freed by their owners, who must have found them intractable as slaves because of their insistence on observing their dietary laws, abstaining from work on the Sabbath, and practicing their exotic religious rites... by the year 59 A.D. the Jews of the city were already a formidable element in Roman politics."

The politically ambitious Julius Caesar recognized the power of the Jews, which stemmed from one incontrovertible fact - Rome was made up of many opposing political groups and sects. In order to win, the politician needed the support of one group which would stick by him steadfastly, and thus influence other groups to support him. Just as in our present-day democracies, this group was the Jews. They would guarantee their support to any politician who in turn would do what they asked.

When Caesar discovered this simple truth, he sought out the Jews, and won their support. On page 8 of "Jews of Ancient Rome", Leon says,

> "The Jews in the 'Populares', the liberal-democratic or people's party, supported Caesar and he issued verdicts in their favor."

Things have not changed much in two thousand years. We still have the liberal-democratic party in every country, and it always represents the ambition of the Jews.

With the Jews behind him, Caesar soon became the dictator of Rome and the unchallenged ruler of the world. Alarmed by his increasing subservience to the Jews, a group of loyal Senators, led by Brutus, a former friend of Caesar's in his pre-Jewish period, resolved to assassinate him. On page 9, Leon says,

"In return for the support which he had received from the Jews, Caesar showed them his favor conspicuously, and his decrees in their behalf, which, fortunately, were recorded by Josephus, have been called the Magna Carta of the Jews. Caesar exempted them from compulsory military service, allowed them to send shipments of gold to the Temple in Jerusalem, and recognized the authority of the special Jewish courts."

Thus we find that Caesar made the Jews a privileged group who were above the laws of Rome. The traffic, in gold between nations was the cornerstone of Jewish international power two thousand years ago, just as it is today. It was carried on under the guise of being a "religious" occupation, and if we understand that the religion of the Jews was and is gold, this was an accurate description. The Jewish Temple in Jerusalem was still the headquarters of Baal, the Golden Calf, although he was now called Jehovah. Several Roman Senators tried to ban the traffic in gold, only to be overthrown by Jewish power,

On page 10, of "Jews of Ancient Rome," Leon says, "For many nights after Caesar's murder, groups of Jews came to weep at the site of his funeral pyre."

Here too, nothing has changed. We saw the Jews weeping at the funeral of Roosevelt, at the funeral of Kennedy, at the funeral of Churchill, They will always be weeping when a politician who has committed himself to the machinations of world Jewry meets his end.

Leon states that Emperor Augustus, who inherited the empire after Caesar's generals fell out among themselves, restored the special privileges of the Jews. This probably explains why he emerged stronger than the other factions which divided Rome alter Caesar's death. As Jewish decay continued, the empire rapidly weakened. After the death of Domitian in 96 A.D., the emperors of Rome were no longer of Roman birth; hence forward, they were all foreigners.

The power of the Jews was such that no Roman politician dared to attack them. Leon quotes the speech of Cicero in October, 59, before a Roman jury. Cicero was defending Lucius Valerius Flaccus, a Roman aristocrat and the former governor of Asia. Flaccus had tried to enforce the ban on the Jewish shipments of gold, with the result that the Jews of Rome had him removed from office and brought back to face a trumped-up charge of embezzlement. Cicero said,

> "We come now to the libel involving the gold, the Jewish gold. This is obviously why the present case is being tried close to the Aurelian Steps. It is because of this particular charge that you have sought out this location, Laelius (the prosecutor), and that mob (referring to the noisy crowd of Jews whom Laelius had assembled to create a commotion at the trial). You know how large a group they (the Jews) are, and how influential they are in politics. I will lower my voice and speak just loudly enough for the jury to hear me; for there are plenty of individuals to stir up those Jews against me and against every good Roman, and I don't intend to make it any easier for them to do this. Since gold was regularly exported each year in the name of the Jews

from Italy and all our provinces to Jerusalem, Flaccus issued an edict forbidding its exportation from Asia. Who is there, gentlemen of the jury, who cannot sincerely commend this action? The exportation of gold had been forbidden by the Senate on many previous occasions, and most strictly of all during my consulship. Further, that Flaccus was opposed to this barbarous Jewish superstition was proof of his strong character, that he defended the Republic by frequently denying the aggressiveness of the Jewish mobs at political gatherings was an evidence of his high sense of responsibility."

This speech of Cicero's is one of the few revelations of Jewish subversion which survived the burning of libraries. The great consul of Rome, Cicero, had to lower his voice to avoid stirring up the Jews. A Roman aristocrat, Flaccus, was removed from office and dragged back to Rome to face a false charge. Why? Because he had tried to enforce the Roman law banning the Jewish traffic in gold. The outcome of this trial was that Flaccus was acquitted of the charge of embezzlement, but the Senate ban on the shipping of gold was removed. Thus the Jews won their objective, and Flaccus was lucky to escape with his life after he had opposed them.

In the face of this power of the Jews, the Roman aristocrats were no longer able to keep order in the empire, and Rome fell to the barbarians.

CHAPTER 5

THE JEWS AND THE PASSION OF JESUS CHRIST

Now that many civilizations had fallen prey to the Jews, what recourse did humanity have? There was only one answer, and that answer was and is Jesus Christ. It was Christ's mission to effect a complete spiritual rebirth of all peoples, and only one people on earth proved deaf to his message. That people is the Jews.

The prophets of the ancient world were well aware of the destructive effects of the Jewish parasitic communities. John denounced the Pharisees as "a generation of vipers" (Matthew III: 17). Jesus called the Jews "the Synagogue of Satan", and told them He was well aware that they were born of the devil". The Passion of Jesus Christ is the greatest moment in the history of mankind. Today, faced with world destruction from the Jewish bomb, we realize that it is the only way to salvation, just as it was two thousand years ago. And what is this passion? It is, first of all, the willingness in one's own heart to renounce evil in oneself; second, to criticize evil in others; and third, to bring to other people the message of Jesus Christ as He brought it to the world, uncontaminated by the distortions which Jewish propagandists have added to it to serve their own purposes.

In His physical presence, Jesus Christ was a blonde, blue-eyed native of Galilee, born of Joseph and Mary. The Biblical scholar Williamson states that Jews formed only a minute portion of the Galilean population, and they were seldom seen in the province. Williamson also says that "the region was entirely Hellenistic in sympathy", meaning that the inhabitants of Galilee, the family and friends of Jesus, preferred Greek culture and opposed Jewish barbarism. Jesus spoke Aramaic to the people, with a Galilean accent. All of these facts are well-known to Christian scholars, yet they insist on confusing people with the terrible Jewish lie and blasphemy that "Christ was a Jew". Why do these self-styled "Christians" do this? Such men actually have no belief in anything, but they find that religion is a good business, and that peddling Jewish lies is the most profitable business of all.

They have even invented a new word to describe the entire Western culture. They call it "Judaeo-Christian" civilization, and no scholar can obtain a university post today unless he writes articles which praise the pluralist "Judaeo-Christian" culture.

What does "Judaeo-Christian" culture mean? It means two diametrically opposed forces. It is like saying "black-white" culture, or "Asiatic-European" culture. And most of all, it means "evil-good" culture, with the Judaeo standing for evil and the Christian, coming in second, meaning good. This is the codeword by which the professional Jewish propagandists in our churches and universities identify each other. They seldom if ever, mention the name of Jesus Christ, except in a sneering aside about a "ragged preacher" or "an itinerant revolutionary".

Why do these self-styled Christians hate Jesus Christ so much? Because He knew them and he named them for all time.

He said, Matthew VI: 24-25,

"No man can serve two masters: for either he will hate the one, and love the other; or else he will hold to the one, and despise the other. Ye cannot serve God and mammon."

These so-called "Christian" ministers in their chauffeur-driven limousines can only serve one master, and they serve him willingly. Their master's name is mammon. They tell their congregations that Christ was a Jew, and that we live in a Judaeo-Christian culture, and the words of Jesus Christ never cross their lips.

When Jesus resolved to go out and preach to the Jews, the devil hurried to dissuade Him from His mission. Matthew IV: 8-11,

"Again, the devil taketh Him up into an exceedingly high mountain, and sheweth Him all the kingdoms of the world, and the glory of them; and saith unto Him, All these things will I give thee, if thou wilt fall down and worship me. Then saith Jesus to him, Get thee hence, Satan; for it is written, Thou shalt worship the Lord Thy God, and Him only shalt thou serve. Then the devil leaveth Him, and behold, angels came and ministered unto Him."

Having spurned the devil, Jesus now went into the towns and preached against the Synagogue of Satan, the Pharisees and scribes who comprised the Elders of Zion, and whose lives were devoted to evil. He said, Matthew XXIII: 13,

"But woe unto you, scribes and Pharisees, hypocrites! for ye shut up the kingdom of heaven against men; for ye neither go in *yourselves*, neither suffer ye them that are entering to go in."

Jesus continued his criticism of Jewish hypocrisy, saying, Matthew XXIII: 27-28,

"Woe unto you, scribes and Pharisees, hypocrites! For ye are like unto whited sepulchres, which indeed appear beautiful outward, but are within full of dead men's bones, and of all uncleanness. Even so ye outwardly appear righteous unto men, but within ye are full of hypocrisy and iniquity."

When the Elders of Zion heard that Jesus was preaching these words to the multitudes, they met and planned to kill Him. St. John VII: 1, "After these things Jesus walked in Galilee: for He would not walk in Jewry, because the Jews sought to kill Him." "The Jews sought to kill Him!" How can anyone believe that Christ was a Jew, after reading these words in the Bible?

Jesus went to the temple of the Jews, and overturned their money tables,· for the temple was merely their stock exchange, and their religion was gold. They traded before the idol of Baal, the Golden Calf. Jesus went into the temple, and preached to the scribes and Pharisees, who were amazed at His courage. At last, the Elders of Zion could stand no more of this, and, plotting in secret, they resolved to make a complaint to the Roman ruler and to have Jesus executed.

Jesus knew that all of this was taking place, and He was praying in the Garden of Gethsemane when the soldiers came to take Him away. When He was brought before the Elders of Zion, He said, Luke XXII: 53,

"When I was daily with you in the temple, ye stretched forth no hands against me: but this is your hour, and the power of darkness."

With these words begins the Passion of Jesus Christ, the greatest moments in the soul of man. *This is your hour, and the power of darkness,* He said to the Jews, and so can each of us say, in this terrible time of crisis and of Jewish power, This is your hour, and the power of darkness. But the light of Christ will shine forth again, and the darkness will pass away.

Jesus was tried three times, because there were three temporal powers in Palestine. Although the Romans ruled 'through King Herod, whom Kastein describes, page 114, as "a bestial and tragic Jewish half-caste", and through a Roman governor, Pontius Pilate, the real power in Palestine was exercised by two rival groups of Jewish rabbis. One set, led by Ananias, was backed by the Romans, and the second, led by Caiaphas, was backed by the Jews. Jesus was tried before each of them so that both Romans and Jews would be satisfied.

The New Testament describes Jesus' appearance before Caiaphas, head of the Jewish Sanhedrin, or priestly court. Mark XIV:56,

> "And the chief priests and all the council sought for witness against Jesus to put Him to death, and found none. For many bare false witness against Him, but their witness agreed not together."

The Jews were such fantastic liars that their lies conflicted with each other, and so none of them could be used to testify. Consequently, the Jewish Elders of Zion decided to persuade Jesus to testify against Himself. Mark XIV: 61-65,

> "Again the high priest asked Him, and said unto Him, Are thou the Christ, the Son of the Blessed? And Jesus said, I am: and ye shall see the Son of Man sitting on the right-hand of power and coming in the clouds of Heaven. Then the high priest rent his clothes, and saith, What need we any further witnesses? Ye have heard blasphemy: what think ye? And they all condemned Him to be guilty of death. And some began to spit upon Him, and to cover His face, and to buffet Him, and to say unto Him,

Prophesy: and the servants did strike Him with the palms of their hands."

Thus we see the Jews spitting upon Christ, and mocking Him, because they were overjoyed that they could now have Him killed. When He was tried before Pontius Pilate, a formality because the proceedings of the Jewish court had no legal standing, Pilate ignored the first two charges, stirring up the people, and forbidding the people to give tribute to Caesar. The third charge, that Christ claimed to be king, he found harmless, because Christ did not claim royalty in the Roman sense of the term. Therefore he found Christ innocent, but in order not to incur the wrath of the Jewish leaders, he sent his prisoner to Herod. Herod sent Him back, and Pilate pronounced Jesus innocent for the third time and washed his bands of the matter. The Jews demanded that Christ be crucified, and Pilate was forced to give in to their demands. This scene is described in Matthew XXVII: 20 26,

"But the chief priests and elders persuaded the multitude that they should ask Barabbas and destroy Jesus. The governor answered and said unto them, Whether of the twain will ye that I release unto you? They said, Barabbas. Pilate saith unto them, What shall I do with Jesus which is called Christ? *They all* say unto him, Let Him be crucified. And the governor said, Why, what evil hath He done? But they cried out the more, saying, Let Him be crucified. When Pilate saw that he could prevail nothing, but *that* rather a tumult was made, he took water, and washed *his* hands before the multitude, saying, I am innocent of the blood of this just person: see ye *to it*. Then answered all the people, and said, His blood *be* on us, and on our children. Then released he Barabbas unto them: and when he had scourged Jesus, he delivered *Him* to be crucified."

The yelling multitude of Jews, incited by the Elders of Zion, were determined that Jesus should die, even though He was innocent. And the Jews gladly assumed the blood guilt for the crucifixion of Christ. Despite the expenditure of millions of dollars by Jews in recent years to bribe Christian leaders to call the Bible a lie and to sell themselves for thirty pieces of silver, these words remain true. It is a sad fact that much of the Christian church today has fallen into the hands of these modern Judases.

After the crucifixion, when Jesus was resurrected, the Jews also did everything to deny that He had risen. Matthew XXVIII: 11-16,

> "Now when they were going, behold, some of the watch came into the city, and shewed unto the chief priests all the things that were done. And when they were assembled with the elders, and had taken counsel, they gave large money unto the soldiers, Saying Say ye, His disciples came by night, and stole Him away while we slept. And if this come to the governor's ears, we will persuade him, and secure you. So they took the money, and did as they were taught: and this saying is commonly reported among the Jews until this day."

Schaffs Commentaries on the New Testament, a standard work, Scribner's, 1879, says of this passage,

> "Had taken counsel refers to a meeting of the Sanhedrin to discuss this alarming development. "gave large money", meaning more than they had paid Judas to betray Christ. This is the lowest depth of their (the Jews) malice."

Schaff also notes that the soldiers risked a death sentence by declaring that they had slept at their posts. To offset this danger, the Jews promised to bribe Pilate if he sought to make an issue of it.

After the Resurrection, the Jews continued their evil work, but retribution was not long in coming. Jewish bandits attacked a slave of Caesar's on the high road about eleven miles from Jerusalem, and robbed him of all his baggage. The Romans decided to put an end to this banditry, and they began a campaign against the Jews which ended when Titus destroyed the temple in 70 A.D. Josephus describes the Jews of that period in his book, *The Jewish War*,

> "On the one side was a small minority of revolutionaries, insurgents, bandits and assassins, led by wicked tyrants and unscrupulous gangsters, on the other the property owners and bourgeois."

Such were the Jews in the time of Jesus, bandits and assassins, led by unscrupulous gangsters. Josephus claims that the Jewish war began as a civil war among the Jews, and that the Romans, attempting to restore order, found it impossible and had to wipe them all out. When Agrippa's palace was burned by the bandits, destroying all tax records, the Roman Emperor gave the order to finish off the Jews in Palestine.

Chapter 6

Jews and Ritual Murder

At the dawn of civilization, the blood rite, in which human blood is drunk from the body of a still-living victim, was known to many tribes. However, only one people, that has never progressed beyond the Stone Age, has continued to practice the blood rite and ritual murder. This people is the Jews. We have already noted that Arnold Toynbee, a noted scholar, has called the Jews "a fossil people". In so doing, he must have been aware of the fact that they still practice ritual murder and the drinking of human blood. As a scholar, he could not have failed to note the many attested incidents of this practice of the Jews, for hundreds of examples of ritual murder by the Jews are cited in official Catholic books, in every European literature, and in the court records of all European nations.

It is the official historian of the Jews, Kastein, in his "*History of the Jews*", who gives the underlying reason for this barbaric custom. On page 173, he says,

> "According to the primeval Jewish view, the blood was the seat of the soul"

Thus it was not the heart which was the seat of the soul, according to the stone-age Jews, but the blood itself. They believed that by drinking the blood of a Christian victim who was perfect in every way, they could overcome their physical shortcomings and become as powerful as the intelligent civilized beings among whom they had formed their parasitic communities. Because of this belief, the Jews are known to have practiced drinking blood since they made their first appearance in history. Civilized people find this practice so abhorrent that they cannot believe it, despite the hundreds of pages of evidence against the Jews which are found in court records. Historical records for five thousand years have provided irrefutable proof of the blood guilt of the Jews.

As other people became more civilized, the blood rite became a symbolic one, and a symbolic form of blood, usually wine, was drunk during the ritual, while the barbaric practice of killing a victim was given up altogether. Only one group, the Jewish cult, has continued to practice the blood rite in modern times. Authorities on the blood rite, such as the noted Catholic scholar, James D. Bulger, state that the Jews practice the blood drinking rite because they are a parasitic people who must partake of the blood of the gentile host if they are to continue to survive. Bulger also states that the drinking of blood is a rite of black magic which enables the Jewish rabbis to predict the future as the blood of their gentile victim courses through their veins.

Therefore, Jewish leaders from time to time entice a gentile child, preferably male, and from six to eight years old. According to Jewish ritual, the gentile child must be perfectly formed, intelligent, and without blemish. He also must be younger than the age of puberty, because the Jews· believe that the blood becomes impure after the beginning of puberty. When the child is enticed into the synagogue, or, if the Jews are under observation, into some more secret gathering-place, the kidnapped child is tied down onto a table, stripped, and its body pierced with sharp ritual knives in the identical places where the nails entered the body of Christ on the cross.

As the blood is drained into cups, the Jewish leaders raise the cups and drink from them, while the gentile child slowly expires in an atmosphere of unrelieved horror. The Jews call down curses upon Christ and on all the gentiles, and celebrate their symbolic victory over the gentiles as they continue to drink the blood of the dying child. Only by performing this rite, so the Jews believe, can they continue to survive and prosper among the gentile host.

Although all Jews are aware of the blood rite and its importance to the Jewish cult, only the most important Jewish leaders, the rabbis and the wealthiest members of the Jewish community, are allowed to participate in the blood-drinking rite. Kastein states, on page. 173, that the ordinary Jews are forbidden to participate in the rite. One reason for this is the fact that the practice of ritual murder is fraught with danger for the entire Jewish community. Most uprisings against the Jews during the past two thousand years have stemmed from the discovery of this practice, and the resulting attempts of the gentiles to punish the Jews for murdering gentile children.

The principal reason that this crime is so often discovered is that the naked, pierced body of the gentile child, once it has been drained of blood, must be thrown on a trash heap. The Jewish rite forbids burial of the body, even though this would conceal all evidence of their crime. The Talmud, the Holy Book of the Jews, defines all gentiles as beasts, and by Jewish law, the burial of beasts is forbidden. Therefore, the Jews try to conceal their crime by throwing the corpse of the murdered child down an abandoned well, where it may not be discovered, or by hiding it in some manner which will not constitute burial. In many cases, the body is discovered, and then the Jews either are attacked by the gentile, or they spend thousands of dollars bribing witnesses and officials, and attempting to frame some gentile as a "sex murderer". Bribery and intimidation of public officials and newspapermen is always the first step in this campaign. In the United States, since many of these are Jews, no bribery is necessary, as every Jew knows that it is his first duty to conceal the evidence of ritual murder. It is also customary for the Jews to pay off the murdered child's parents with a large sum of money, which in many cases means that they will not prosecute.

There are so many thousands of well-attested examples of Jewish murder of children that we need only cite a few. In "Excavations at Gezer", the archeologist R. A. S. Macalister notes that the bodies of sacrificed young children are found in every strata of Jewish remains from the earliest times. Photographs of the children's bodies are published in Macalister's book, although the book itself, like most works which attest to the criminal nature of the Jews, is now almost unobtainable. It is classified as a rare book, and most rare book dealers are Jews.

In the Bible, Isaiah LVII, 3-5 the prophet says,

"But draw near hither, ye sons of the sorceress, the seed of the adulterer and the whore. Against whom do ye sport yourselves? Against whom make ye a wide mouth, and draw out the tongue? Are ye not children of transgression, a seed of falsehood? Inflaming yourselves with idols under every green tree, slaying the children in the valleys under the cleft of the rocks?"

By the phrase, "ye sons of the sorceress", Isaiah calls attention to the fact that Jewish ritual murder is a black magic rite.

It is customary for the rabbi, as he drinks blood, to invoke the presence of Satan, who will then presumably carry out the wishes of the Jews. The drinkers of blood also swear eternal obedience to Satan during the blood rite.

Isaiah also calls attention to the fact that here the children are slain "under the cleft of the rocks". This refers to the Jewish ban against burying the slain gentile child, and to hiding the body in the rocks in the hopes that the gentiles will not discover their crime.

In the Cyclopaedia of Biblical Literature, published in 1895 Rev. J. Kitto says of the Jews,

> "Their altars smoked with human blood from the time of Abraham to the fall of the kingdoms of Judah and Israel"

The Jewish Encyclopaedia, Vol. VIII, page 653, published in 1904, says,

> "The fact, therefore, now generally accepted by critical scholars, is that in the last days of the kingdom, human sacrifices were offered to Yhwh (Yahu, or Jehovah), as King or Counsellor of the Nation, and that the Prophets disapproved of it."

Yahu also is interchangeable with Baal, the Golden Idol, and Satan, who is thought to have been a minor god of the Jews, and an instrument of Baal. The two themes of Jewish history are blood and gold, and every practice of the Jews is inextricably bound up with these two factors.

Jesus denounced the Jews as ritual murderers, and also made a point of protecting little children from them. "Suffer the little children to come unto me", as a means of saving them from the Jews. He also says, St. John VIII: ",

> "Ye are of your father the devil, and the lusts of your father ye will do; he was a murderer from the beginning."

This passage refers to the blood lust of Satan and the Jews. As has been customary throughout Jewish history, whenever a gentile criticizes them for their practice of ritual murder, the Jews officially resolve to kill him, and alter this accusation, the Eiders of the Zion met and resolved to crucify Jesus.

Among the Jews themselves, the blood rite is an integral part of the ceremony of circumcising Jewish males. According to the Jewish Encyclopaedia, Vol VI, page 99, when performing the circumcision, the mohel, or circumciser, "takes some wine in his mouth and applies his lips to the part involved in the operation and exerts suction, after which be expels the mixture of wine and blood into a receptacle provided."

What the Jewish Encyclopaedia does not tell us is that this mixture of wine and blood is then drunk by the rabbi, as a great delicacy. No other people in the world today enacts such a weird blood rite, save, perhaps, some Stone-Age natives in the deepest jungles of the Congo or New Guinea.

The connection between Jewish ritual murder and the practice of black magic is touched upon by Bernard Lazare. A Jew, Bernard Lazare wrote a book, "Anti-Semitism" , in France, which tries to examine this phenomenon. In the 1934 edition, Vol. II, page 215, he says about ritual murder,

> "To this general belief are added the suspicions, often justified, against the Jews addicted to magical practices. Actually, in the Middle Ages, the Jew was considered by the people as the magician *par excellence;* one finds many formulae of exorcism in the Talmud, and the Talmudic and Cabbalistic demonology is very complicated. Now, one knows the position that blood always occupies in the operation of sorcery. In Chaldean magic it had a very great importance... Now it is very probable, even certain, that Jewish magicians must have sacrificed children; hence the origin of the legend of ritual sacrifice."

Thus Lazare tries to absolve the Jews of the ritual murder charge by saying that they were guilty, but that it was done from motives of sorcery, rather than as a key element in the practice of the Jewish religion. He apparently has not read the Bible, or noted Isaiah's denunciations of the Jews as sorcerers and murderers of children. Of course the Jews killed children during their rites of sorcery, as Lazare admits, but these horrors were committed as essential rites of the Jewish religion.

Dr. Eric Bischoff, a famous German scholar, has found the explicit authorization of the practice of Jewish ritual murder in the *Thikunne Zohar*, Edition Berdiwetsch, 88b, a book of cabalistic ritual, as follows,

> "Furthermore, there is a commandment pertaining to the killing of strangers, who are like beasts. This killing has to be done in the lawful (Jewish) method. Those who do not ascribe themselves to the Jewish religious law must be offered up as sacrifices to the High God."

Murders of Christian children by the Jews usually occur during the important feast-days, Purim, one month before Easter, and Passover, at Easter. Jewish law prescribes that the gentile victim at Purim, a Jewish holiday described in a previous chapter as the Jewish victory over the gentiles, may be an adult. Also if no gentile victim can be obtained, dried blood from a previous victim may be used. However, Jewish law is quite specific that the victim at Passover must be a white child under seven years of age, who must be bled white, crowned with thorns, tortured, beaten, stabbed, and finally given the last blow by being wounded in the side, the dagger prescribed to be in the bands of a rabbi, in a complete re-enaction of the crucifixion of Christ. This vindictive ceremony reassures the Jews that even if a few of the gentiles are alerted to the nature of this people, as Christ talked against them, the Jews will always win out by murdering the critic.

Consequently, many critics of the Jews are slain in these terrible ceremonies. In the United States, perhaps the most famous victim of Jewish ritual murder was the son of Charles Lindbergh, on March 1, 1932, during the time of the annual Jewish celebration.

Lindbergh's son was chosen because Lindbergh himself was the most logical person to lead the gentiles against the Jews. His son was slain as a warning to him to decline this service. Lindbergh's father, a Congressman, had led the fight against Paul Warburg of Kuhn, Loeb Co., when Warburg succeeded in getting a subservient Congress to pass the Federal Reserve Act. The elder Lindbergh had published a book which was burned by Federal agents during World War I, even though he was a Congressman at the time. He was well aware of the nature of the Jewish problem. Now that his son was a world-famous man, after his feat of flying alone across the Atlantic, the Jews feared that he might be persuaded to lead a gentile revolt against their power. They were already planning World War II, in which Germany was to be the sacrificial victim, and now they brought in an almost illiterate German, Gerhart Hauptmann, and convicted him of the killing. Symbolically, Hauptmann, like Christ, was also a carpenter, a profession which made him a logical victim for the Jews. Hauptmann's defense was that a Jew named Isidor Fisch had hired him to do some carpenter work, and had paid him with the bills which proved to be from the Lindbergh ransom money. Although the existence of Fisch was proved, he could not be located during the trial. This court was like the one which had convicted Jesus, for it only accepted evidence which the Jews allowed to be presented. In reality, of course, one cannot believe anything which is accepted as evidence in an American court, due to the facility of the Jews for manufacturing evidence and due to the prevalence of Jewish lawyers and judges in all American courtrooms.

Although one could cite thousands of pages authenticating famous ritual murders of children by the Jews, we shall mention only two. In Lincoln, England, stands one of the most magnificent Gothic cathedrals in the world, its soaring arches a marvel of engineering and art. Tourists are told that it was built to commemorate a local child named Hugh of Lincoln, but they are not told why he was martyred, or by whom. Nevertheless, the story is well known, and it was told by many prominent writers, including the great poet, Chaucer, who told the story of Hugh O'Lincoln in his poem, The Prioress' Tale.

Saint Hugh was murdered by the Jews in Lincoln in the year 1255, and the townspeople resolved to erect a great cathedral which would serve as a warning to all gentile parents to protect their children from the Jews. Hugh's body had been found in a well on the property of a Jew named Copinus. King Henry III himself directed the investigation, as proof of its fairness. He refused to allow mercy to be shown to Copinus, after the evidence had been gathered against him, and Copinus was executed, but the other Jews involved in the act escaped punishment. Tourists are now told that no such child as Hugh ever existed, and the story has been expunged from the guidebooks about the cathedral.

Many professors of English have also dropped Chaucer from their courses because he exposed this Jewish crime.

Many other European churches were erected to commemorate the victims of Jewish ritual murder, some four hundred in Europe alone. Many of these children were elevated to sainthood because of their sufferings at the hands of the Jews. One of these was Saint Simon of Trent. We cite his story from an official Catholic parochial book, Father Alban Butler's *Lives of the Saints,*

"In the year 1472, when the Jews of Trent met in their synagogue on Tuesday in Holy Week, to deliberate preparations for the approaching festival of the Passover, which fell that year on Thursday following, they came to a resolution of sacrificing to their inveterate hatred of the Christian name, some Christian infant on the Friday following, or Good Friday. A Jewish physician undertook to procure such an infant for the horrid purpose. And while the Christians were at the office of Tenebrae on Wednesday evening, he found a child called Simon, about two years old, whom by caresses and by showing him a piece of money, he decoyed from the door of a house, the master and mistress whereof had gone off to Church, and carried him off. On Thursday evening the principal Jews shut themselves up in a chamber adjoining to their synagogue, and *at midnight* began their cruel butchery of this innocent victim. (Ed. note, Did not Christ say to the Jews, 'This is your hour, and the power of darkness'). Having stopped his mouth with an apron to prevent his crying out, they made several incisions in his body, gathering his blood in a basin. Some, all this while, held his arms stretched out in the form of a cross; others held his legs. The child being half dead, they raised him to his feet, and while two of them held him by the arms, the rest pierced his body on all sides with their awls and bodkins. When they saw the child had expired, they sung round it: 'In the same manner did we treat Jesus the God of the Christians; thus may our enemies be confounded forever.' The magistrates and parents making strict search after the lost child, the Jews hid it first in a barn of hay, then in a cellar, and at last threw it into a river. But God confounded all their endeavours to prevent the discovery of the fact, which being proved upon them, with its several circumstances, they were put to death, the principal actors in the tragedy being broken upon the wheel and burnt. The synagogue was destroyed, and a chapel was erected upon the spot where the child was martyred. God honored this innocent victim with many miracles. The relics lie in a stately tomb in St. Peter's Church at Trent; and the name occurs in the Martyrology."

During this ceremony, the Jews identify Christ as the God of the Christians; they do not claim Him as a Jew, as do so many of our so-called Christian religious leaders. Also, they could not conceal the body and hide their crime, for the Talmud forbids the burial of a gentile "beast". As in many such cases of ritual murder, a Jewish physician obtained the gentile victim, because Jewish doctors have many opportunities to steal away gentile children. There are now many Jewish hospitals in the United States, which are owned and operated by Jewish doctors and nurses. Parents who place their children in these institutions for minor ailments are stunned to be told, a day or two later, that the child has suddenly passed away. In many such cases, the child has been removed to a synagogue and murdered by the prescribed ritual. The bloodless body of the victim is then turned over to the parents. This procedure also obeys the Jewish prohibition against the burial of a gentile, for the Jews simply allow the parents to take care of the burial.

It therefore behooves American parents to avoid leaving their children unguarded in the presence of a Jewish physician or placing the child in a hospital run by Jews. Any parent should think twice about abandoning a helpless child to a people which has a history of five thousand years of murdering children under such horrible circumstances. And any parent should be able to visualize the horror of the handsome, perfectly formed body of the child on which they have lavished such loving care, being stripped and laid clown on a table while Jews, their eyes filled with blood lust and hatred of the gentiles, gather round the child and pierce its flesh, and drink its blood, and call down curses upon the name of Jesus Christ. Can any parent really wish to place its child in such danger and to have it die in such terrible circumstances?

In the United States, Jews have been able to practice ritual murder of gentile children with impunity, because they control the press, and because they hold so many high public offices. It has been estimated by a leading police official that four thousand children disappear in the United States each year. There is no question that the majority of them are victims of Jewish ritual murder. So prevalent has the custom become in this country that Jews are able to ship large quantities of the children's blood to Israel for use in their ceremonies there. One of the problems of the Jewish homeland in Israel has been a shortage of gentile children who could be used in the ritual ceremony, and the United States, which has also furnished most of the money to Israel, has also provided much of the required children's blood.

Because most of these children are taken from poor families, no mention is ever made of their disappearance in the press. Only in rare instances do the Jews dare to take the child of a well-known public figure, as they did in the Lindbergh case, and then it is done for a specific political purpose, and as part of a larger policy.

Because of the terror that strikes the Jewish community when the body of a gentile child is found murdered in the ritual manner, and the public outcry from the gentiles, many gentiles have found fame and sudden fortune by biding with the Jews in these instances. Typical was the case of Jan Masaryk, the President of Czechoslovakia. Masaryk was an obscure lawyer when the body of Agnez Hruza was found in Bohemia in 1899. A Jew named Hilsner confessed to the murder and implicated two other Jews. Nevertheless, a new trial was ordered. Dr. Bua, attorney for the murdered girl's mother, who was seeking justice in this case, made a speech in the Bohemian Diet, or Parliament, Dec. 28, 1899, accusing the Government of having shown extreme partiality to the Jews in this case. A second body was found, that of Maria

Klima, who had also been murdered with a ritual knife which was found in Hilsner's possession.

Hilsner's defending counsel at this trial was Jan Masaryk. At the Versailles Peace Conference, twenty years later, the Jews showed their gratitude by making a new nation, Czechoslovakia, and appointing Masaryk President, with the title, founder of Czechoslovakia. Throughout his life, Masaryk was an eager and willing tool of Jewish leaders.

In the United States, many gentiles have found large sums of money suddenly available to them for campaign purposes, after they have aided in hushing up some new scandal of Jewish ritual murder. The path to the Governor's mansion, the Senate, and the White House has been magically eased when the candidate proves that he is willing to cover up for the Jews in their murders of gentile children.

The director of the Federal Bureau of Investigation, J. Edgar Hoover, annually conducts a scare campaign warning children in the United States never to talk to strangers, or to get into a strange car. It is not generally known that Hoover has to do this because of the prevalence of Jewish ritual murder. Hoover's campaign is ostensibly directed at molesters of children, although only a dozen such cases are reported annually in the entire country.

The real reason behind Hoover's campaign is that Jewish leaders fear the recklessness of some of the lesser Jews, who try to seize gentile children for ritual purposes without covering their tracks. Therefore, J. Edgar Hoover spends hundreds of thousands of dollars annually of taxpayer's money to warn children against all strangers, although he should only be warning them against Jews. He does not dare reveal the true purpose of this campaign, which is intended solely to prevent children from falling into the hands of unauthorized Jewish murderers. Not only does this cause the

American child to be brought up in an atmosphere of fear and horror, so that it is taught to mistrust all adults, and causes much neurosis in later life, but it also refuses to face the real issue, the taste of the Jews for gentile blood..

Some journalists suppose that J. Edgar Hoover performs this annual task, and many other favors, for the Jews because he is grateful to the Anti-Defamation League for having ghostwritten a book for him called *Masters of Deceit*, and for having peddled hundreds of thousands of copies for him. The book was written by a Jewish communist named Jay Liebstein, who claims to have shocking personal information about the Great Deceiver himself.

The real reason why Hoover uses the FBI to harass all gentiles who know the truth about Jews may lie in Liebstein's hold over him.

Because the city of Chicago is a center of Jewish financial power, and is completely controlled by the Jews, some of the most flagrant cases of ritual murder of gentile children have occurred there in recent years. Chicago is said to have become one of the world centers of the supply of children's blood used in Jewish rites. The Chief of Police recently admitted that three hundred gentile children disappear each *month* in Chicago, but he claims that they are all "runaways". It is odd that these runaways never turn up, either in Chicago or anywhere else. In October, 1955, the rash of ritual murder cases was at a height when the bodies of two Schuessler boys, a Peterson boy, and the two Grimes girls were discovered.

Police officials immediately labeled these killings "sex crimes", as the Jews had taught them to do. Frantic efforts were made to railroad several poverty-stricken and ill-educated gentiles to the electric chair, but no evidence could be manufactured against them which would hold up in court, and they were released. As in the trial of Christ, the lies of the Jews conflicted with each other.

Although these murders occurred in the heart of a great city, NOT ONE CLUE HAS EVER BEEN DISCOVERED IN THESE CASES! Or rather, we should say that no clue was ever announced to the public. Although hundreds of police and detectives worked day and night, due to the public horror over these crimes, nothing was ever admitted to have been found. There were many charges that there had been a cover-up, and that Chicago officials had destroyed or concealed all the evidence that was uncovered.

Due to this public interest, the Chicago press published many stories about these killings, which were seen at once to be typical Jewish ritual murders. In these cases, the bodies had been stripped and thrown onto garbage heaps. Pathologists agreed that not one of them had been sexually molested. However, there were many strange punctures on the bodies, which could not be explained. The Daily News published an early afternoon edition in which a diagram of the Peterson boy's body showed puncture marks in each of the places where the body of Christ had been wounded on the Cross. Within ten minutes, the edition had been taken off the newsstands and rushed back to the News building, where it was burned. However, eight copies of this issue were obtained by Mrs. Lyrl Clark Van Hyning, the courageous publisher of a patriotic journal called *Women's Voice*. When she called the News office to ask why the edition had been taken off the stands, she was told that there had been complaints about it, and that it was likely to cause "racial unrest". During this entire episode, Mrs. Van Hyning printed the truth about the murders. Police reports showed that the bodies of the Grimes girls bore puzzling wounds on their chests, which were too shallow to cause death. Also, no cause of death could be agreed upon. It was even claimed that they had died of fright! Actually, as Mrs. Van Hyning pointed out in her paper, they died from a very simple cause, loss of blood, for the News had already published the strange fact that there was no blood in their bodies, when they were found.

A copy of Arnold Leese's definitive work, *Jewish Ritual Murder*, was sent to Arnold Schuessler, father of the murdered boys. He read it, and began to ask questions of the police. The Jewish Sheriff of Chicago, Lohman, had assigned a Jewish deputy, Horowitz, to stay with the Schuesslers night and day in case they raised the question of ritual murder. When Mr. Schuessler asked Horowitz if his boys had been killed for their blood, in a Jewish religious ceremony, the Jew immediately accused him of murdering his own sons! He was taken to police headquarters and given a lie detector case, which completely cleared him. Instead of releasing him, the police turned him over to a Jew named Dr. Steinfeld. He was spirited away to a "sanitarium" operated by Steinfeld in the nearby town of Des Plaines, Ill. Mr. Schuessler was given electric shock *treatments* and died that same afternoon.

An inquest was held, and Dr. Steinfeld was forced to testify. He claimed that Mr. Schuessler had been suffering from "hallucinations", but he refused to describe these visions. He also refused to give any further information, and it was obvious to Dr. Thomas McCarron, the City Coroner of Chicago, that Steinfeld was concealing the truth. McCarron denounced Steinfeld, and told the newspapers that the case was very strange. Patients were never given shock treatments immediately upon being admitted to a sanitarium. McCarron knew that Schuessler had been murdered, but he could do nothing about it, and city officials ordered him to say nothing further about the case. For a few days, there was a very real danger that he too would be murdered. He has since refused to discuss the case with anyone.

Dr. McCarron knew Steinfeld's sinister history. During World War II, Dr. Steinfeld had been convicted of giving special drugs to Jewish boys in the Chicago area which caused their hearts to flutter. They were exempted from military service as 4-F. Steinfeld received $2000 fee for each of these cases. After the war, Steinfeld opened his sanitarium in Des Plaines, which became the production center for Jewish ritual murder in the Midwest. It was ironic that Mr. Schuessler, supposedly being protected by the police, was murdered in the same place his boys were killed, and his murder, like that of his sons, went unavenged, except for one later development. Several patriots went to Des Plaines the next afternoon and distributed five hundred copies of a pamphlet charging Dr. Steinfeld with the murder of Mr. Schuessler, and accusing him of operating a Jewish ritual murder center. One of these pamphlets was handed to the chief of police, yet nothing was done. The distributors of these pamphlets could have been arrested and charged with criminal libel, with a possible ten-year sentence; yet Steinfeld refused to make any charge against them. A few days later, he flew to Switzerland, and it was announced that he was taking a "rest cure". The next day, his body was found banging in a closet in his hotel room. The verdict was "suicide", although he may have been a reluctant one. Strangely enough, no Chicago newspaper carried the notice of this well-known local figure's death.

A few weeks later, Arnold Leese, who had been preparing a book about the Schuessler case as a classic example of Jewish ritual murder, died suddenly. He had been airmailed copies of all newspaper accounts of the case during the long investigation, some one hundred pages of newspaper clippings, but these were not found in his effects after his death. Meanwhile, a Jewish columnist for the *Sun-Times*, Irv Kupcinet, whose daughter died a drug addict in a Hollywood pad, raised $100,000 among the Jewish community and presented it to Mrs. Schuessler. The Jewish deputy had continued to stay with her, and a few days later, Mrs. Schuessler revealed to a reporter that he had taken all the money and gone to Las Vegas. Sheriff Lohman also left

Chicago, being given a $20,000 sinecure as consulting criminologist at the University of California.[1] The position had been endowed by a prominent Jewish banker. The Schuessler and Grimes cases are still marked "Unsolved" in Chicago.

It is the duty of every American parent whose child disappears to make every effort to find it. However, many poor families with too many children to feed take it for granted that a child has gone out into the world to make his own way, and they are unaware of the probability that the child has been murdered by the Jews for his blood. Consequently, no effort is made to investigate these Jewish crimes, despite the fact that they have been going on for many centuries. It is necessary for us to use every weapon to arm ourselves against the Jews, and to observe the divinity of Our Lord and Saviour Jesus Christ, in Whose Name salvation awaits us.

Another horrible involvement of an official American agency in the widespread practice of Jewish ritual murder was hushed up recently. A deputy chief of the Central Intelligence Agency committed suicide in Washington. The verdict was "over-work", thereby concealing a terrible tragedy. This official had been off from work for three months, following a nervous breakdown. He had suffered a fit of remorse over discovering that he had inadvertently been responsible for the murder of many gentile children in the Jewish religious ceremonies. This man, a gentile, had become known for a special talent in an agency that was sixty percent Jewish. Most

---

[1] A few weeks after an earlier edition of this book had been circulated in California, which recounted the story of the Schuessler murders in full, another name was added to the list of those who had died. Joeeph Lohman died suddenly in Los Angeles of unknown causes. The obituary notice, strangely enough, did not mention Lohman's term as Cook County Sheriff, but identified him incorrectly as "a former State Treasurer of Illinois"!

of the Jewish agents travelled around the world with unlimited expense accounts, staying at the best hotels, a la James Bond, while they carried out spy missions for Israel, with the American taxpayer footing the bill.

The gentile's special talent was a gift for picking up boys who could be used as homosexuals for the pleasure of foreign officials. At least, that was what he had been told, and he saw no reason to suspect otherwise, for the use of boys in international espionage was an old story, and most governments employed them at one time or another in order to blackmail high-ranking officials of other governments. In the early evening hours, this CIA official would stroll about downtown until he saw a handsome lad. He would strike up a conversation, and if the boy was not otherwise engaged, he would take him to a hotel room, where he would turn him over to another agent. This CIA official would then leave, after promising the boy a sum of money, usually about twenty dollars.

During the period from 1947 to 1952, this CIA official picked up eighty-six boys on the streets of Paris and Vienna in this manner. He heard nothing further from any of them although it must have seemed odd that he never saw any of them again after leaving them in the hotel room. In 1963, a Jewish agent in CIA headquarters in Washington, who had learned of this official's former specialty, asked him if he would pick up a boy for him. By this time, the gentile had risen much higher in the hierarchy of the CIA, and he refused, saying that he did not have to engage in such activities any longer. The Jew then astounded him by saying that since he already had eighty-six murders on his conscience, one more wouldn't hurt him. He could not believe that the gentile did not know that every one of these boys had been used as the victim of a Jewish ritual murder, and he described for him the entire ceremony. The Jew ended up by threatening him, saying that if the gentile did not get him a boy for a ceremony planned for the approaching Passover holiday, he would be exposed. The gentile went home that evening, and collapsed with a complete nervous breakdown, from which he never recovered. Some months later, he committed suicide.

However, most gentiles who aid the Jews in committing ritual murders, covering up for them in police departments, on newspapers and in government offices, are not so squeamish. It has been estimated that at least one-third of all office holders in the United States are well aware of the prevalence of Jewish ritual murder of children, and that their continuing to hold office depends on aiding and abetting the Jews in the practice of these crimes.

During a conversation with Father Bulger in 1956, this writer was told that he had been working all his life on a book which was to be the definitive work on Jewish ritual murder. Father Bulger furnished much of the information contained herein. However his superiors had forbidden him to have his own book published. In former years, most of the information about this type of crime had been published in Catholic encyclopaedias and official parochial works, but further writings on the subject of Jewish ritual murder had been banned because of Jewish pressure on the Vatican.

Father Bulger told this writer that according to his estimates, six million gentile children had been clone to death in the ritual manner by Jews since the crucifixion of Christ. These six million victims have not only gone unavenged, but each one of them, deserving to be elevated to sainthood for their sufferings at the hands of the Jews, has died without gentile society making the slightest effort to protect other gentile children from becoming victims in the same manner. Father James E. Bulger said, "The blood lust of the Jews and their hatred of Jesus Christ are combined in this horrible ceremony. Not only have six million innocent souls been done to death in ritual murder by the Jews, but each of us must ask himself, What kind of Christian, what kind of human being, am I, if I do nothing to protect children from such horrible sacrifice in a supposedly Christian and modern society?

Chapter 7

Jews in Europe

After the fall of Rome, the Jews dispersed over the civilized world, swarming along the trade routes which the armies of Rome had opened up for them. In every city which had contact with the rest of the world, a Jewish entity would be found, firmly encysted as a parasitic growth which the gentile host hated and feared, and frequently tried to drive out, in a characteristic biological reaction.

These efforts proved to be useless, as the Jews always came back. For purposes of collective security, the Jews packed themselves into tight little residential areas, which were called ghettoes. In recent years, with typical effrontery, the Jews have claimed that they were forced to live in the ghettos because of the prejudice which their hosts exhibited against them, but every Jewish scholar of repute agrees that it was the Jews themselves who insisted on living in a separate area, probably to conceal their evil customs from the gentiles.

Because Europe was the center of the wealth of the world, the Jews gathered there in great numbers. Every European nation made repeated efforts to oust them, and the history of the Middle Ages is a chronicle of gentile protests against the Jews. The scholar Williamson wrote of this problem,

"Why was there this bitter hate? Why have the Jews, in country after country, in age after age, been hated and despised, herded into ghettos, concentration camps and torture chambers, accused of monstrous crimes, and saddled with responsibility for the perplexities of nations'? Have they deserved these things, or have they been the victims of misunderstanding, prejudice or envy? Such a question is beyond the scope of this book, but it demands an answer."

Indeed this question does demand an answer, yet no gentile scholar dares to answer it. As we have seen, the only answer that the Jews can offer is that the gentiles do not like them because of their religion. What are the facts?

The Jews have advanced the claim that during the Middle Ages, the rulers of Europe adopted the vicious practice of allowing the Jews to accumulate vast wealth, and then inspiring pogroms against them, so that the rulers could seize this wealth. Even if this claim were true, we still face the question, how did the Jews manage to accumulate great fortunes in country after country, in a very short time? Of course, the Jews do not wish to discuss this aspect of the problem.

The facts are quite different. It is true that in country after country, the Jewish community came into possession of most of the monetary wealth in a short time. Gold, jewels, and other items of great value, all seemed to be pulled into little Jewish ghettos as if by some unseen magnet, white the gentiles soon found that they did not have enough money to carry on their daily activities. In every case, it was not the ruler who protested against the Jewish oppressors; it was the working people.

The ruler found the Jews useful to him in many ways. He used them for arranging loans, for spying in foreign countries, for making deals with other nations, and most important of all, for tax-collecting. Because of his avarice, his ruthlessness, and his lack of all human compassion, the Jew made the ideal tax-collector. Throughout the ages, it has been the Jew who demanded the pound of flesh for the government, with, of course, a few ounces for the Jew. As the United States has moved closer to becoming a Jewish dictatorship, the most recent Commissioners of Internal Revenue have been the Jews, Morris Caplin and Sheldon Cohen. Therefore, the ruler had many reasons for protecting the Jews and allowing them to remain in his country. But in every case, the people would be on the brink of revolution as the Jews oppressed them and murdered their children, and the ruler would have to agree to their expulsion. As soon as the Jews were expelled, they began to conspire to return. They met with the ruler's agents in other countries, or they sent their own agents back to make fantastic promises to the ruler or to his heirs. Why this desperation to get back to where they were hated and despised? The Jewish parasite could not exist unless he was feeding on the gentile host, both symbolically, in day-to-day life, and in reality, by drinking the blood of the gentile children.

The European ruler was always happy to welcome back his Jews, and he would readmit them. Once again, the vicious cycle of host and parasite would begin, as the Jewish tax collectors ruthlessly oppressed the people, and the rabbis would seize the gentile children and murder them for their blood. As always, the Jews would meet in their Synagogue of Satan and conspire against the working people, as they called down curses on the name of Jesus Christ. As the pawns of the aristocrats, the Jews were always enemies of democracy. The eminent historian, Charles Beard, has estimated that democracy would have come to Europe three hundred years earlier, had it not been for the Jews. The aristocrats were too inbred and tainted with hereditary insanity to rule without their vicious Jewish overseers.

The affinity between the Jews and the aristocrats is simple to explain. Like the Jews, the European aristocrats were a small, international community, closely inbred over a period of centuries, with strong ties transcending geographical boundaries. In 1914, the King of England, the Czar of Russia, and the Kaiser of Germany were all three cousins. The aristocrats and the Jews have always had the same purpose, to brutally oppress and exploit the working people. Indeed, the continent of America was settled solely because of the desire of the European workers to escape further exploitation by the Jews.

The centuries during which the alliance of Jews and aristocrats held Europe in bondage have been termed "the Dark Ages" by historians. Due to Jewish intrigue, the nations were periodically involved in senseless wars which resulted in great loss of life, and great profits for the Jews. Frederick the Great, who is considered the most enlightened monarch ever to rule in Europe, wrote of this era,

> "The study of history leads one to think that from Constantine to the date of the Reformation, that the whole world was insane."

And indeed it was, governed by insane aristocrats and schizophrenic Jews. Not only were the Jews schizophrenic because of their unnatural way of life, existing on the gentile host, but the aristocrats showed a strong strain of hereditary insanity. This may have been due to racial contamination, because the aristocrats intermarried with Jews and Negroes in a process of self-degradation beginning with the downfall of the Roman Empire.

The result showed all too plainly in the many European aristocrats who had broad fiat noses, kinky hair, and dull gray skin. They were also renowned for their senseless cruelty.

Many European aristocrats were more Jewish in appearance than the Jews. As a native born German,

Frederick the Great was free of this racial taint, and he was disgusted by the fact that so many of his fellow monarchs showed strong traces of Jewish and Negro blood. The aristocracy of Spain, Italy and France were particularly Jewish in their physiognomy. In the past fifty years, a strong Jewish strain has shown up in the English monarchy, so that Elizabeth the Queen looks much like the Yiddish movie queen, Elizabeth Taylor.

Time after time, the kings of England, facing revolution if they refused, were forced to expel the Jews in response to the demands of the working people. In October, 1290, sixteen thousand Jews boarded vessels, leaving England to live with their fellow-parasites in France, Flanders, Germany and Spain. They were kept out of England for three hundred years, and during this period, England became the greatest nation in the world.

The Jews finally succeeded in returning, by financing a revolution for a fanatic named Oliver Cromwell. With unlimited funds at his disposal, Cromwell hired troops and seized the country. He beheaded the King, Charles I, and began a campaign of ruthless extortion and crime against the people of England. Ostensibly, the Cromwell party was Christian, and it was called the Puritans, but in fact, it was Jewish from its very inception, financed with Jewish money for the purpose of regaining a foothold in England. Its every precept was Jewish, and its adherents worshipped the Jews as the Chosen People of God. Cromwell's lieutenant, a Major Gordon, introduced a resolution before Parliament that the English language be forbidden and that henceforth Hebrew should be the language of the land. The resolution failed by only four votes, as four members who had previously agreed to the measure, were stricken with conscience and voted against it. As a result, this book is being written in English instead of Hebrew. So cruel was the oppression of the Christians by Cromwell and his Jewish group that the English people rebelled and restored King Charles II to the throne. The first thing they demanded was that he expel the Jews, whom Cromwell had brought back to the. country. Charles II was a dissolute profligate who cared only for the company of prostitutes. He needed money for his sex orgies, and he needed the Jews to help him raise the money. He refused to expel the Jews, and they stayed in England and consolidated their power, even though they were hated and feared by every decent Englishman.

Throughout the Middle Ages, the gentile hosts reacted biologically against the Jews, periodically rising up and driving them out because of anger and fear. In no case did the gentiles attempt to examine the problem intelligently, or to set up a program for controlling the Jews. As we have seen, during this same period, the Byzantine Empire had no Jewish problem because no Jew was allowed to hold government office or to teach the young. The nation was securely protected against Jewish treason and subversion of the people. Unable to do any real damage to the Byzantine people, the Jews lived quietly, merely one more minority in a vast empire.

In Europe, however, the Jewish problem was considered only from the religious standpoint. It was never examined biologically. The Jews bore the blood guilt for the physical execution of Christ, and this was the principal objection to them. As a result, the expulsion of Jews from country after country occurred without any real understanding of what was going on. It was a reaction to a particularly horrifying ritual murder, such as that of Saint Hugh of Lincoln, or because of some other temporary problem. There was no study of the destructive effect which the Jews had on the gentile community.

Jews were also feared because of their practice of medicine. In the year 833, the Mohammedans forbade the Jews to adopt the profession of medicine, and in 1335, the Holy Synod of

Salamanca declared that Jewish physicians entered this profession solely for the opportunities which it offered them to kill Christians.

One of the greatest calamities which befell mankind was the bubonic plague, or the Black Death, as it was known during the Middle Ages. The Jews were known to have brought this plague to Europe and to have wiped out one-fourth of the population but the gentiles believed that the Jews had done it out of malice. In this instance, the Jewish parasite came perilously close to destroying its gentile host, but it was not deliberate. The story of how the plague came to Europe has been researched by the scholar, Jacques Nohl. He writes that a group of Jewish traders from Genoa and Venice had established a settlement in the Crimea, at a place called Kaffa. Here the Jews stored furs and jewels and other valuables which they had obtained in trade, until Genoese merchant ships could carry them back to Europe.

Knowing of these riches at Kaffa, nomadic tribesmen frequently raided the town. As a result, Kaffa was heavily fortified. In the year 1346, an army of Tartar tribesmen attacked the town determined to seize it and carry off its riches. However, the Jews were well-entrenched, and weeks went by, with little chance of the Tartars achieving their objective. Bubonic plague broke out among Asiatics in their crowded cities, which had no sanitation, and now this disease appeared among the besiegers. Their commander devised a particularly diabolical plan to smoke out the Jews. He put the corpses of the diseased soldiers on his catapults, and flung them over walls into Kaffa. The plague soon broke out among the defenders, and more than half of the Jews died. The survivors retreated to a ship and sailed for home, carrying the plague bacillus with them.

Their first port of call was Constantinople. This city of one million was soon swept by the plague, and one third of its inhabitants died within two months. The Jewish death ship next landed in Sicily, where its terrible cargo spread death among the gentiles. Then to Sardinia, and Genoa; finally the Jewish death ship docked at Marseilles. The Jewish survivors set out for their settlements in many European cities, and wherever they went, the people were decimated by the plague.

The gentiles soon realized that the plague only appeared where there were Jews, but they had no idea that the Jews had brought the disease with them from Asia Minor. Their first reaction was that the Jews had poisoned their wells, for the plague affected its victims like the symptoms of well-known poisons of that age. The victim was seized with horrible pains, vomited blood, and died within two days. The corpse immediately turned black, suggesting the presence of a virulent poison.

A rumor circulated among the gentiles that the Sanhedrin, a secret council of ruling Jews, had met at Toledo, Spain, and had given orders to destroy the gentiles by poisoning their wells. There was some basis for this rumor, as the Jews quickly disposed of Jewish victims of the plague by throwing the bodies down a well, to avoid being accused of spreading the plague. This, of course, infected hundreds of people who used this water. As many communities took action against the Jews, they began to flee from country to country, which spread the plague more rapidly. In Naples, a horde of Jews was driven into the ocean and drowned by the angry gentiles. Their bodies washed up for miles along the Italian coast, and further infected the people. Ship loads of Jews cruised along the coasts of Europe, forbidden to land, as every country had been warned that the Jews were carriers of this disease. As Jews died on board, their bodies were thrown into the water, and they too, washed up on shore, infecting the very towns which had refused to let them land. The Jews continued to wander about Europe, and the plague raged unabated for fifty years. Twenty-five million people, one-fourth of the population of Europe, died the horrible death of the plague. It was the most awful calamity ever endured by a civilization and, in this case, the Jews nearly succeeded in wiping out their host.

The plague, however, was only one incident of Jewish history during the Middle Ages. Many shocking events of this era proved to have Jewish origins. The pattern which the Jews followed was a consistent one. They would live in a country for perhaps a hundred years, they would be driven out by the enraged gentiles, and they would bribe their way back in. In the year 1066, the Jews were expelled from Granada, Spain on the charge of murdering a boy, drinking his blood; and eating his heart. In 1254, the French people expelled the Jews. In 1290, they were driven out by the English. The Germans expelled the Jews in 1283 and 1298. In the year 1306, King Philip IV expelled the Jews from France. In 1394, the King of France again ordered that all Jews be expelled from France 'forever'. A few centuries later, the Jews were in complete control of France. The Spanish people expelled the Jews in 1492, and Portugal expelled them, in 1496. The scholar John William Draper states that scandals concerning the practices of Jewish doctors had caused the expulsion of all Jews from France in 1306.

In all of recorded history, there is nothing remotely comparable to this list of Jewish expulsions. No other racial or political group has ever aroused such hatred. How, then, did the Jews survive? The Jews survived because survival is their business, and it is also their religion. Knowing that sooner or later, they would be expelled, their first acts, on entering a country would be to make allies among the gentiles, through gifts and bribery, and later on, through blackmail. No matter where they were, the Jews always had gentile supporters who would hide them during pogroms.

When the Jews were driven out of one country, they would go to Jewish communities in other countries, or they would enter a country which was not aware of their destructive habits. During the Middle Ages, Amsterdam became a constant Jewish haven for refugees from other countries, and it also became the bank for their wealth. Most of the money for outfitting Cromwell's armies came from Amsterdam, the funds being supplied by the Amsterdam Jews.

The Jews survived because they maintained an iron discipline over their own people. Cramped into small quarters in the great European cities, every Jew became a Fagin, a concentrated instrument of evil. So terrible was their reputation as emissaries of Satan that good Christians crossed themselves as a protective measure when they met a Jew on the street. Few gentiles were bold enough to look a Jew in the face, for they were always met by the hateful glare of the Evil Eye.

The precept of Jewish discipline, known for thousands of years, was rarely committed to writing. At last, the gentiles found its manual and published it after the discovery of the Dead Sea Scrolls, much to the discomfiture of the Jews. The Manual of Discipline as recorded in the Dead Sea Scrolls, says,

> "If a man's spirit wavers from the institutions of the community, so that he becomes a traitor to the truth and walks in the stubbornness of his heart; if he repents, he shall be punished two years. During the first, he shall not touch the sacred food of the masters, and, during the second, he shall not touch the drink of the masters."

We may note that the Manual prescribes this punishment if the member of the Jewish community only "wavers", that is, if he even considers the dictates of his own heart. If he actually turned against his fellow-Jews, he would, of course, be killed. The punishment here prescribed, forbidding him to touch the sacred food of the masters, refers to the wafers used in the ritual murder ceremony; the drink of the masters, of course, is the blood of innocent gentile children.

As a tribal unit under absolute discipline, the Jews were able to survive in the most hostile gentile areas. The Jewish scholar, Kaufmann, in the book, *"Great Ideas of the Jewish People"*, says, page 38,

> "The Israelite socio-political unit after the (Roman) Conquest, as before, was the tribe. The tribe itself is the autonomous territorial unit."

Note that the Israelite unit underwent no change despite the efforts of the Romans to eradicate their bandit groups in Palestine. They have been a tribe with a Stone-Age mentality since the beginnings of recorded history. They have never been able to make the progression to city, city-state, and nation which the gentiles have made. Instead, the Jews have sought to extend their tribal form of government over the entire world, through such institutions as the United Nations, which is governed by a Council, just as the Stone Age Jews are governed by a Council of Elders, the Sanhedrin.

Kaufmann also states, page 80,

> "The Jewish Diaspora (or Dispersion) was a religious-nation body the like of which the pagan world had never seen."

This is quite an understatement. No other group in the world has ever been able to exist like the Jews, who have maintained their parasitic growth in the gentile countries.

The Greek historian Strabo stated that in the ancient city of Alexandria, the Jews were ruled by an ethnarc, or high priest, "who governs the people and adjudicates suits and supervises contracts and ordinances, just as if he were the head of a sovereign state".

Throughout history, scholars have been amazed at the manner in which the Jews have ruled themselves as a separate community, no matter under what form of government they found themselves. Their Manual of Discipline forbids them to recognize the courts of the gentile "beasts". This is one reason that Jews are always revolutionaries. Since they do not recognize the gentile government, they are always in revolt against it. Their first order of business is to undermine the laws and the legitimate government of any gentile state in which they settle, and they do this by any means at their disposal. Corruption, bribery, betrayal, these are standard weapons in the Jewish arsenal of treason. As a result, Kaufmann says, page 12, "The religion of Israel effected a revolution in the world view of man."

In reality, the Jewish manual sought to destroy the gentile's faith in his own institutions, and thus weakened him for Jewish control.

In one of the most striking comment about the essential secrecy of the Jewish "religion", Kaufmann says, page 12, "Nowhere in the Bible is the Israelitic idea stated explicitly, nor, for that matter, is it ever so stated in later Jewish literature. It appears rather as a primal intuition informing all of Jewish creativity."

What strange admission about a "great culture"! It is not an idea, says Kaufmann, but an intuition. He is correct, because the Israelitic idea of a parasitic group of criminals existing on a gentile host, is purely intuitive. It is not a conscious idea, but an instinct, and therefore it is not written down. Animals do not write down their heritage of knowing how to avoid traps and seeking food in the jungle, and Jews do not write down their techniques for surviving among their gentile host. Kaufmann does call attention to the fact that no one really knows what the Jewish religion is. Consequently, not only could the gentiles be incapable of hating the Jews for something of which they knew nothing, but also, the Jewish culture can hardly be such a tremendous achievement, if we have to be detectives to find any traces of it. Of course Jewish culture does not exist, nor has it ever existed, for a criminal conspiracy is not a culture. Kaufmann explains another aspect of the Jewish passion for secrecy about their customs. Conspirators do not like to broadcast their methods to the world. As a result, the Jewish religion is the only one in the world which is famed for its secrecy. Its aims and purposes, as well as its traditions, are shrouded in mystery. For all practical purposes, the scholar finds that the Jewish religion is an unwritten code, which can be best compared to the unwritten code of the Italian gangster group, the Mafia. The Jewish code is principally concerned with protecting a criminal group, and it too invokes the Mafia rule of Omerta, or death to anyone who talks about their activities.

The Jewish code is principally concerned with protecting wrongdoers from punishment and allowing them to continue their criminal pursuits. In order to carry out such a program, the rights of the individual must be destroyed. Consequently, the member of the Jewish community, like the member of the Mafia, has no personal rights or freedoms. He can only do as he is told, and if his superiors decide that he may merely be thinking of betraying them, he is killed at once. This is the only manner in which the parasitic community can avoid destruction.

With such a code, the Jews found themselves in opposition to every people among whom they lived. They were particularly distasteful to the Greeks, who had perfected a code of human rights. Kastein, in *The History of the Jews*, says, page 39,

"To the Greek, incapable of founding a community, everything was a question of form for the individual, or at best, to a number of individuals; but the Jews immediately inquired how it affected the community as a whole. Thus their peculiar problem of form - theocracy, or a temporal state, was again raised."

Thus Kastein criticizes the Greeks for not setting up a parasitic community like the Jews. The Greeks could only have done this if they were capable of ignoring their basic instinct for human freedom. The Greeks perfected the greatest human civilization the world has ever known by making the rights of the individual more important than the power of the central government. The Jews, on the other hand, were able to perpetuate a vicious criminal state by destroying the rights of the individual. The Jew has always lived as the faceless member of a collective state, and he has no feeling for the rights of the individual. If the individual protests against the state, he must be destroyed. This is the method used in every country where the Jews have brought about a Communist revolution, and it is the type of government they intend to set up in every country in the world.

Not only is the denial of individual human rights a basic part of Jewish culture, but it also raises the artificial above the naturel in life. The Jew hates nature, and prefers any sort of artificial environment, however sordid, to that of clean healthy living. Kaufmann says, page 8, "The basis of pagan religion is the deification of naturel phenomena." Kastein says, page 19, "The Canaanitish cults were closely connected with the soil and expressive of the forces of nature, particularly the force of fertilization... Whenever any question arose involving their existence as a nation, they (the Jews) knew only one God, and recognized but one idea - the theocracy."

What was this Jewish theocracy? It was the rule by the Elders of Zion, the iron dictatorship exercised by the Sanhedrin, the Synagogue of Satan, the same Elders who met to demand the crucifixion of Jesus Christ. The Elders have power over every member of the Jewish community. The word "community" itself is a new word in all Jewish activities, as its companion word, "solidarity". One hears the phrase "community relations" on all sides. Where did it come from? It is the Jewish impact upon gentile social institutions, which are now carried on in Jewish modes. During Communist upheavals, the word "solidarity" is used as a password. It is a Jewish password to protect Jews who are not part of the uprising.

During the Middle Ages, as they were expelled from country after country, the Jews revised their survival techniques. However, the basic Manual of Discipline remained the same. The Jewish scholar, Gerson Cohen, page 191, *Great Ideas of the Jewish People*, remarks with surprise,

> "It has often been remarked with amazement that a culture so theocratically oriented as the Talmudic should have so relatively little to say of its God."

The fact is that the Jews have never been much concerned with God. In the Old Testament, God speaks most frequently to reproach the Jews for their crimes against humanity.

Cohen continues,

> "In the ensuing centuries, new Jewish communities sprang up throughout Southern and Western Europe. While their growth is generally veiled in darkness, they all come to maturity with the assumption of a community structure patterned after the Talmudic type... Everywhere the Talmudic law became the constitution of Jewish origin."

It is interesting to note Cohen's observation that the growth of Jewish communities is "generally veiled in darkness". Did not Christ say to His Jewish prosecutors, "This is your hour, and the power of darkness,"? Certainly the Jewish communities sought to conceal themselves as much as possible. They maintained iron discipline over their members, because they could survive only if they observed the Mafia principle of Omerta, silence of death. No wonder that the Jewish poet Heine remarked, "Judaism is not a religion, it is a misfortune."

Although the Jewish code is seldom found in written form, scholars occasionally set down some of its principles. Thus the Jewish writer, Joseph Albo, published a Book of Roots, in 1414, in which he set down six dogmas of Judaism, as follows:

1. The creation of the world in time, out of nothing.
2. The superiority of Moses to all other prophets, including Jesus or Mohammed, or who would ever arise.
3. The Law of Moses will never be changed or repealed.
4. Human perfection may be attained by fulfilling even one of the commandments of the Law of Moses.
5. Belief in survival of the Mosaic community.
6. The coming of the Messiah.

This was a legalized version of Jewish dogma, meant for gentile publication, which made no reference to the iron dictatorship of the Jewish community, drinking the blood of gentile children, or other essentials of the Jewish dogma. Number 5, the survival of the Mosaic community, was the most important item of this dogma. No reference is made to cursing Jesus Christ, which is called for by the secret Jewish law, the Talmud. The Law of Moses referred to is the Jewish law of *lex talionis*, the law of claw and fang, which was invoked on the gentile world at the Nuremberg Trials, when ex post facto law according to the Law of Moses, became the law of gentile nations.

In speaking of their conquest by the Romans, Kastein says, *The History of the Jews*, page 188, "The Jews were forced to react to the death of the collective state by standardizing the behaviour of the individual, by a general attack upon the individual, in which the doctrine of a Christian state beyond centered. Thus the Jews became a people in whom the idea of discipline reached its highest expression. This discipline was rigid to the point of death as far as the individual was concerned."

This is one of the most revealing passages in Jewish writings.

Kastein points out the crucial and irreconcilable difference between Christians and Jews. The gentile, with his love of freedom, has little idea of the Jewish hatred for the individual. Christ preached the individual salvation of the individual soul, but the Jew declares that the individual cannot even be allowed to survive on earth, much less in Heaven. The Jews do believe in survival, but only the survival on earth of the parasitic Jewish community. They deny all of the basic tenets of the Christian religion, which was built upon Christ's love for the individual human being and His promise of Salvation. Yet so-called Christian ministers have the audacity to tell their congregations that Christianity is a "Jewish" religion, and that the Jews gave us Christianity. This is as absurd as saying that the Mafia wrote our code of laws, or that Al Capone wrote the United States Constitution, yet the congregations listen to these blatant Jewish lies without a word of disapproval.

Although the Talmud, the Jewish Holy Book, revealed some aspects of Jewish religion, it was principally devoted to their barbaric ideals and their Stone Age way of life. Consequently, the Jews had to keep its contents secret from the gentiles, and any gentile caught reading it had to be killed. Few gentiles had any interest in reading such filth, but some Catholic scholars occasionally obtained a copy of the Talmud and set about translating it. They were horrified by its terrible blasphemies against Christ, by its descriptions of incredible sexual rites, and by its revelations of the true nature of the Jew. These scholars were usually murdered before they completed their translation. The person who sold them the Talmud, usually a renegade Jew, was also killed. *Lex talionis*, the cruel Law of Moses described in Exodus, XXI: 18-25, has always been the basis of Jewish life. The law of the talon - what could be more descriptive of the Jew's attitude towards his fellow-man, the claw extended to maim and kill all who dare to oppose him?

Because of its filth, the Talmud also gave rise to another custom, that of book-burning. Books were rare and precious things during the Middle Ages, and no one would think of willfully destroying a book, but when the knowledge of the filthy contents of the Talmud was made known to the gentiles, they would invade the ghetto, drag out the copies of the Talmud, and burn them.

Whenever possible, after a victory, as during the Cromwell Puritan reign in England, the Jews exercised their law of the talon against the helpless gentiles. History is filled with stories of Jewish atrocities against women and children, from the Book of Esther down to the atrocities which they committed against the Arabs in Israel One of the most terrible examples of this Jewish viciousness was the Spanish Inquisition. Although usually denounced as a "Catholic" phenomenon, the Inquisition from its very inception was a Jewish exercise, and most of its victims were good Christians. The original purpose was to discourage members of the Jewish community from becoming "marranos", or rice-Christians. Many Jews had become nominal Christians in order to improve their chances of doing business with the gentiles. In Spain and

Portugal, the marrano movement had become widespread, and the Elders of Zion decided that they must put a stop to it. As usual, they would use the gentiles to do their dirty work for them. What was more natural than for the Elders to use the Church for their evil purposes?

At this time, Torquemada had risen rapidly in the hierarchy of Spanish Catholicism. The Church was not anti-Jewish, as was proven by the fact that many Jews were able to become high-ranking Catholics. At this very time, in 1483, the Spanish government had appointed a Jew, Isaac Abrabanel, as Administrator of the State Finances, in order to raise money to drive the Jews out of Granada. Thus, Spain could hardly be said to be an anti-Jewish nation at the time of the Inquisition. However, the Jews were able to devise a plan which would force the Church to persecute the marranos.

Torquemada informed his superiors in the Church that many marranos were not Christians at all, which was quite true, and that they still kept Jewish holy objects in their homes and sacrificed to them. The bishops were horrified at such treachery, and they asked Torquemada what should be done. He suggested that the marranos should be brought before a Catholic board of inquiry, and questioned about their betrayal of the Christian faith to which they pretended to belong. The bishops agreed, and since it was Torquemada who had originated the idea, they put him in charge of the Inquisition.

Within a few weeks, Torquemada had summoned hundreds of Jews, and many Christians as well, to his Inquisition. The bishops were horrified to learn that he had set up a secret police throughout Spain, in the name of the Catholic Inquisition, and that he was subjecting people to the most hideous tortures.

When they remonstrated with him, and begged him to stop carrying out such iniquities in the name of Jesus Christ, he merely smiled philosophically at them, and murmured,

"Perhaps you too are wavering in your faith?"

At this bold threat that they too might be brought before his Inquisition, the bishops were forced to let him continue his work... He financed an army of spies by confiscating the fortunes of everyone brought before his Inquisition, for the victims always confessed.

For centuries, the Church has been denounced for the crimes of the Inquisition, yet those bishops who tried to prevent Torquemada from carrying out these atrocities were themselves burnt at the stake. As usual, the Jews have fastened the responsibility for their crimes upon someone else.

The influence of Torquemada soon permeated the highest councils of the Catholic Church, and in some countries, converted it into an instrument for the oppression of the working people. Not only did this have nothing to do with the teachings of Jesus Christ, but it was also abhorrent to most Catholic leaders. Nevertheless, they were powerless to change matters. While the Jewish bishops wallowed in luxury, and extorted vast sums from the people through the use of heavily armed troops, one man finally risked his life to protest. He was Martin Luther.

It was never Luther's intention to effect a schism in the Church, or to lead a separate religious body. He simply wished to reform the Church from within, expel the Jews, and put an end to their unchristian practices. In 1524, he published one of a series of attacks on the Jews, "Letters Against the Sabbatarians, Concerning the Jews and Their Lies, Concerning the Shem-Ha-Mephorash".

Had Luther been able to prevail against the Jews, and reform the Church from within, there might never have been a Protestant Church. However, the Jews were too powerful and he was unable to dislodge them. He had translated the Talmud, because he was one of the greatest scholars of all time, and he knew exactly what the Jews were and what their purposes were.

One of today's leading scholars, Father James E. Bulger, told this writer,

> "If Luther had been able to reform the Church from within, the people would have been spared the terrible religious wars which devastated Europe for so many centuries. The Jews sought to destroy Luther by massacring ail of his followers, and these so-called religious wars which they instigated are one of their most vicious crimes against humanity."

The country of Poland has one of Europe's longest histories of biological reactions against the Jewish parasites. As a corridor nation between two great powers, Germany and Russia, Poland has been overrun more often than any other country. It has also been subjected to more treachery by the Jews. For this reason, the Poles have always been known for their anti-Jewish sentiments. The principal objection to the Jews arose during Charles X of Sweden's invasion of Poland in 1655. He conquered the Poles because the Jews came to his tent and gave him complete information on the Polish defenses. After he conquered Poland, Charles X made the Jews high officials of his occupation government. So viciously did the Jews abuse their power that a Polish patriot, Stephen Czarniecki, led a revolt against the conquerors and drove Charles X from the country.

No sooner had the Swedes gone than the Poles fell upon the Jews and massacred 300,000 of them in payment for their treachery. It was a scene which has been repeated many times in history. We have only to remember that Stalin evacuated the Jews from border regions as the Nazis advanced into Russia, and that he allowed two million of them to die on cattle trains in Siberia. for fear that they would betray his military positions to the Germans, and that he ordered the Russian armies to halt outside of Warsaw for two weeks while the Germans wiped out the Warsaw ghetto. No matter who the enemy is, the Jew will always betray the people to him. Then after the invaders are driven out, the Jew has to pay for his treason. The Poles have never forgiven the Jews for their subversion, and even today, while Premier Gomulka has a Jewish wife, and is a practicing Jew, he cannot still the murmurings against the Jews. It takes the entire might of the Soviet Government to uphold his Jewish Communist government.

During the eighteenth century, the Jews perfected new techniques for gaining power over their gentile hosts. These methods were joint stock ventures, banks, and stock exchanges. With these devices, the Jews were able to draw most of the wealth of the gentile world into Jewish nets, or banks. The headquarters of these ventures was Amsterdam, until the Jews financed the conquest of England by Cromwell. They then moved their enterprises to London, because the English fleet controlled world trade. Despite the anguished outcries of the suffering English people, the Jews have been in London ever since.

With great ingenuity, developed through centuries of inbreeding in the ghettoes of Europe, the Jews used the gentiles' own money to control and strangle them. As parasites, the Jews brought nothing to England on their return except their wits, but in less than a century they had secured control of the wealth of a great Empire. In the year 1694, William of Orange, the King of England, needed money to pay his troops. He feared an attempt by the Stuarts to regain the throne, and he had to maintain a large standing army. His advisors suggested that he confer with the merchants of London, many of whom were Jews, because they could afford to lend him the money. They were willing to lend William the money on one condition, that he allow them to issue bank notes against the indebtedness. Hardly understanding this unusual request, William agreed. Thus was born the first central bank of issue, and now the gentiles became enslaved by interest-bearing bank notes issued by the Jews.

Although William did not realize it, the Jews had usurped the authority of the English Crown, with his permission. Sovereignty has always meant the authority to coin money, and now the Jews obtained this right for their Bank of England. The history of the world since 1694 is the record of the Jewish manipulation of their central banks to finance ever-larger wars and revolutions against the gentile powers. Millions of gentiles have died violent deaths because William of Orange, not knowing what he was doing, issued the charter of the Bank of England to the Jews.

With the monetary power at their disposal, the Jewish parasites soon gained control of the British Empire. They then used the empire to rule other European nations. Baron, in *"The Great Ideas of the Jewish People"*, says, page 319,

"As early as 1697, the London Stock Exchange, soon to become the world's leading bourse, reserved permanently for Jews twelve of its 124 seats."

Was not this racism? Was it not discrimination? Not one seat was reserved for gentiles, but approximately ten percent were reserved for Jews, who at that time numbered but a few thousand in all England. They also used their money to agitate for "equal rights". One of their hirelings, a black named John Toland, published a pamphlet in 1714, *"Reasons for Naturalizing the Jews in Great Britain and Ireland, on the Same Footing as all other nations.*" In 1721, James Finch publicly espoused conquering the Holy Land and giving it to the Jews, a goal which English stooges of the Jews sponsored for two hundred years before it became a reality.

In 1723, King George I acknowledged Jews as British subjects; in 1753, King George II passed a Naturalization Bill allowing Jews to become national subjects, which would have meant they could never be expelled again. There was such an outcry from the British working people that he was forced to repeal the bill the following year, no doubt after he had spent the money the Jews paid him to enact it.

Kastein says, *History of the Jews*, page 377,

"In 1750 the stock exchanges of bath Amsterdam and London were controlled by Jews."

In 1775, King George III laid the foundation of the Rothschild fortune by paying the Elector of Hesse of Hessian mercenaries to fight against the American patriots and put down their revolution. When Napoleon later marched against Germany, the Elector of Hesse asked his good friend, Mayer Amschel Rothschild, a Jewish coin-dealer from Frankfurt, to hide the money for him. Rothschild was glad to do so, and he lent the money in other countries at high rates of interest. When Napoleon retreated, Rothschild gave the Elector his money back, with interest. The Elector was so pleased that he begged Rothschild to keep the money and to continue to lend it out for him. As court banker for the Elector, Rothschild began to specialize in international loans.

Jewish power and finance now grew by leaps and bounds. A Jew, D'Israeli (meaning, of Israel), became Prime Minister of England. He was also a writer of bad novels, in which he expounded his theory that Jews were superior to all other peoples. "All is race, there is no other truth," declares the hero of his novel, Tancred, in explaining the natural superiority of the Jews.

In 1871, William Gladstone elected the Jew, Sir George Jessel, as Solicitor General of England. Another Jew, Rufus Isaacs, became Lord Chief Justice of England, Ambassador to the United States, and Viceroy of India.

If Germany provided the manpower for the Jewish rise to wealth, and England provided the money, it was in France that the Jews found the most fertile soil for their activities. It was Jewish money which paid for the rioting mobs who set off the Revolution in Paris and brought down the gentile leaders, with their King's head rolling into a basket beneath the guillotine. In no country did the Jews do so well in wiping out the gentile leaders as they did in France, with the result that the country has been flopping around like a headless chicken for two hundred years. The Jews achieved the same goal during the Communist Revolution in Russia. *"The best of the gentiles kill!"* has always been the terrible motto of the Talmud.

The French have always feared the Jews. The great philosopher, Voltaire, wrote of them, in his Philosophical Dictionary,

> "Jews - In short, we find in them only an ignorant and barbarous people who have long united the most sordid avarice with the most detestable superstition and the most invincible hatred for every people by whom they are tolerated and enriched."

No wonder that Voltaire has been dropped from the courses in philosophy at American universities! He was one of the few gentiles intelligent enough to see that it was not the gentiles who hated the Jews, it was the Jews who hated the gentiles. He would have been pleased to see Kastein's observation that the Jews hated Romans with "an almost inhuman hatred". And so they have hated every people by whom, as Voltaire says, "they are tolerated and enriched."

When Napoleon became the master of Europe, be discovered, to his dismay, that the Jews were the only force over whom he could exercise no control. In an attempt to limit their international activities, he issued a decree in 1808 which the Jews termed the *Décret Infame*, the Infamous Decree, because he sought to make them obey the laws which governed other people in France. Throughout history, we find that the Jews do not consider themselves subject to the laws of the gentiles, whom they consider to be mere ignorant beasts. When a ruler tries to force them to obey the law, he is reviled through the centuries as a cruel tyrant. If he lets them do as they please, he is recorded as a liberal, gracious monarch who is devoted to human rights. The phrase "human rights", as used. in modem history, means "Jewish rights", because, according to Talmudic law, gentiles are not humans and have no rights.

In most cases, European monarchs have found it advantageous to them to let the Jews have their own way. In every case, it has been the exploited working people who have risen up against the Jews. Kastein says, page 322, *History of the Jews*,

> "The Russian government regarded the activities of the village Jews as exploiting the rural population."

Consequently, the Czar issued a decree that the Jews should not go beyond the Pale, an agricultural area. Jewish bankers in the United States immediately demanded that the President declare war against Russia and force the Czar to rescind the decree, but President Taft refused, with the result that the Jews split the Republican Party in his next campaign, and elected their preferred candidate, the Democrat, Woodrow Wilson.

Kastein also states, page 390,

> "In Switzerland, which became the Republic of Helvetia in 1798, there was also a Jewish problem, although there were only two hundred Jewish families in the country, and there was much anxious debate as to whether this handful of people should be granted equal rights. In the end, they were refused."

Even Switzerland, the most democratic state in Europe, could not afford to grant equal rights to the Jews. Most European nations still followed the precepts of the Byzantine Empire. Jews were not allowed to hold public office or to educate the young. The Jews had to rely on bribery and blackmail of gentile officials to gain their ends, and the results were often unpredictable. The Battle of Waterloo signified the end of gentile independence from the Jews in Europe. Napoleon was unshakable in his determination that the Jews should obey the laws of his Empire. The other European nations were governed by aristocrats who were indebted to the Jews. When Napoleon made his triumphant return from Elba, the Rothschilds immediately guaranteed huge loans to every European country which would send an army against him. As a result, Napoleon faced a vast coalition at Waterloo. It was the first instance of the Jewish technique of enlisting "Allied" nations to fight their enemies for them.

During the Battle of Waterloo, the London stockbrokers were fearful of the outcome. Despite the tremendous force arrayed against him, Napoleon was still known as the most brilliant general in Europe. Because the Jews specialized in exchanging information, Nathan Mayer Rothschild, head of the House of Rothschild, had made arrangements to learn the outcome of the battle from London. No sooner had

Napoleon's troops been defeated than a lieutenant of Rothschild hurried to a bill overlooking the Channel; and late that night, he sent the message by winking lights, "Napoleon has lost". Then he released a carrier pigeon bound for the London Stock Exchange with the message, "Napoleon has won."

When Nathan Mayer Rothschild came swaggering into the Stock Exchange the next morning, all was pandemonium. At the news that Napoleon had won, everyone tried to unload their stocks at any price. Only Rothschild knew the truth, and he bought everything that was offered. Prices fell nine hundred per cent in a few minutes, and he bought at his own price. When the Exchange closed that afternoon, he owned sixty-two per cent of all shares listed on the Exchange. Many of the great names of England were ruined that day. The next morning, London awoke to learn the truth - Napoleon had been crushed. The London aristocrats who had been ruined on the Exchange now hurried to do Rothschild's bidding. The Duke of Marlborough, who had led the British Army to victory at Waterloo, became Rothschild's ally, after Rothschild had raised a large purse, from the public, of course, and presented it to him. Marlborough became a loyal henchman of the Jews, just as, one hundred years later, his descendant, Winston Churchill, or W. C., as he was known to his subjects (meaning water-closet), became the faceless tool of Baruch and the Rothschilds.

As the master of Europe and the victor over his gentile enemy, Napoleon, the merciless Rothschild had the fallen Emperor shipped to a remote Atlantic island and slowly poisoned with arsenic until he died. Now Rothschild forced all the European nations to take large loans from him. As soon as the nations borrowed the money, the Jews moved into official positions. The real celebration of the Jewish victory was the Congress of Vienna in 1815. Rothschild ordered the European rulers to meet in Vienna and draft a plan which would make it impossible for another Napoleon to rise to power. They developed the "balance of power" plan, whereby, if any European nation began to get too powerful, the other nations would rally and attack it. In effect, it meant that any future enemy of the Jews would have to face the armies of the other nations, as later occurred against Hitler.

The Congress of Vienna swept away the last restrictions upon the Jews. It guaranteed them "equal rights" in every European country, and they poured out of the ghettoes, seizing government offices, educational positions, and banking posts. The Jewish parasite had become the unchallenged ruler of the gentile host. It was inevitable that the gentile host should face a terrible future, with its destiny in such cruel, avaricious bands.

Within one hundred years after the Congress of Vienna, all of Europe was embroiled in a calamitous world war. The Jews ended this war in such a manner that a second world war was inevitable. Over one hundred million gentiles lost their lives in these two Jewish wars. The aristocrats of every country except England, which was then Jewish world headquarters, were swept from their thrones. They were cast aside because the Jews had no further use for them, and the Jews now set up their own form of communist government. These Jewish Communist governments stripped the gentiles of all personal property and individual human rights. Only Jews could have a voice in these governments, and those gentiles who opposed them were sent to concentration camps, tortured, and murdered by the millions. In Russia alone, the Jews murdered twenty million Christians between 1917 and 1940.

After the Congress of 1815, the next wave of Jewish revolts occurred in 1848. Every country in Europe was alarmed by the spectacle of hordes of yelling Jews demanding that the gentiles surrender all of their private property. This was known as Communism. The Jew Karl Marx wrote and issued the Communist Manifesto, and he became the founding father of the Communist Party, whose membership has since been dominated by Jews. After the 1848 uprisings, the Jews assumed cabinet posts in many European countries. Baron says, page 329, *Great Ideas of the Jewish People*,

> "It is less surprising that France, where Jewish emancipation had been in effect for a century, also included two prominent Jews in its new cabinet. One of them, Michael Godchaux, became Minister of Finance... The equally crucial Ministry of Justice was handed over to the staunch champion of Jewish rights, Adolphe Crémieux."

Note that Baron says this post was "handed over". At this time Baron James de Rothschild had a fortune sixty times larger than the fortune of the King of France. Baron also does not mention that Crémieux was head of the Alliance Israelite Universelle, the Zionist world power movement. He also does not mention that Jewish emancipation had been in effect for a century because the Jews had massacred the gentile leaders of France during the Revolution. In England, Nathan Mayer Rothschild controlled the majority of the empire's wealth. Other Rothschilds controlled the nations of Germany and Austria-Hungary. The Jewish spider of international finance had now spun its web over the gentile world, and soon its poison would paralyze all the gentiles and make them helpless slaves of the Jews.

Jewish officials now filled the halls of government in all European nations. Baron hails D'Israeli as "one of Britain's great empire builders", and "the regenerator of the Conservative Party". The foreign Minister of the Austro-Hungarian Empire was Baron Alois von Aehrenthal, a Jew who created the perennial "Balkan crises" and paved the way for the big kill, the First World War.

During the late 19th century, the Jews realized with growing excitement that the moment was approaching to set up their world empire. Jewish international bankers controlled all of the governments of Europe, and they needed only to wreak further havoc on the gentiles before conquering Palestine, for it was their superstition that they could not rule the world until they owned the little patch of desert where they had started out as bandits five thousand years ago.

A typically prominent Jew during this period was Basil Zaharoff, who for fifty years was known as the Mystery Man of Europe. He is credited with having started many small wars and to have played the leading role in setting off World War I. There was never any real mystery about Zaharoff. His biographers state that he was born Manel Sahar, of Russian Jewish parentage, in the ghetto of Wilkomir, Russia. His parents moved to Constantinople when he was four years old, and at the age of six, he became a brothel tout, leading tourists to houses of prostitution. As a young man, he was a well-known pimp in Constantinople, and at the age of twenty-four, he fled to Athens after murdering a sailor on the docks during a robbery.

After eking out a dishonest living in Athens for several years, Zaharoff became an armaments salesman for the firm of Maxim Nordenfeldt. The transition from pimp to salesman was a simple one, for government contracts were customarily arranged by furnishing beautiful prostitutes to the contracting officer. Through his talents for pimping and blackmail, Zaharoff was extraordinarily successful at persuading governments to buy his wares, and he soon became a millionaire. He spent many thousands of dollars to erase his criminal record, but in 1911, his past was revealed when his son, Haim Sahar, a Jew living in Birmingham, England, sued him for part of his fortune. Although Haim proved that he was Zaharoff's son, he got nothing from Zaharoff, who by this time had amassed a fortune of one hundred million dollars.

In the 1890's the largest munitions firm in the world was Vickers of England, which was owned by the Rothschilds. In 1897, Vickers purchased the Naval Construction and Armaments Co., and also the Maxim Nordenfeldt Co. Zaharoff was the biggest stockholder, and the Rothschilds placed him on the board of Vickers. The Jews then loaded up all of the governments of Europe with munitions. The Rothschilds forced the governments to whom they lent money to allot most of it for the purchase of armaments. The stage was set for a world war, and as Werner Sombart, the economic historian, said "Wars are the Jews' harvests". The Jews began to spew out of their Balkan ghettoes, entering England at the rate of 600,000 a year, and the United States at the rate of one million a year. They took over government offices so completely that the English Foreign Office was known as "the Too-Foreign Office", in reference to the great number of Jews with thick accents who filled its ministries became ministers of finance and justice in many countries, so that they could control the nations through these positions. The Minister of Finance in France was Klots; in Italy, Luzzatti; in Germany, Demberg; in England, Isaacs. Of 355 English salaried consular officials, 200 were foreign born, and 120 readily identified as Jews, although the total was undoubtedly higher.

Every European Government was rocked by financial and espionage scandals as the Jews sold state secrets and patents to the highest bidder. When the gentile, Marconi, invented radio, the Jewish Isaacs family obtained possession of it, and the American branch RCA, was headed by the Russian Jew, David Sarnoff. On March 7, 1912, the English Postmaster, Sir Herbert Samuel, of the Jewish family which owned Shell Oil; and Charles Isaacs, president of Marconi, Ltd., split 100,000 shares of stock as a gift to his brother Rufus Isaacs, Minister of Finance, and Lloyd George, the Prime Minister. When the scandal broke in the press, not only did Lloyd George remain in office, but, with typical effrontery, the Rothschilds forced Lord Asquith to appoint Rufus Isaacs as Lord Chief Justice of England, with the title of Baron Reading of Erleigh. Rudyard Kipling commented on this appointment, "Three years ago you would have said that the Marconi scandals and the appointment of the present Lord Chief Justice were impossible."

Not only did the Jews control Lloyd George with bribes, but Zaharoff sent his ex-wife over to have an affair with the Prime Minister. An aide of Zaharoff was an Hungarian Jew named Trebitsch who had come to England, added Lincoln to his name, perhaps in memory of the murdered St. Hugh of Lincoln, and as Trebitsch-Lincoln, he became a Church of England clergyman and a member of Parliament, while working as an agent for Zaharoff. Trebitsch-Lincoln died during the 1930s as a monk in Tibet. His career typified the homeless, cosmopolitan Jew, able to go anywhere and to assume any role.

Zaharoff also died during the 1930s, as a multi-millionaire on the Riviera, while planning the Second World War. Before he died, he had had murdered the only person who knew all the secrets of his criminal past, a Jew named Nadel who had been a member of the French Surete, and who had come into possession of documentary evidence against Zaharoff. Nadel blackmailed Zaharoff for ten years, and was finally found dead in his suite on the Riviera with one million francs in cash in a bureau drawer, apparently the last installment that Zaharoff was willing to pay. The First World War had broken out on schedule, carefully planned by Zaharoff and the other Jewish munitions tycoons. Tremendous fortunes were made during the slaughter of the gentiles. A Jewish scientist in England named Chaim Weizmann invented a deadly poison gas during the war, and the Jews agreed that the British could use it if they would support the Zionist movement to seize Palestine. The British accepted the offer, which Lord Balfour made formal in a letter to Lord Rothschild on November 2, 1917. However, T. E. Lawrence, known as Lawrence of Arabia, had persuaded the Arabs to revolt against the Turks and support England. In exchange, the English had agreed to keep the Jews out of Palestine. Lawrence was so disgusted by this betrayal of the Arabs that he left public life forever. Ironically, this double-cross marked the beginning of the decline of England as a world power, and she soon sank to the role of a second-class nation.[2]

Chaim Weizmann became known as the Founder of Israel, and the Jewish nation owed its origin to the invention of a weapon so horrible that most countries have agreed never to use it. During the Second World War, Jewish scientists again

---

[2] "Desmond Stewart and other English writers have recently compiled evidence that T. E. Lawrence's death in a motorcycle 'accident' was really cold-blooded murder. The Jews understood that their plans to take over the Arab lands could never be carried out as long as Lawrence was alive to testify to the pledges of territorial integrity which the British made to the Arabs in exchange for their support during World War I. A line was stretched across the road down which Lawrence was accustomed to travel at high speed, and when his cycle struck it, he was thrown and killed instantly. The story was then circulated that he had swerved to avoid striking some children in the road, although there were no children in the area at the time of the 'accident'. Because of his intelligence connections, Winston Churchill was one of those privy to the fact that Lawrence had been murdered, and it was this information, demonstrating to Churchill the power of the Jews, plus his failing financial standing, which led him to reverse his previous contemptuous attitude toward the Jews and to seek their support. He travelled to New York to petition' Bernard Baruch for a loan, but the Jews, uncertain that he could be trusted, had him struck down by a car outside Baruch's apartment, nearly killing him. After some months in the hospital, Churchill returned to England. The Jews then advised him that since he had survived his 'accident', and was aware that any deviation from their line would result in a second, and fatal, one, they would pick up his outstanding notes. In return, he began to campaign for 'preparedness' and war against Germany, a stand which mystified those who cited his previous references to Hitler as 'the George Washington of Europe'. Hitler might be George Washington, but it was the Jews who held the mortgage on Chartwell, the Churchill estate."

cooperated to invent a deadlier weapon, the atomic bomb, which became known as the Jewish Hell-bomb.

During the war, the Jews sang their anthem,

"Onward Christian soldiers,
Marching as to war;
We will make the uniforms,
As we did before."

Although the Jews obtained most of the contracts for supplying the struggling gentile armies, the real money was made by the Rothschilds, in interest on the enormous debts piled up by all of the warring nations. The Jews also took advantage of the war to stage a successful revolution in Russia. At the conclusion of the war, Jews from all over the world flocked to Paris for the Peace Conference, which could well have been conducted in Yiddish, as every nation was represented by a Jewish delegation. Political observers were amazed at the reckless manner in which the Jews carved up Europe so as to make a second world war inevitable. They created a new state, Czechoslovakia, and presented it to their friend Masaryk, as a reward for having defended them against punishment for crimes of ritual murder. They demanded huge sums in reparations from the Germans, knowing that this would goad the Germans into fighting again.

During this Peace Conference, one of the great statesmen of France, Senator Gaudin de Villain, made a speech on May 13, 1919, in the French Senate, in which he denounced the subversive acts of the Jews. Among many other points, he said,

"The Russian Revolution and the Great War of 1914-1918 are only phases of the supreme mobilization of the cosmopolitan powers of money, and this supreme crusade of Gold against the Cross is nothing more nor less than the furious aspiration of the Jew for domination of our world. It is the High Jew Bank which has fomented in Russia the revolution prepared by the Kerenskys and finally perpetrated by the Lenins, Trotskys, and Zinovievs, as was yesterday the Communist coup d'état in Hungary, for Bolshevism is nothing but a Talmudic upheaval."

Chapter 8

Jews and Communism

With their usual talent for confusing the issues, the Jews have created a number of smokescreens to hide their latest gift to the world, the philosophy of Communism. What is Communism? In some millions of words written on this subject in thousands of books published by the Jews, you will not find the one sentence which will explain Communism - Communism is the modern form of the Jewish collective state.

What are the principles of Communism? First of all, Communism is international in scope. It denies the principles of nationalism. Second, Communism denies Jesus Christ and His love for the individual. It also denies the principle of salvation of the soul, which is the basis of all Christian belief. Third, Communism denies to the individual all human rights, such as private property, a voice in the government, or the right to question the authority of the collective state.

These, then, are the fundamental principles of Communism. Oddly enough, these are also the fundamental principles of the Jews. Internationalism, hatred of Jesus Christ, hatred of the individual, the denial of human rights, the dictatorship of the collective state, these are equally basic to both Jewish political movements and Communist political movements. One should not be surprised, then, to find that a Jew, Karl Marx, is the father of the philosophy of Communism.

We have already discussed the iron discipline under which the individual Jew lives, the dictatorship exercise by the Elders of Zion over every aspect of Jewish life. This Jewish dictatorship, extended over the gentiles, is then called Communism.

But, one may ask, why do the Jews attack the principle of private property when the Jews already own 80% of the private property in the Western nations? First of all, by the term private property the Jew means property which is still owned by the gentiles. Under Talmudic law, gentiles are beasts who cannot be allowed to own anything, neither homes, nor land, nor personal property. Therefore in carrying out the seizure of private property from the gentiles, the Jews are simply following a basic principle of their religion.

When Communists take over a country, the first thing they do is to murder all of the gentile leaders - the professors, doctors, government officials, and any other gentiles who might lead opposition against them. This follows the basic Jewish command,

"The best of the gentiles kill!"

Since the Jewish people do not believe in individual rights, the concept of private property is alien to them. Every Jew considers the wealth of other Jews as part of the Israeli national wealth. Although individual Jews may have the use of their money during their lifetimes, they must contribute heavily to Jewish institutions, finance Jewish revolutionary movements, bribe officials to cover up Jewish ritual murders, and spend most of their income on purely Jewish matters. After their death, their money must go to Jews, and under no circumstances is it allowed to pass into gentile bands. Therefore, the Jews set up Zionist foundations, avoiding all taxes on their money, despite the punitive Marxist taxation laws which they enact and enforce on the gentiles.

But how can Jewish bankers be Communists, asks the earnest citizen? Everyone knows that Communists attack bankers, and confiscate their wealth. Nevertheless, tons of documents prove that all funds for the growth of Communism throughout the world have come from Jewish bankers. The chief source has been the Jewish-controlled Bank of England, and the Bank of France. These are departments of what Senator de Villain called "the High Jew Bank", which is administered by the Rothschild family. Thus we find that a supposedly private Jewish fortune is used principally in Jewish activities and in financing the international Jewish Communist revolutionary movement.

Also, despite the fact that the Jews own or control most of the property in Christian nations, it is the peculiar characteristic of the Jew parasite that he must dominate every action and detail in the life of the gentile host. Without this complete dictatorship over the gentile, without the fury and the schizophrenia of the Jew which makes it necessary, modern life would lose much of its direction, for the Jew can never feel wholly secure. A Rothschild with his billions has the same nightmare as the little Jewish tailor down the street, the fear that some day, he may be driven off of the gentile host, that he may be denied his parasitic existence. Therefore, he has to attain a life and death power over the gentile host.

Most gentiles make the error of supposing that the Jew is interested only in money. This is a dangerous oversimplification. If the Jew were only interested in money, he would no longer be a problem, for he already has our money. The Jew is interested in money primarily as a weapon, an instrument of power over the gentile host. With money, the Jew spends hundreds of thousands of dollars to cover up brutal ritual murders of innocent Christian children; he bribes gentile officials, bankrupts those gentiles who dare to oppose him, buys evidence and witnesses to send gentiles to prison or to insane asylums on trumped-up charges.

Communism is merely the next step in the Jewish parasite's furious desire to subdue and control the gentile host. First comes the financial power, then the government dictatorship of Communism. Under Communism, the Jew does not have to bribe gentile officials. He merely signs their order of execution. Weak gentiles are sent to concentration camps; strong ones, who might become leaders, and who might present a threat to the rabbinical theocracy which rules the state, are tortured and murdered. After a few years of Jewish Communist rule, there are no gentile leaders left, and the gentile survivors sink into a state of hopeless apathy, for the tension which brought the Communist state into being, the need for the Jewish parasite to control the gentile host, no longer exists. Jews and gentiles alike slip into a life of shabby hopelessness. What sort of life is this? It is the life of the ghetto. A Communist state is merely a ghetto of a nation.

All visitors from the West who enter a Communist country remark immediately on the drabness of people and cities alike. Everything is shabby and rundown. The spark of life has been extinguished. The gentiles exist in a zombie half-world of fear and poverty, while fat Jews travel from one vacation resort to another, accompanied by blond mistresses in sable coats. Despite their obvious pleasures, the Jew also finds Communism a boring existence. Why is this? Every stroke of invention, every bit of creative life, bas come from the gentile, because the earthbound Jews, living collectively and hating the individual, lack any imaginative or creative instinct. They have always had to get this from the gentiles. Now it is gone, for under Communism, the gentiles have no money or leisure to develop new inventions or works of art.

Consequently, the Jew loses his reason for existence. The driving purpose of Jewish life for five thousand years has been to subdue or control the gentile host. Once this has been achieved, the Jew has nothing left to live for. He has destroyed the spark of life in the gentile host, and he is horrified to discover that he has, by so doing extinguished the spark of life in himself, for his own life was wholly dependent on the life of the host.

In a recent book, *Floodtide in Europe*, the eminent journalist, Don Cook, states that all newspapermen who go to Communist countries speak of "the smell of Communism". He says, "Worst of all to me was the peculiar and unmistakable *smell* of Russia and the Communist world which pervaded Leipzig."

Thirty years ago, Leipzig was a spotless German city. Under Communism, it soon reverted to the grime of a medieval Jewish ghetto. Cook continues,

> "Everyone who has ever set foot the Soviet Union knows that smell -a stale, heavy, unwashed smell." Cook calls it "a prison smell of hopelessness and despair and indifference." He also describes it as a smell "of old lavatories, carbolic soap, unwashed bodies... a smell that closes in as soon as you enter a building, a smell that nobody can do anything about, a smell that goes with the system."

What is this smell that goes with the Communist system? It is the rank and putrid air of the Warsaw ghetto in the Middle Ages, created by the Jews as they sat, unwashed for years, in tiny rooms pouring over the Talmud and wondering when they would be able to gain power over the gentiles. Baths or a change of linen were unknown to them. One would have had to work for these things, and this was unthinkable to a Jew. Their religion forbade them to work for a "gentile beast", and in any case, the only skill they had was black magic, and this usually failed to come off.

This stale, unwashed smell of Communist hopelessness is not unknown in the United States. We find it on Skid Row, where Jewish hotelkeepers rack up the unwashed bodies of bums at 25 cents a head for the night in stinking cubicles. These are the gentiles who have lost their fortunes to Jewish entrepreneurs and who now drink themselves into a state of hopeless inertia; and we also find this smell in the insane asylums where the Jewish psychiatrists have sentenced so many gentile critics of the Jews to be imprisoned for the rest of their lives, without a trial and without having committed a crime, except for the unpardonable crime of having opposed the Jews. The poet Ezra Pound, who criticized the Jews for plunging the world into the horrors of a second world war, spent thirteen years in the Hellhole of St. Elizabeth's, a Federal mental institution in Washington, D.C. for political prisoners. Pound won a number of prizes for his writings while the Jews had him locked up as a madman. Many visitors to the ward, including this writer, commented that the stench of the place was exactly like that of the cities in Europe which had fallen to the Jewish Communists.

Not only does Communism bear the awful smell of human despair, but it also exhibits all of the inhumane aspects of the Jew. The French writer, Simone de Beauvoir, in her recent book, *The Force of Circumstance*, stated that she had visited Brasilia, a city in Brazil which had been designed by an architect named Oscar Niemeyer, whom she describes as a "Communist Jew". She said of the architecture there, page 533, "This inhumanity is the first thing that strikes one." She also quotes Lacerda's comment on Brasilia, "It is an architectural exhibition-life size". de Beauvoir fails to add that the American taxpayer put up five hundred million dollars to build this dream city of the Jews in the midst of a Brazilian jungle.

Inhumanity and bloodthirstiness - these are the hallmarks of Jewish Communism. To incite the French revolution, Jewish bankers paid agitators to work up the crowds in the streets, while the French king was appalled, unable to understand what was happening. The well-known scholar, Stanton Coblentz, on page 126 of his book, *"Ten Crises of Civilization"*, mentions "the secret directing force which seems to have been at work" in the French Revolution. Either he feared to mention that this force was the Jews, or it was deleted from his manuscript by a Jewish editor. Many other scholars have named the Jews as the secret force behind the French Revolution.

After they had incited the crowds to murder the gentile leaders, the Jews dragged thousands of nuns and priests out of the churches, and chopped them to bits with axes and hatchets, or they murdered them before the altar of Christ, so that the Christian cathedrals became hell-changed into traditional Jewish synagogues reeking with gentile blood and echoing with the screams of dying women and children. Hundreds of helpless Christian men and women were stripped naked, tied together in couples, and thrown into the rivers to drown, while Jews stood on the banks and jeered at the victims of these "Revolutionary weddings". The French Revolution had been hailed as the greatest triumph of the Jewish Communists. Why, then, did the gentile Napoleon take over? Why could not the Jews set up a Communist dictatorship in France?

The Jews have never been able to retain political power over a North European people, whose intelligence and courage had made them the masters of the world. The Jews could win with their cunning, but cunning could not administer a nation nor forge the chains of slavery about the North Europeans. As a result, throughout the nineteenth century, Karl Marx and other Jewish Communists were able to incite revolutions, but they could not win the power. It was in Russia that the Jews finally found their victim, and even then they could not have won if the Russian leaders had not been distracted by the tasks of war. Baron says, *"Great Ages and Ideas of the Jewish People,"* page 329,

"During the Revolution (of 1848), Jewish leadership came to the fore in a most dramatic fashion. In Vienna, where the Metternich system was suddenly overthrown, two young Jewish physicians, Adolf Fischof and Joseph Goldmark, became the chief architects of the revolutionary movement. As head of the Comite on Security, Fischof appeared as the uncrowned emperor of Austria... In Italy, too, the Revolution was often led by Jews. The head of the new Venetian Republic was a converted Jew, Daniel Manin, but his cabinet included two loyal Jews."

Loyal to whom, one must ask. To the people of Venice? Baron does not say, but obviously he means, loyal to international Jewry. It was merely another Jewish revolution. A Jew was "the uncrowned emperor of Austria", as the result of a Jewish revolt, but he could not hold the power. The gentile governments had to be weakened another seventy-five years before the Jews could keep control.

Russia gave the Jews their opportunity. The Slavic people were much like the Jews, in that they had little cultural life. Archaeologists find no artifacts of civilization in Russia. Like Palestine, the home of the Jews, the soil yields only fragments of clay pots and other evidences of a Stone-Age culture. Russia too was the home of nomadic bandits until recent times. Two Greek monks travelled to Russia and set up the Cyrillic alphabet, named after one of them. In 908 A.D., the Slavs asked the Germans to come in and rule them, for they stated that they were incapable of ruling themselves. The Germans founded an aristocracy, known as White Russians, who administered the country for one thousand years, until the Jews took it over in 1917. The Slavic peasants had never made any trouble, but in less than a century, the Jews achieved their revolution. As Baron states, page 332, *Great Ages and Ideas of the Jewish People*,

"The realization increasingly dawned upon the growing Jewish intelligentsia that the Jewish question could not be solved without the total overthrow of Russia's established order."

What an interesting decision! It was hardly a new one. In Fact, the Jews have come to this inevitable conclusion in every gentile country in which they have established a community of parasites. They must devote themselves to the overthrow of the established order. This is a typical *"Great Idea of the Jewish People"*. It is the only idea they have ever had.

On page 416, Baron tells us that "The rise to power of Jewish banking firms led some socialist writers to join in the anti-semitic outcry against so-called Jewish financial domination."

For a hundred years, this posed an embarrassing dilemma for the Jewish Communists. On the one band, they had to attack all gentile landowners, factory operators and bankers as "enemies of the people". On the other band, they had somehow to exempt Jewish landowners, factory owners and bankers from these attacks. They also walked a constant tightrope to conceal the fact that all Communist funds came from Jewish bankers. In the entire Communist literature, one finds not a single criticism of the Rothschilds, but many pages of fulmination against gentile bankers such as J.P. Morgan.

"The Jewish problem" in Russia, of course, was the exploitation of the peasants by the Jews, and the measures taken by the White Russian leaders to protect the peasants from further exploitation. All scholars agree that the "pogroms" or attacks on the Jews by the peasants came about because the Jews cornered the grain markets and ruthlessly exploited the peasants. The Jews became so rich that many of them had no occupation of any kind. The famous Jewish writer J.L. Peretz wrote of the Jews of Odessa during this period, "Alas, we have become a nation of luftmenschen." This is Yiddish for "people who live without visible means of support".

During the nineteenth century, thousands of Jewish agitators worked to promote Communist revolutions. With the publication of Karl Marx's Communist Manifesto in 1848, the Jews split into two groups. The Bolshevist Marxists followed the hard line that all gentile landowners must be exterminated. The Socialist Marxists argued that conquest of the gentiles should be done gradually by acquiring control of all government and educational facilities, leaving the gentiles helpless to govern themselves. Edward Bernstein led the "soft" line. He is described as "one of the leaders of Marxian ideology, but as an exile in England he had become a Fabian gradualist". Bernstein is the father of the present socialist Labor government in England. Lenin was the leader of the "hard line" group, and he carried on a propaganda war against the "Bernsteinians".

In 1905, the Leninists made their first attempt to seize power in Russia. They won, but, being theoreticians, they had no idea of how to administer the government. The wild-eyed Jewish intellectuals stood on the street haranguing the crowds for days after their victory, until the Czarist officials went back into their offices and began issuing orders. The revolution was over.

In 1917, the Leninists had learned their lesson. In March, a group of "Bernsteinians", led by the Jew Kerensky, set up a liberal socialist government of Jews, but they did not murder anyone. Trotsky, as Lev Bronstein liked to call himself, and Lenin led a Bolshevik seizure of power in October of that year. Copying the example of the French Revolution, Trotsky initiated a Reign of Terror. During the next three years, he murdered eighty-eight per cent of the White Russians. Only two gentile officials were known out of 312 leading

Communists in Russia. All of the others were Jews. Their first official act was to pass a law that anti-Semitism, or criticism of the Jews, was the worst crime one could commit in Communist Russia. It was perishable by death, and might be as insignificant as telling an anti-Jewish joke. Even the possession of books about the Jews, such as the *Protocols of the Learned Elders of Zion*, was a crime punishable by death. The seizure of power by the Jewish Communists was characterized by the slaughters of the gentiles such as occurred during Esther's heyday in Persia, the French Revolution, and other scenes of horror. Thousands of brutal Jewish Mordecais and Esthers seized White Russians, including priests and nuns, and tortured them in an unspeakable manner before delivering them to the firing squads. Between 1917 and 1940, the Jews murdered twenty million Christians in Russia.

A Jewish brute herded the Czar of Russia, his wife and children, into a cellar and shot them down in cold blood. It was the most heinous political assassination in European history, yet the Czar's first cousin, King George V of England, made no effort to save his relatives. Why was this? Did he have no feelings?

Of course he had feelings. He also had a Privy Council who refused to let him make an appeal to the Bolsheviks to spare the Czar. This Privy Council in 1919 was composed only of Jews. It was headed by Lord Rothschild and consisted of Sir Edwin Montagu, Sir Edgar Speyer, a Jewish banker born in Frankfurt, Germany, and inexplicably raised to the highest council in England, Sir Matthew Nathan, Sir Alfred Moritz Mond, head of Imperial Chemicals Ltd., Sir Harry Samuel, owner of Shell Oil, Sir Ernest Cassel, and Earl Reading, Rufus Isaacs. The King's fortune was entirely in the hands of these Jewish bankers. He dared not open his mouth, even to save his blood relatives. A few years later, the British Crown welcomed Soviet envoys to London. After all,

England had provided a home for Karl Marx while he formulated his theories of Communism, working them out while sitting at a desk in the British Museum, and he is buried in England.

It was also a crime punishable by death in Communist Russia to have been a Czarist official. For years, Russian officials had warned the Czar that Jews were attempting to overthrow the government. It was imperative that these officials be killed before they could get away to warn the rest of Europe against the Jews. In 1903, Minister Wenzel von Plehve had made a written report to the Czar, drawing upon police files, that ninety per cent of all Communist revolutionaries in Russia were known Jews. The Czar tried to appease the Jews by granting them special privileges, but this was like throwing gasoline onto a fire. They sowed their gratitude by murdering him and his family. The officials who had warned him died before the firing squads. Lenin wrote that they had to park rows of trucks in Moscow at night, with the engines running full blast, to drown out the continuous roar of the guns of the firing squads.

The Russian ruling class, the White Russians of German descent, were wiped out, with the exception of a few who escaped to the West. It was the French Revolution over again. The Jews forced the populations of entire towns to march through inspection lines. If the men had no callouses on their hands, they were not workingmen, and they were shot. If the women spoke good grammar, they were shot. In this manner, the gentile intelligentsia was exterminated, leaving a horde of illiterate peasants ruled by a minority of Jewish bandits and assassins. The Jews had their slave population, as Nietzsche had written of them in 1871, commenting upon the Jewish culture set up by the Elders of Zion in the ancient city of Alexandria, which became known as the Alexandrian or Utopianist movement:

"But let us note that the Alexandrian culture requires slavery in order to maintain its existence."

The Jews realized this too late when they drove the Arabs out of Israel, and had no gentile slaves to do their work. Now they are trying to entice them to return.

With the extermination of the White Russians, within a year, the country was on the brink of collapse. There were no schools - the Jews had murdered the teachers. There was no medical care - the Jews had murdered the doctors. There were no roads, and the factories were not operating - the Jews had murdered the engineers. There were no merchants, there were only Jewish black marketers. Communist Russia was saved only by a massive inpouring of money from the Western democracies, just as it was saved during the Second World War by one hundred billions of dollars of military supplies paid for by the American taxpayer. As in every Communist nation, famine soon threatened to wipe out the people. The Jews begged for food from the free nations, while at the same time maintaining a vast army of spies and assassins in these same countries. The Chief of MI-5, the British Intelligence Service, recently stated that his files contained the names of 4326 persons definitely known to have been murdered in the United States and Europe by Communist assassins since 1920. This international network of Jewish assassins was exposed by the murder of a defector Walter Krivitsky, in Washington D.C. in 1938. Flora Lewis tells the story in the *Washington Post*, Feb. 13, 1966:

A Polish Jew named Schmelka Ginsberg, born in 1899 and only 18 years old at the time of the Bolshevik Revolution, distinguished himself as an executioner of gentiles. Squads in his command shot 2341 people, and he himself usually delivered the coup de grace with a pistol bullet in the head. He changed his name to Walter Krivitsky, and by 1935, he was Chief of Soviet Military Intelligence for all Western

Europe, with headquarters in Paris. After twenty years of a career as a professional assassin, his nerves began to crack and Moscow ordered him to murder a fellow Jew, a Communist assassin named Ignatz Reiss. The Fourth Bureau had discovered that Reiss had banked large sums of money in Switzerland and intended to defect to the West. This had become a common practice of Jewish Communist spies, and orders had gone out that anyone else who attempted it must be killed at once.

Krivitsky-Ginsberg tried to stall the operation, and the OGPU, the secret police in Moscow, which was at that time completely in Jewish hands, sent an agent named Israel Spigelglass to carry out the murder. Reiss was shot and his body dumped on the road in Switzerland on September 4, 1937, in typical gangland style. Krivitsky knew that he was next on the list, because he had tried to shield Reiss. The Communist Party, like the Mafia, always executes a member who refuses to carry out a murder. Krivitsky hurried to the office of the Jewish Premier of France, Leon Blum, who promised to protect him. Another Jew, named Paul Wohl, smuggled Krivitsky out of France to the United States. Another Jew, Isaac Don Levine, got Krivitsky a contract to write nine articles for the *Saturday Evening Post* for five thousand dollars each. Other Jews who aided Krivitsky were Boris Shub and Adolf Berle. Krivitsky was found shot in his Washington hotel room a short time later. Exit Schmelka Ginsberg, a typical Jewish assassin who had lived and died by lex talionis, the Jewish law of the jungle.

During the 1920s, Russia staggered along under the dictatorship of lunatic Jewish commissars, until it was obvious that something must be done. Josef Stalin, who had been chosen by the Jews to be Commissar of Minorities and to prosecute any gentiles who opposed the Jews, was made Chairman of the Central Committee of the Communist Party. His first task was to get rid of the wild-eyed Jewish revolutionaries led by Trotsky. While Soviet Russia was falling apart, the Trotskyites still wanted to use all of the Soviet funds to promote revolution in other countries, despite the fact that the Jewish Communist bid for power had been defeated in every country in Europe. A madman named Bela Cohen had been released from a Hungarian insane asylum to head a short-lived Jewish Communist reign in Hungary; Rosa Luxemburg and another crowd of Jewish hysterics had promoted a brief Communist government in Germany; Mussolini had shoved the Communists aside in Italy, and although he had Jewish intellectuals in his camp, his regime was a practical gentile operation.

At a meeting of the Party, Stalin asked that Trotsky and his band of lunatic Jews be expelled. The delegates agreed and Trotsky was asked to leave Russia. Stalin himself had murdered his second wife during a drunken brawl and was now married to Esther Kaganovich, sister of the Jewish Commissar of Heavy Industries. He was safely in the bands of the Jews, and he married his daughter to another Kaganovich. Jews have never worried about inbreeding. Stalin's right-hand man was Molotov, whose wife was Rebecca Karp, sister of the Jewish realtor Sammy Karp, in Connecticut. Karp's influence there promoted the first Jewish Governor of Connecticut, "Abie the Rib" Ribicoff.

Thus the Stalin government was a group of more conservative Jews who replaced the hysterical Trotskyite Jews. Since 1917, only one man has survived all Party purges. He is Ilya Ehrenberg, a Jew who has directed the policies of the Soviet government from behind the scenes for half a century. Newsweek recently called him "the richest man in Soviet Russia". During the Second World War, he and another Jew named Litvinov-Wallach actually directed the military operations of the United States! Against General MacArthur's wishes, they forced us to concentrate our military strength in Europe, in order to aid the Jews, while

American soldiers in the Pacific theatre of war were slaughtered by the thousands, because they could not get ammunition and air cover. Ehrenberg is the leader of a group of Jewish millionaires, the new Russian aristocracy, who have villas on the Black Sea, mistresses in all of the satellite countries, and who cannot be removed from office because they hold no official position.

Another revolt of Jew against Jew occurred during Khrushchev's regime. The Jewish head of secret police, Beria conspired with Kaganovich and Molotov to remove Khrushchev's, but Khrushchev's group of Jews murdered Beria and retained power. Soviet Russia continued to be the promised land of the Jews. The *New York Times* reported on July 8, 1965, that a Jew named Shakerman had led a band of Jews who forced inmates of a mental institution to work at hard labor manufacturing knitted goods, which the Jews sold on the black market for four million rubles. The Jews were sentenced to death "in absentia", as they had miraculously escaped before the trial and had become refugees to the United States. Shakerman is now operating a knitted goods factory in Union City, New Jersey.

The Soviet Jews occasionally have trouble controlling their intellectuals, even though they imprison them whenever they dare to disagree with the Talmudic concept of Communism. The columnist Joseph Newman wrote in the *Roanoke Times*, Sept. 6, 1965, commenting upon the plight of Soviet writer Valeriy Tarsis, who had been put into a mental institution, as per the law of Purim, because he criticized Jewish Communism. Newman quoted Tarsis as follows:

> "All great thinkers have been aristocrats of the spirit, and not one of them, from Heraclitus to Nietzsche, could have fathered the wretched doctrine of that bearded Jewish philistine Marx - nor does anyone follow him except our blockheaded Talmudists and the demagogues who make

up our ruling junta... But I firmly believe that man will triumph and not the ape."

Thus Tarsis equates the Talmudic Communist state with the ape, a valid observation, since it is a Stone Age culture. However, it is dangerous to have schizophrenic Jews controlling a great modern power with its store of deadly weapons. We narrowly escaped a Third World War in October, 1956, when the Rothschilds plotted to take back their Suez Canal, which had been seized by President Nasser of Egypt after the British had broken thirty-three treaties concerning Egypt and the Canal. The plot was to have English paratroopers descend upon Egypt while French jets bombed and strafed the Egyptian defenses, and Israeli troops moved in for a mopping up operation. The Jews saw nothing wrong in an unprovoked attack upon another country, and their power was demonstrated by the fact that they could order the British Army and the French Air Force to support the Israeli Army. At the same time, the Soviet Union decided to take advantage of this distraction to wipe out Hungarian patriots who had temporarily overthrown the Jewish Communist government there. The Hungarians were massacred while Jewish advisors to Eisenhower ordered him not to send them any aid, but the Israelis were forced to withdraw from Egypt. Nevertheless, for several days, the world was on the brink of atomic war, a situation which had been precipitated by the State of Israel.

A key figure in this plot was Marcel Bloch, a Jew who survived the detention camp of Auschwitz and who suddenly became one of the richest men in France. He owned the influential newspaper *Jours de France*, and he manufactured the Mystere jet fighter. It was these fighters which had attacked Egypt. Another figure in this plot was the former Premier Mendes France, a radical Jew who "successfully negotiated an end to the war in Indochina," according to journalist Don Cook. Mendes France's solution was to surrender to the

Communists and to give up French investments in Indochina worth billions of dollars. Mendes France led the French delegation to Bretton Woods, where the Jewish bankers set up a World Bank and International Monetary fund in 1944, dividing up the money of the gentiles at the very time that the gentiles were saving them from the Germans. Although murder is one of the accepted Jewish techniques, blackmail and kidnapping are also widely practiced. Castro kidnapped Americans in order to promote his Communist revolution in Cuba. In This Week, October 16, 1965, a feature story described how a Jew named Henry Jacober, who was high in the ranks of the Soviet Secret Police, obtained dollars to finance Soviet activities in Europe. He allowed American Jews to ransom their relatives out of Soviet concentration camps, where they had been sentenced for various crimes, for $3000 each. Seventy thousand Russian Jews were purchased from Soviet Russia and brought to the United States, which gave the Soviet espionage forces $210,000,000 in operating funds. The West German government disclosed that it had purchased 25,000 German Jews from East Germany for $25,000,000 to bolster the economy of that Communist satellite.

The unthinking citizen might say, if Soviet Russia is a paradise for the Jews, how is it that some of them are being put into concentration camps, and others shot? Few gentiles have any conception of the vicious inter-tribal warfare which is waged constantly among the Stone Age Jews. They do not know how often Jewish leaders conspire to ruin or murder each other, in their unending struggle for power. The chaos of Jewish community organizations in the United States gives some indication of the viciousness of these inter-Jewish conflicts. However, one should not mistake the murder of one Jew by another as an outbreak of "anti-Semitism".

The power of Jews in other countries to protect the Jewish Communist government in Soviet Russia was demonstrated during World War II. Hitler believed that the Western democracies, who ostensibly were free-enterprise economies, would be glad to see him destroy the Russian experiment in Communism. Apparently he did not believe his own statements that the Western democracies were controlled by Jews. This situation dated back a hundred years, to the problems which had been created when the Jews burst out of their ghettos after the Congress of Vienna in 1815, and swarmed like a plague of locusts over Europe. Baron says, page 400 *"Great Ages and Ideas of the Jewish People,"*

> "Even in Jewish circles immigrants were not altogether welcome. A Circular Letter issued in 1849 by the Anglo-Jewish leaders asked the German Jews to restrict their immigration to England. Representatives of American Jews at the Paris Conference in 1878 publicly sounded a warning against indiscriminate Jewish migrations."

Jews who had become established in one country frequently found their wellbeing threatened by a horde of later Jewish immigrants, dirty, uncouth, with fleas in their beards and lice in their hair. It was this problem which gave rise to the Nazi Party in Germany. The German Jews, prosperous and accepted by the German people, were horrified by a flood of lower-class Galician Jews into Germany after the First World War. *The national Jewish Post*, official organ of the German Jewish community, expressed indignation in an article in June, 1923:

> "These people are quite right from their own point of view when they try to shake the dust of the pogrom countries from their shoes and flee to the milder West. The locusts are also right from their own point of view when they descend in swans upon our fields. But the man who is defending his own land, which gives him his own bread and his well-being, is also in the right. And who can deny that they come in swarms? They laugh at rents, they laugh

at officials. Above all, they laugh at the wishes of the tenants. They have only one purpose in view, and they use every opportunity to further it. But they are far from making houses the sole object of their rapacity. Whatever money can buy is, in their eyes, a proper subject for greed. Nobody knows how many Jews from Eastern Europe there are in Germany.

We only know that all statistics lie, public and private equally. The workers relief committees of the Jews lie. The people of whom we speak do not go to these committees. Out of Tarnopol and surrounding districts they have conquered Vienna and are now conquering Berlin. When they have become masters of Berlin they will stretch out their strategic lines and conquer Paris. The vacuum created by the fall in the rate of exchange sucks them in."

The panic of the German Jews at the invasion of the aggressive, lisping Galician Jews who were wrecking the German economy soon found a political expression. Baron Oppenheim, a conservative German Jew, and Max Warburg, a Jewish banker whose brother Paul was head of the Federal Reserve System of the United States, found an anti-Jewish politician named Adolf Hitler and financed his movement in its early years. The initial payment was one million marks. With this money, Hitler formed a uniformed body of storm troopers and attempted a coup d'état in 1923. When this failed, the Jewish bankers continued to support him. As a result, Max Warburg lived quietly in Germany until 1939, during the period of Nazi "pogroms", and when he saw war approaching, he decided to emigrate to the United States. The journalist George Sokolsky states that Max Warburg was allowed to leave Germany with his entire fortune, despite the stringent currency regulations.

After 1928, most of Hitler's financing came from gentile German businessmen who feared that they would lose their factories to the Communists, but the fact remains that the initial impetus for the Nazi movement, as documented by many scholars, was Jewish money. This is not so fantastic as the uninformed reader might believe. A sizeable portion of the scattered anti-Jewish groups in the United States are financed by grants of money from the Anti-Defamation League of B'nai B'rith, which in turn raises the money from American Jews who fear the specter of anti-Semitism. The ADL keeps them constantly aware of this specter by publicizing the anti-Jewish groups out of all proportion to their importance. Most Americans have no knowledge of the Jewish problem, and the few who do have no money to contribute to these groups, or they fear to do so because they would lose their jobs or businesses. Consequently, the ADL, as exposed in the newspaper *The Independent*, finances its own anti-Jewish movement. It spends four hundred thousand dollars a year for this purpose, but it annually collects from the Jewish people five million dollars! This is not a bad annual return. This enables the ADL to maintain a tight control over the Jewish community, and over the anti-Jewish groups as well. They know at any time the exact extent of anti-Jewish feeling in the United States. This practice accords to the traditional Jewish pattern of contributing money to all political parties and movements, a basic technique of the Jewish parasite for gauging the temper of the gentile host, and for exercising control over its every activity.

Another Jewish technique, pluralism, was overcome by Hitler, as Mann noted in his book, *Diagnosis of Our Time*, Oxford Univ. Press, 1944, page 104,

> "There are two main stages in Hitler's group strategy: breaking down the traditional groups of civilized society and a rapid re-building on the basis of an entirely new pattern."

Pluralism is the technique of the Jew for maintaining power over the gentiles, by setting up a host of groups in the gentile society, each of which had almost equal power, and contend against each other, dividing the gentile leaders' support among a dozen or so groups, while the closely knit and cohesive Jewish group finds it easy to wield power. Thus, in the United States, a typical Jewish democracy, we have, first of all, the executive, legislative, and judicial branches of the government all contending against each other for power, while many other large groups, such as the trade unions, the underworld, the religious groups, the education, the journalists, the entertainment world, and many others, exercise their individual influence. Also, Jews tend to make their desires known and attended to in each of these groups, while the basic Jewish direction of the country goes unchallenged.

Jewish writers are constantly sounding the praises of our "pluralistic democracy", but the gentiles have no idea what this means. The Jews know very well what it means, a host of groups dividing power among themselves while in the background the Jew retains all the power that he needs to further his own interests. They thrive upon the ignorance of the gentiles, and the growing Jewish influence in our universities is making a mockery of education. The colleges are turning into boy-meets-girl clubs which offer opportunities for dances, games and sex, while all intelligent activity is shoved aside. This fulfills the basic Jewish feeling about the gentile, as expressed in the Talmud, that gentiles are stupid beasts who cannot be educated anyway. The graduate schools are filled with Jews who toil over their rabbinical dissertations; in less than a quarter of a century, American universities have been lowered to the level of a medieval ghetto, and the proportion of Jewish professors and students increases each year. "Philosophy" classes consist solely of wild harangues against the Nazis and recruiting students to plant trees in Israel; assignments are made to study Spinoza instead of Nietzsche; Sassoon instead of Pound; Schwartz instead of Eliot.

To return to Hitler; Dr. Hermann Eich, a prominent German editor, stated in a recent book that Germans were less anti-Jewish than any other people in Europe, which was true. The Storm Troopers had to carry out their raids on German shops at night, lest the Germans attack them in defense of the Jews. When bombers began to kill women and children, the mood changed. Hitler ordered all Jews to be interned in camps for the duration of the war, because many Jews had been caught posting signal lights to guide the bombers in the destruction of German cities and residential areas. The Elders of Zion in each Jewish community cooperated with the Germans in rounding up the Jews. Hannah Arendt, the eminent Jewish scholar, stated that only in Denmark did the Jewish community escape, because Denmark had no group of Jewish elders who could hand them over to the Germans. Dr. Rudolf Kastner, head of the Zionist Organization in Budapest, turned over the Roumanian Jews to the Nazis in exchange for their allowing 1683 of his friends and relatives in the Jewish community to emigrate to Switzerland with all of their fortunes. Needless to say, all of the important Jewish bankers in Europe survived the war. Kastner was later murdered in Israel by a Jew whose family had been sent to a concentration camp because of him.

In these camps, the Jews soon began to die of typhoid, because of their refusal to maintain clean living conditions among themselves. The Germans were fighting a two-front war, and had no personnel to serve the Jews. The camp officials were soon faced with disposing of hundreds of corpses of diseased Jews. There was only one solution - to burn them - and crude ovens were used for this purpose. After the war, Jewish propagandists regaled the world with fantastic tales of millions of Jews having been burnt to death in two tiny ovens which could only dispose of six bodies a day. Virginius Dabney, editor of the *Richmond Times* Dispatch, wrote in the Saturday Review, March 9, 1963, of a visit to Dachau,

> "The gas chamber, surprisingly enough, never got into operation, since it was constructed late and successfully sabotaged by the inmates."

Dabney also states that inmates were "allowed to die of typhus and other diseases." At Auschwitz, a "reconstruction" after the war showed gas chambers and ovens which were built by German slave labor in 1946, as part of the Jewish campaign to tell the world about the missing "six million". There was a sound economic reason behind this story of six million Jews supposedly killed by the Nazis out of Germany's prewar Jewish population of 300,000. The State of Israel, which had not been in existence at the time of the supposed massacres, levied "reparations" against the German people of $800,000,000 a year for ten years, in payment for these "killings". The majority of the dead Jews were Polish Jews who had been killed by Stalin to prevent their betraying his defenses to the oncoming Nazi armies in 1941, but Israel did not ask any reparations from Russia. With the German reparations, the Jews in Israel were able to live comfortably without working, as they lounged in the homes seized from the hardworking Arabs who had built them."

Germany, the only nation which has ever sent military forces against the Communist government of Soviet Russia, was resoundingly defeated, thanks to the frenetic activity of American Jews, who, urged on by Ehrenberg in Moscow, and personally led by Wallach-Litvinov, got the United States into the war to save Jewish Communism from the German attack. Thousands of Germans living in America, who were loyal to the United States, were herded into concentration camps and kept there until long after the war was over, while four billion dollars worth of their property was seized by the Alien Property Custodian's office and given to the Jews.

After the war, the United States appointed a High Commissioner of Germany, one John McCloy, who had worked all his life as a lawyer for the firm of Cravath and Henderson, the firm which represented the Jewish bankers, Kuhn, Loeb and Co. The Assistant High Commissioner, and real power, was Benjamin Buttenweiser, a partner of Kuhn, Loeb, whose wife Helen was the lawyer representing Alger Hiss during his trial. General Lucius Clay commanded the American Occupation Army, and later accepted a lucrative position with the Lehman Corporation, a Jewish banking firm. Obviously he had done nothing to offend the Jews while serving in Germany. German businessmen found that they were compelled to hire a Jewish lobbyist, General Julius Klein, commander of the Jewish War Veterans, or the Occupation Government would refuse them a license to do business. Klein used Senator Thomas Dodd as a flunky in arranging some of these connections. Dodd also accepted ten thousand dollars from A. N. Spanel, a pompous Jew who headed a panty girdle empire in the United States. The money was intended to pave the way for Spanel's appointment as ambassador to France. Dodd took the money but Spanel never got the appointment.

Jews also took sizeable percentages of every German firm which was given a permit to operate by the McCloy, Kuhn, Loeb occupation government. The Jews swarmed in to seize valuable German patents and to fasten themselves onto the helpless German populace. One of the first laws passed by the Occupation made it a crime to criticize a Jew (Bavarian Stute No. 8). An economist recently estimated that the Jews had taken two hundred billion dollars in net profits out of Western Germany since the war. The Nazi movement in which Oppenheim and Warburg had invested had finally paid off. Another Jew, Dr. Hans Deutsch, specialized in submitting false evidence about works of art which the Nazis had supposedly requisitioned from the Jews. He got ten million dollars from the German Government for one of his clients, Baron Edmond de Rothschild of Paris, but when Deutsch went back in 1965 for another $105,000,000 for paintings which he claimed had been taken from a Hungarian Jew named Hatvany, who had gotten a sugar monopoly in that country, he was arrested for fraud. The paintings which he had listed had been hanging in the Hermitage Museum in Moscow for many years, and the Nazis had never seen them!

The Jews also conduct annual "anti-Semitic" campaigns in Germany, in which tombstones in Jewish cemeteries are tipped over. The German people are then herded out to clean the cemeteries, and other indignities heaped upon. them, while the Jews raise more millions with his foolproof fund-raising device. This provocateurism of the Jew is also a basic technique for controlling the gentiles.

Although the Jews saved Russian Communism from the German armies, Communism continues to be a farcical failure. Poland has decollectivized 85% of the farms, Hungary bas decollectivized 90% of them, so that the people can grow enough to eat. Nevertheless, the Communist countries continue to face annual threats of famine. Everyone admits that the Communist system cannot work; but few people have the courage to add what is painfully obvious; that it cannot work because it is the ideological creation of schizophrenic Jews.

Chapter Nine

Jews and the United States

Of all the gentile nations in the world, not one has suffered more at the hands of the Jews than the United States. The two greatest calamities which struck this country were the Civil War and the Crash of 1929. The first laid waste the entire Southland and massacred its youth; the second wiped out two hundred billion dollars worth of investments and ruined most of the gentiles of the country, leaving a clear field for the Jews.

Both of these calamities were caused by Jews, as literally tons of documentation proves. The Civil War was provoked by the Rothschild bankers in order to split the United States into two weak republics. The stock market crash of 1929 was provoked by the Jews in one of their most familiar operations, transferring a large shipment of gold out of the country, in order to effect a sudden contraction of credit. At least once in every generation, millions of Americans have been impoverished by a financial panic caused in the same way, yet the remedies for these panics, such as the Federal Reserve System and the other monetary panaceas which the Jews have devised for us, have only succeeded in making the Jews richer and the gentiles poorer.

In all fairness to the Jews, let us ask, "Why should it be otherwise?" If we fall for the same trick at least once in every generation, why shouldn't Jewish tricksters use it over and over? We know that the Jews are a highly compact racial unit

- why shouldn't they take advantage of our diversity? Why shouldn't they take over our government, if, as they claim, we are too stupid to run it ourselves? Why shouldn't they dominate our banks and our universities, if gentiles are too dumb to operate them?

Unfortunately, it is not quite that simple. According to this argument, we can only win over the Jews by becoming more Jewish than they are. Many gentiles do just that. There are numbers of gentile businessmen who can and do skin the Jews in every business transaction they have with them. Jewish cleverness is much over-rated; their real power is not their intelligence, but their solidarity, the phalanx of treachery and cunning which they have formed to repel the gentile. Even when the gentiles outwit them in business, the Jew wins the last battle, because the gentile dies, and his fortune winds up in Jewish bands. Henry Ford is a typical example. The Jews could never win out over Henry in a business transaction, and he despised them wholeheartedly, yet the Ford Foundation has spent two billion dollars of old Henry's money to flood the country with Jewish propaganda, underwrite enormous projects for the Jews, such as Mortimer Adler's twenty million dollar study of the "meaning of philosophy", one of most ludicrous boondoggles ever proposed, and a long list of other equally insane and equally Jewish projects. The Jews used the United States government to force the Ford family into setting up this foundation as a Jewish propaganda vehicle, threatening to destroy the Ford Company if they refused.

Why does the Jew win the last battle in the money struggle? First of all, money is the Jew's first choice of weapons. He knows everything that can be done with it, including pyramiding of credit, inventing systems of accounting which conceals profits, setting up foundations so that the government never gets a cent of Jewish money, and many other techniques which were sharpened during centuries in the ghetto.

When a gentile sets out to make money, he sweeps aside all other personal considerations. When a Jew sets out to make money, he is doing it not only for himself but for his race. Every dollar he can get his hands on is a gun which the Jew can aim at the gentile. It is the natural advantage of a faceless member of a collective state over a state in which every member prides himself on being an individual. We might remember that the United States has no culture of its own. It is a North European culture which, over the past fifty years, has become heavily tainted with Jewish viciousness.

Americans are easily influenced, because we are a generous hardworking, unthinking people. Henry Ford boasted that he didn't need to know history because he could afford to hire the best historians in the country. This is a typical hired man's attitude towards education. All that Ford would get would be that particular historian's version of history, and he would have no way of knowing whether he was getting what he was paying for. As a result, we have Mortimer Adler and a host of other Jews having a picnic at Ford's expense. But do we hear of any Jewish billionaires subsidizing a group of gentiles? Of course not. When Gerard Swope, the leftwing Jew who was president of General Electric, died, he left his entire estate, eight million dollars, to the Israel Institute of Technology. Money which he had sweated from the gentile employees of General Electric was going to Israel. Not only that, but the United States government lost $4,500,000 inheritance taxes on this money. E. J. Kahn writes, page 439, *"Herbert Bayard Swope,"*

> "That obstacle was neatly circumvented when Congress, before Gerard died, passed a bill permitting certain individuals - individuals whose circumstances were precisely tailored to his - to choose a charity to receive a decedent spouse's money without having to pay any tax on it."

Thus Marxist inheritance taxes are only levied against gentiles. The Jewish money goes intact to Israel.

We have mentioned that the American people do not like to think about anything. However, people who do not think are often taken advantage of by those who do, and the Jewish brain is always active. For a Jew to attain wealth in the United States is like taking candy from a baby; it is such a simple matter to rook the American suckers. The Jewish parasite has found in this people the ideal gentile host - enormously productive and hard working, and almost oblivious to the cancerous presence of the parasite which is poisoning every aspect of its life. Our entire foreign policy is dictated by Jews, and from a native American point of view, that policy is insane. Fifteen years ago, we refused to use Chiang Kai-Shek's anti-Communist Chinese troops to fight Communist Chinese in Korea, even though we had paid for all the equipment of Chiang's army, because our government preferred to have our own boys slaughtered over there. As a result, the Communists called our intervention "white imperialism" and "racism", which they could not have done if he had used Chiang's army. Now we are doing the same thing in Vietnam. Chiang's army, ready to fight, will never be used in Vietnam, despite our mounting casualties. The Jews order us to attack Rhodesia. Why? Because Rhodesia followed our example, and declared her independence from British injustice. No people in the world has more in common with native born Americans than the white people of Rhodesia, yet our Jewish-controlled government is spending millions of dollars to harass the Rhodesian people. Hundreds of other examples could be cited to prove this insanity. Twenty years ago, we concluded a bitter war against Germany and Japan. Now they are our only reliable allies.

Sixty per cent of the American people do all the work, earn most of the money, pay all the taxes, and support a considerable portion of the rest of the world. This is our white

Christian people, yet they have no lobby, no voice in the government, and are always caricatured as boobs on television shows. Any attempt to set up an organization to represent them is immediately crushed by the government, while the entire newspaper, radio and television empire scream about "racism"! The press never seems to notice the racism of the Jewish organizations. Jews and Negroes are sacred cows on television. They are always portrayed as kind, angelic human beings who patiently endure the outrages of the ignorant white people. Of course white business people pay for these shows. As the Senator from Texas, Tom Connally, remarked in a public toast a few years ago, "The United States, here's to it! The white people work for it, the Jews own it, and the Negroes enjoy it!"

Economists recently revealed that the white Christian middle class pays 84% of its income in taxes. Oh, no, says Mr. American, I only pay 46%, and I have an average job, an average home, and an average family. But, Mr. American, you haven't figured the hidden taxes you pay on every consumer product which you and your family use. Add that to your 46% income tax, state, federal, and local, and you arrive at the figure 84%. By a startling coincidence, the eminent economist, J. J. Cavanagh, recently concluded a study for the National Zionist Foundation which showed that American Jews own 84% of the real wealth of the United States. Is it not remarkable that the American wage earner pays 84 cents of every dollar he earns in direct and hidden taxes, and the Jews own 84% of the nation's wealth? Even the slowest-witted Americans must dimly perceive some sort of connection. After a career of forty to fifty years of unremitting labor, the average American worker leaves an estate of $2500, according to the American Inheritance Society. Yet, according to the Jewish Independent, an economists' newsletter, the average American Jew leaves an estate of $126,000! This, of course, is reported wealth. The actual figure is probably closer to $500,000. As we pointed out in the

Swope case, the Jewish wealth goes only to the Jewish state. The Jews have set up hundreds of foundations to siphon off their enormous fortunes into Jewish Communist goals. China was lost to the Communists because of the activities of the Institute of Pacific Relations. The IPR was financed by donations from General Electric Corp. through Gerard Swope. General Electric continues to give large sums to the IPR today, in defiance of Congressional reports tracing its long and successful record on behalf of Communist goals.

The Rockefeller fortune has been split among a number of foundations, nearly all of which have been notable for their vicious pro-Communist agitation. Few people know that John D. Rockefeller was merely a gentile shill for Jacob Schiff and Kuhn, Loeb Co. the American representatives for the Rothschilds. If Rockefeller made a billion dollars, how much do you suppose the Jews made? Not only that, but Rockefeller had to agree that his fortune would always be administered by a partner of Kuhn, Loeb Co. Thus the *New York Times* publishes the fact that Kuhn, Loeb partner L. L. Strauss is "the financial adviser to the Rockefeller brothers." This means that the millionaire Rockefellers will be millionaires only as long as they do what they are told.

How did this happen? How did the freedom-loving American people become slaves of the Jews? First of all, Americans do not stick together. Second, many sincere and misguided Americans believe the blasphemy that Christ was a Jew, and that the Jews are our natural rulers because our God is a Jew. Third, the Jews spend fortunes every year to cover up their crimes, while Americans spend nothing to find out what the Jews are doing. Our history has been falsified to conceal Jewish guilt for starting the Civil War and many other American disasters.

The story of the Jewish control begins with the founding of America. The new continent was settled by European

Christians who fled the terror and the devastation of the religious wars incited by the Jews, or they fled the tyranny of Jewish overseers who administered the large estates in Europe, while the aristocratic owners gambled and wenched in the large cities. Suddenly the Jew realized that many of his Christian slaves were disappearing. He soon found that they had gone to America. If the gentile host moves, the Jewish parasite must move after him and regain his parasitic hold. In no time, the Jews were pouring into America. They were merchants in the cities, and they travelled into the farthest regions of the wilderness to ply the Indians with liquor and take all their belongings. They also sold the Indians guns with which to massacre the white settlers.

When King George III of England could not meet the demands of the Jewish moneylenders, to whom he was heavily in debt, he had to place higher taxes on all goods sent to America. This did not satisfy the Jews. They informed him that the American people were printing and circulating their own paper money, and this had created great wealth and prosperity in the colonies. King George III was forced to issue an order banning this interest free money and stipulating that the colonists could only use Bank-of-England money which was printed by the Jews. Within a few months after this order went into effect, the colonists were in the throes of a terrible financial depression. Trade slowed to a standstill, and many Americans were ruined. The colonists decided to fight back, and the result was the American Revolution. Benjamin Franklin commented that the colonists had no objection to the little tax on tea, but they could not stand the curtailment of trade which followed the banning of the native currency. However, it suited the Jews to publicize a minor incident, the Boston Tea Party, and to obscure the real reason for the revolt.

When the American patriots rebelled, King George was again in a predicament. The much vaunted British Army was in no shape to take to the field. Badly outfitted by Jewish suppliers, and badly led by career aristocrats who were drunkards, homosexuals and sadists, the troops were completely demoralized. The officers thought nothing of ordering a young soldier flogged to death because he had refused some drunken homosexual overture. It seemed that the Americans would win by default. Once again, the Jews offered a solution. A Jewish moneylender named Montefiore suggested to King George that the Germans had plenty of good soldiers for hire; as usual, the Jews were active as flesh-peddlers. Montefiore ascertained from a German Jew, Mayer Rothschild, that the Elector of Hesse had fifteen thousand firstline troops whom he would send to King George for twenty million dollars. King George borrowed the twenty million dollars from Montefiore, and the money was sent to the Elector of Hesse. The Elector dispatched the mercenary troops to America to crush the rebellion, and he handed the money over to his court banker, Mayer Amschel Rothschild for safekeeping. Rothschild sent the money back to Montefiore for reinvestment, and within a month, Montefiore had another twenty millions available for loan, although it was the same twenty millions he had before, and which King George now owed him, and which belonged to the Elector of Hesse. Anyone who cannot understand this cannot understand how a Jew can have twenty million dollars one day and forty millions the next. The money was lent out several times during the next ten years, and Rothschild returned the money, with interest, to the Elector, but the delighted ruler insisted that Rothschild continue to handle it for him, thus the basis of the Rothschild fortune was the sale of troops to crush the American people and the Rothschilds have been profiting from their attempts to crush us ever since.

As usual, the Rothschilds bet on both sides. Through an American agent, A Polish Jew named Haym Salomon, the Rothschilds lent money to the American Army. The American representative was Robert Morris, and the sum was said to have been $600,000. Although the entire transaction is shrouded in mystery, for more than a century, the Jews have peddled the fantastic lie that Haym Salomon financed the entire American struggle for independence. Kastein says, page 376, *The History of the Jews*, "As might almost have been expected, it was a Jew, Chaim Solomon (sic) who was obliged to finance the revolution."

Kastein offers no evidence to support this claim, because there is none. The Jews have stated that a poor Jewish tailor, Chaim Salomen knowing that the Americans had no money to continue their fight donated his entire fortune of $600,000 to them, and that he was never repaid a cent. First of all, a poor Jewish tailor can hardly be said to be poor if he had a fortune of $600,000 (equivalent to twenty million dollars in today's purchasing power), nor is there any explanation as to how he acquired such a fortune. Second, no one has ever been able to establish that anyone named Haym Salomon lived in America during the Revolution. The likelihood is that this was one of a number of aliases used by a Rothschild agent in carrying out various missions for the Jewish bankers. We do know that there was a Robert Morris, that he obtained a charter for the Bank of North America in 1781, that he was an agent of the Rothschilds, and that the bank's capital of $200,000 in gold was sent from the Rothschilds via the French fleet which bottled up Cornwallis at Yorktown. We also know that the Rothschilds made $14,000,000 in profit in speculating in Continental currency, after driving the price down and that even if they had made a loan to the American Army of $600,000, and even if this loan was not repaid, they suffered no loss.

The victorious American patriots were well aware of the monetary issue, and also the Jewish problem. Benjamin Franklin and George Washington solemnly warned the American people to keep out the Jews, or they would regret it forever. Although it was debated whether they should hold citizenship, the issue was turned down because most of the Americans did not believe they would ever threaten our prosperity. We can hardly blame them, in retrospect. After all, the Babylonians, the Egyptians, the Persians, the Greeks and the Romans had made the same mistake. What a pity that our forefathers knew so little of ancient history! To safeguard the people from Jewish bankers, however, the framers of the Constitution specifically stated, Article 1, Section 8, part 5,

> "Congress shall have power to coin money and regulate the value thereof; and of foreign coin."

From the moment the Constitution was adopted, the Rothschilds began to spend money to abrogate this provision. They finally succeeded in 1913, when Congress handed over the power to coin money to the privately owned Federal Reserve Banks. This was the official end of American sovereignty, as Charles Lindbergh Sr. pointed out.

The present-day Jewish parasitic control of the gentile host depends largely upon the Jewish monetary system of private money, issued by Jewish banks and bearing interest, so as to enslave the debtor. The American people handed over this power because of the greed of a few gentiles and the ignorance of the majority. The Attorney General of the United States, speaking of the Legal Tender Acts, said (12 Wallace U.S. Supreme Court Reports), page 319,

> "This legislation assumes that, in contemplation of law, money of every species has the value which law fixes upon it. We repeat, money is not a substance, but an impression of authority." As an impression of authority, in the opinion of the Attorney General, money represents the power, the sovereignty of a people. The Jews obtained this authority through the Federal Reserve Act, and they obtained it through the venality of a few Congressional leaders, among them Carter Glass, Cordell Hull and other "great

Americans", according to the Jewish propaganda machine. Only Congressman Charles Lindbergh, father of the famed aviator, dared to oppose this measure.

One of the advantages of the parliamentary system is that the Jews have a large number of gentiles to choose from in selecting their stool pigeons. They have never lacked for Senators and Congressmen who would do their bidding, for quite small sums, considering the billions of dollars at stake. One of the first and most able advocates of the Jewish monetary system was Alexander Hamilton, who is revered today on Wall Street. Hamilton was the bastard son of a Jewish merchant in the West Indies, named Levine; and his mulatto mistress, whom he never bothered to marry. When Hamilton was killed in a duel at Weehawken, New Jersey, the Rothschilds found an able replacement in Nicholas Biddle of Philadelphia. Biddle was fought to a standstill by President Andrew Jackson after Baron James de Rothschild of Paris had commissioned Biddle to establish the second Bank of the United States.

Because of this opposition to their bank, the Rothschilds determined that the free republic of the American people must be destroyed. They decided the best way to achieve this was to split the country into two weaker nations. The issue was a ready-made one, the dissension between the North and the South over slavery. After Yankee traders had loaded the South with slaves, they turned against slavery. Alexis de Tocqueville, a French traveler, had observed in 1832 that,

> "The presence of the blacks is the greatest evil that threatens the United States. They increase in the Gulf States faster than the whites. They cannot be kept forever in slavery; the tendencies of the modern world run too strongly the other way. They cannot be absorbed into the white population, for the whites will not intermarry with them, even in the North where they have been free for two

generations. Once freed, they would be more dangerous than now, because they would not long submit to be debarred from political rights. A terrible struggle would ensue."

For more than a century, the Jews have used the Negro problem as a weapon against America. The Rothschilds poured millions of dollars into New England to finance the Abolitionist movement, which was a revolutionary group dedicated to violence against the South. The Jews knew that the Achilles heel of the American Republic was the Negro, and the American people had no idea of what was going on. Although Washington had warned his people against the Jews in his Farewell Address, when he issued a solemn warning that they must always be on the alert against this "small, enterprising minority", and Benjamin Franklin had written a long testament begging the American people to beware of Jewish activities, the Rothschilds carried on the Abolitionist agitation and soon brought the nation to the brink of war. As a result, a startling prediction was made by D' Israeli to a great gathering of Jewish leaders in London in 1857, The occasion was the wedding of Lionel Rothschild's daughter Lenora, to her cousin, Alfonso Rothschild of Paris. D'Israeli said,

> "Under this roof are the heads of the family of Rothschild, a name famous in every capital of Europe, and every division of the globe. If you like, we shall divide the United States into two parts, one for you, James, and one for you, Lionel. Napoleon will do exactly and all that I shall advise him, and to Bismarck will be suggested such an intoxicating program as to make him our abject slave."

As a result, the United States was soon embroiled in the Civil War. In London, Lionel Rothschild was a staunch supporter of the South. In Paris, James Rothschild was a staunch supporter of the North. With such friends, neither North nor South needed any enemies. In the beginning, the

Rothschilds revealed their original plan, which was that the North would receive no money to carry on the war. President Lincoln found that he could borrow no money in New York to prosecute the war. Undaunted by this refusal, he confounded the bankers by issuing $346,000,000 in greenback money and equipped his armies. In so doing, he was the first Constitutional President, that is, the first to exercise the principle of national sovereignty. This money, had it been issued by the bankers, would have subsequently earned them eleven *billion* dollars in interest. Obviously, they were disturbed by Lincoln's action. A Rothschild-controlled newspaper, the *London Times*, commented,

> "If this mischievous financial policy, which has its origin in the North American Republic, shall become endurated down to a fixture, then that Government will furnish its own money without cost. It will pay off its debts and be without debt. It will have all the money necessary to carry on its commerce. It will become prosperous without precedent in the history of the world. The brains and the wealth of all countries will go to North America. That government must be destroyed or it will destroy every monarchy on the globe."

The Rothschilds persuaded their agents in Washington to draft the National Banking Act of 1863, which would supersede further need for the government to issue its own paper money and return that privilege to the private bankers. In support of it, the Hazard Banking Circular was issued to all American bankers, as follows:

> "Slavery is likely to be abolished by the war power. This I and my European friends are in favor of, for slavery is but the owning of labour and carries with it the care of the laborers, while the European plan, led by England, is that capital shall control labour by controlling wages. The great debt that Capitalists shall see to it is made out of the war

must be used to control the value of money. To accomplish this, government bonds must be used as a banking basis. We are not waiting for the Secretary of the Treasury of the United States to make that recommendation. It will not do to allow Greenbacks, as they are called, to circulate as money for any length of time, as we cannot control that. But we can control the bonds, and through them, the banking issues."

The American student of economics will find neither the *London Times* editorial nor the *Hazard* circular mentioned in his textbook. He will not likely find the Rothschilds mentioned in his textbook. Indeed, the American student will find very little in his textbook, except what has been agreed upon as harmless for him to know.

The Secretary of the Treasury, Salmon P. Chase, after whom a great bank has been named, later wrote, "My agency in promoting the passage of the National Banking Act was the greatest financial mistake of my life. It has built up a monopoly which affects every interest in the country. It should be repealed, but before that can be accomplished, the people will have to be arrayed on one side, and the banks on the other, in a contest such as we have never seen before in this country."

Although Lincoln had signed his death warrant by issuing the Greenback national currency, he was well aware of his danger. However, he was more concerned with the danger to the country. Shortly before his murder, he wrote,

"I see in the near future a crisis approaching that unnerves me and causes me to tremble for the safety of my Country; corporations have been enthroned, an era of corruption in high places will follow, and the money power of the country will endeavour to prolong its reign by working upon the prejudices of the people, until the wealth is aggregated in a few hands and the Republic destroyed."

A few weeks after writing these words, Lincoln was assassinated. A coded message was found in John Wilkes Booth's trunk, and the key to the code was later found in the possession of Judah Benjamin. Benjamin, a relative of the Rothschild family, was a Jew who had been Secretary of the Treasury for the Confederacy.

Some years later, James Garfield, shortly after becoming President, said, "Whoever controls the volume of money in a country is absolute master of industry and commerce." He opposed some measures put before him for his signature by the international bankers, and a few days later, he was shot down.

Between the end of the Civil War and the outbreak of World War I, the United States endured a series of financial panics. These contractions of credit, in every instance, fleeced the gentiles and concentrated the wealth of the nation in Jewish hands. Many Americans grew enormously rich through land booms, gold mines, railroad booms and the growth of industry. In every case, the gentile money passed into Jewish control. Many Americans have wondered why W. Averell Harriman has been an errand boy for world Jewry. The answer is that his father, a builder of railroads, was merely a gentile employee of Jacob Schiff's, just as Rockefeller had been.

At the outbreak of World War I, Rev. Melvin King, in a little known work called *"Heaven's Magnet for a World Conquest"*, said on page 265,

"Israel's marching towards her goal of universal administration."

Woodrow Wilson created a War Industries Board and placed Bernard Baruch in charge of it, with life and death powers over American industry. Baruch brought in a motley crowd of Jews, including Clarence Dillon-Steinberg, Billy Rose, and the Swope brothers to run the agency. These Jews took over American business. At the conclusion of the war, the Jews packed their bags and hurried off to Paris to divide up the gentile world. Baron says, page 357, *Great Ages and Ideas of the Jewish People*, "Jewish leaders happened to be in a particularly favorable strategic position to bring about the incorporation of safeguards for national minority rights in the peace treaties of 1919." "The favorable strategic position" consisted of the fact that Jews dominated the delegations from all of the Christian nations.

Once again, huge fortunes had been made by war profiteers. Not all of them were Jews. It was time for another "panic". The contraction of credit was decided upon at a secret meeting of the Federal Reserve Board (page 64, *The Federal Reserve Conspiracy*, by Eustace Mullins). But the big killing was made in 1929. After drawing the life savings of schoolteachers and small town businessmen into the stock market, the Jews shipped a large consignment of gold to Montreal, there was a classic contraction of credit, and two hundred billion dollars of gentile savings disappeared (page 99, The Federal Reserve Conspiracy by Eustace Mullins).

After the Crash, the Jews set up many new holding companies for their stocks, such as the Lehman Corporation. By 1933, they owned 69% of the shares outstanding of all stocks listed on the Big Board. Typical of the new rich was a runty little Jewish racketeer named Billy Rose. After working as a secretary for Bernard Baruch, Rose was hired by the Mafia to front for them in the operation of a tourist clip joint in New York called Casino de Paree. The place was netting gangsters $20,000 a week, but they were only paying Rose $1000 a week. He began to hold out some of the cash, and the Mafia passed the usual death sentence. Rose was tipped off, and he rushed to Bernard Baruch. Baruch sent him to J. Edgar Hoover, and four FBI men guarded him night and day until the danger was over. Hoover persuaded the Mafia to forget the whole thing. Rose then went into the production of girly shows. At the time of his death, he was worth one hundred million dollars and was the largest single share owner of American Telephone and Telegraph. The telephone had been invented by a gentile, Alexander Graham Bell, who at his death was worth $18,000.

The Mafia has always found Jews useful to them. Although the inner circle of Cosa Nostra is restricted to the Sicilian Brotherhood, Jews have become important in the mob, such as Longy Zwillman and Mickey Cohen. The Mafia put Moe Annenberg in charge of their national racing wire network, and he amassed a fortune of $150,000,000. His grandson, a dope addict, was recently charged with the murder of his gentile girlfriend. Annenberg owns the *Philadelphia Inquirer* and other newspapers.

A host of Jews has appeared from nowhere to make huge fortunes in the United States; Samuel Newhouse, with a chain of 28 newspapers; O. Roy Chalk, owner of the District of Columbia Transit System, newspapers and other businesses; Norton Simon, owner of the Hunt food empire; Riklis, owner of McCrory dime store empire; and other Jews who as little as ten years ago had never been heard of. The process has accelerated; a recent study by the *Saturday Evening Post* showed that 88% of those who have become millionaires in America since 1950 are Jews. One of them, Moskovitz, alias Moesler, was the star of a particularly nasty murder case in Miami. He had amassed two hundred million dollars through usurious interest charges on automobiles and mobile homes purchased by gentile American workers.

In many cases, these sudden Jewish fortunes represent Mafia profits being channeled into industry, with Jewish fronts ostensibly owning the money. Other sources are "hot" money which is transferred from one country to another, and in some cases these Jewish millionaires are fronts for Soviet investments in American industries, with the purpose of obtaining vital defense plans and formulae.

One of the Jewish giants in munitions is the Olin Industries, another Jewish firm. During World War II, U. S. Cartridge, a subsidiary of this firm, was indicted on many counts of furnishing defective shells, violating the sabotage act, and other crimes. The case dragged along until 1950, when it was finally dropped. However, Department of Justice prosecutions of gentile firms, such as A & P Stores, are unbelievably vicious. Such Jewish owned chains as Food Fair and Giant Stores are ignored by the Justice Department, but the gentile firm of A & P has been undergoing almost continuous prosecution for twenty-five years.

In the same manner, the gentile firm of DuPont, the last stronghold of gentile wealth in the United States, is continually defending itself against Jewish-inspired prosecution by the Department of Justice. DuPont stockholders lost millions of dollars when the Department of Justice ordered DuPont to divest itself of holdings of General Motors. No wrongdoing was charged; the simple fact was that two large gentile corporations had resisted the efforts of the Jews to take them over. The Jews decided that they would have to split them up in order to wrest them from gentile control.³

---

³ "The DuPont family members were finally allowed to keep most of the proceeds from the sale of their stock, at a price. They had to employ Clark Clifford, a leading Zionist lobbyist in Washington, as the attorney for this transaction, thus

The Jews have never lacked for gentile apologists. American poet Robert Lowell states that "This is a Jewish age". Of played out New England stock, Lowell bas had several nervous breakdowns and is a good companion for the schizophrenic Jews. Reinhold Niebuhr, a self-styled Christian philosopher, is the ringleader of the "Christ-is-a-Jew" racket. He attributes everything good to the Jews, and says in his latest book, "I have had a long love affair with the Jewish people." Not surprisingly, the Jews call Niebuhr "the greatest living philosopher".

When Eugene Meyer and Bernard Baruch formed the Alaska-Juneau Gold Mining Co., two of the most sinister men in America joined hands. Baruch appointed Meyer as manager of the War Finance Corporation, handling Liberty Bonds during the First World War. Congressman Louis McFadden, Chairman of the House Banking and Currency Committee, discovered that ten billion dollars worth of bonds had been destroyed, twenty-four million dollars worth had been printed in duplicate and sold, and extensive alterations made in Meyer's records. Meyer bought control of Allied Chemical and Dye Corporation, and later purchased the *Washington Post*. His daughter married a gentile named Philip Graham, and Meyer made him president of the *Washington Post*, but Graham found the things he had to do for the Jews too distasteful, and he shot himself. The Meyer family is worth one billion dollars, which is not difficult to understand, in light of Congressman McFadden's investigations (page 105, *The Federal Reserve Conspiracy*, by Eustace Mullins).

The Meyer family also bought *Newsweek Magazine* and completely staffed it with Jews. The art editor is Jack Kroll; the book editor is Saul Maloff; the film editor is Joseph

---

transferring a large 'fee' to the Zionists, and they had to agree to place a Jew, Irving Shapiro, in charge of all the DuPont companies as president of DuPont."

Morgenstern; the drama editor is Richard Gilman; the music editor is Herbert Saal. No gentiles need apply.

The Meyer family also bought the magazine *Art News*, which promotes the latest fads "in art, and which publicizes pop and op art, the Beer-Can School which replaced the Ash-Can School. Here again the silliest productions of wild-eyed Jewish artiste are given serious review, while gentiles remain unnoticed in their garrets.

Nowhere has Jewish monopoly been more apparent than in the movies and television, and no mediums have been more relentless in flooding the nation with vicious Jewish propaganda. The movies began as a gentile enterprise; the first great director was David W. Griffith, who produced the great film, *The Birth of a Nation*. Griffith was soon shoved aside by a horde of lisping Russian and Polish Jews, the cloak-and-suiters from New York's Seventh Avenue. There were no more Griffiths to be found in Hollywood; instead, the producers were Schulberg, Goldwyn, Mayer, Zanuck, Cohen, Schary and hundreds of other Jews.

The first great comedians were gentiles, Buster Keaton and Laurel and Hardy. Keaton was shoved aside in favor of Charlie Chaplin, a Cheapside Jew whose comic gift seemed to consist of slowly turning his backside to the audience and ostentatiously scratching it. This was one of his less obscene gestures, and his art had apparently been learned while observing the monkeys at the zoo. Laurel and Hardy were replaced by the Marx Brothers - the list is endless.

On television, Americans have the choice of watching programs on three networks: NBC, controlled by the Russian Jew Sarnoff; CBS, controlled by William Paley or Palinsky, whose Polish Jewish father made a fortune from Muriel cigars; or ABC, controlled by Barney Balabanson, of Polish Jewish stock. These Jews have spent millions of dollars to foist off on the American public a score of Jewish comedians who have never found favor with audiences except in Yiddish night clubs-Milton Berle, Red Buttons, Danny Kaye, Jerry Lewis, have been financial disasters on television but two gentile comedians, Jackie Gleason and Red Skelton, go on year after year. Their secret is that they are funny. The Jews spew out a curious combination of perversion, dope addiction and integration vomit, and expect the audience to double up with laughter. Instead, they should get sick.

In 1966, a Congressional Committee found that these Jewish networks were employing all of the usual techniques of Jewish monopoly. They would not allow a show on the air unless the network was given 51% of the profits. This gave them complete control of the contents and a majority of the profits. It was a clear violation of the anti-trust laws, but nothing has been done about it; the Department of Justice is too busy prosecuting gentile firms like DuPont and A & P to worry about what the Jews are doing with their television monopoly. All of the television shows are heavily staffed with Jews; gentiles average only fifteen per cent employment in television production. Needless to say, nothing appears on television except what the Jews want the gentiles to see. The few gentiles who have programs of their own have Jewish wives. Ed Sullivan is married to Sylvia Bernstein; Dave Brinkley, etc. Sullivan is a devout Catholic, but his wife is rearing their children in the Jewish faith.

Despite their prominence in such legitimate industries as theater and television, Jews prefer underworld activities. They are well known for white slavery; pornography, gun-running, liquor, and other businesses. The liquor business in America is dominated by the Bronfman family, who owns Seagram's, and the Rosenstiel's, who own Schenley's. The gun which killed Kennedy was handled first by a Jewish wholesaler named Irving Feldschott, and then by a Jewish retailer in Chicago named Milton Klein. The nation's largest pornographer is said to be Irving Klaw, of New York, although many other Jews are pushing hard for the title. A Jew named Lyle Stuart, earlier known as Samuelson, has printed some of the juiciest items in the trade. The Supreme Court recently upheld the conviction of Ralph Ginzburg as a wholesale pornographer. He had circulated a number of items, among them The Housewife's Handbook on Selective Promiscuity, which featured a series of photographs of a naked Negro man having intercourse with a white woman. And so we could go on for hundreds of pages, listing the vile things which the Jew is doing here today, in our country, to us. We might stop to think about the number of fine old gentile businesses which pass into Jewish hands each year, such as Willoughby' s Camera Shops of New York. Some segments of American business, such as drug stores and both manufacturing and retail clothing, are completely controlled by Jews, and much of the gentile middle class has already been driven out of business.

Samuel Roth, the author of *Jews Must Live*, wrote that he knew a man who employed four thousand people, but he always refused to employ a Jew, because he did not wish to lose his business. Roth asked him how he could spot a Jew, as they seldom identified themselves as such. The man replied, "They always look over your head." Roth then explained to the man that the Jew looks over his head because he is looking up to the invisible God of Israel. Since all wealth is meant for the enrichment of Israel, the Jew is waiting for God to show him how to get the gentile's business away from him. Roth states that be never heard of a gentile who prospered after hiring a Jew.

No satanic practice of the Jew has done Americans more damage than the Jewish promotion of racial warfare in the United States. We have already mentioned De Tocqueville's observation in 1832 that "the presence of the blacks is the greatest evil that threatens the United States." Not only did the Jews use this issue to precipitate the devastating Civil War, but they renewed the Negro issue before the First World War. At the turn of the century, Harlem was an undeveloped area. It was developed by three Jewish speculators - August Belmont, Oscar Hammerstein and Henry Morgenthau. These Jews are responsible for the horrible slums in which the Negroes live, for the Jews only put up buildings which would bring the maximum profit. Also, the Jews own every business in Negro areas. An AP dispatch dated February 19, 1966, gave on interview with one Meyer Bleustein, who owned one million dollars worth of property in the riot area of Watts. Not one journalist has ever revealed the true significance of these Negro riots in Harlem, Rochester, Watts and other Negro slums. These were anti-Jewish riots, in which the Negro smashed into Jewish stores and took by force the liquor and television sets for which the Jews had been charging them four prices. The Negro has been exploited in America, but only by the Jews. Many Negroes began to realize this, and the riots began. The Jews have always controlled the NAACP, which has never had a Negro at the head of it. The Negroes finally saw that the Jews were using fronts to control them. At the same time, the Jews were agitating the Negroes to turn against the white gentiles and slaughter them. Even the most retarded Negro knew that it was a Jew who sold him a pair of badly torn trousers, second hand, for 15 cents, and let him pay 5 cents a week, for thirty weeks, and then took him to Small Claims court to collect the balance (an actual case in Washington, D.C.).

Even while he was exploiting the Negro to a degree which few white people ever realized, the Jew was also using the Negro as his expendable troops in the front line of the Communist conspiracy in America. This dated back to 1912, when the prominent Jewish writer and Communist theoretician, Israel Cohen, wrote an extensive plan called "A Racial Program for the Twentieth Century". We quote in part,

"We must realize that our Party'& most powerful weapon is racial tension. By pounding into the consciousness of the dark races that for centuries they have been oppressed by the whites, we can mold them to the program of the Communist Party. The terms colonialism and imperialism must be featured in our propaganda. In America, we will aim for subtle victory. While inflaming the Negro minority against the whites, we will endeavour to instill in the whites a guilt complex for their exploitation of the Negroes. We will aid the Negroes to rise to prominence in every walk of life, in the professions and in the world of sports and entertainment. With this prestige, the Negroes will be able to intermarry with the whites and begin a process which will deliver America to our cause."

When the Jews denied that there was a writer named Israel Cohen, two writers named Israel Cohen were found listed in Who's Who in World Jewry.

Writers such as Israel Cohen have continued to lead the Negroes in racial agitation. One of the leading newspapers favoring integration is the *Chicago Sun-Times*, which is owned by the Marshall Field family. This newspaper came into being because the grandson of the original Marshall Field, an alcoholic and sexual degenerate, was being attended by a Russian Jewish psychiatrist named Gregory Zilboorg. Zilboorg advised Field to become a newspaper publisher and to fight for "racial justice". Field then founded the *Sun-Times*. Field had become an alcoholic because of shame over the death of his father, the circumstances of which were known to everyone in Chicago. This Marshall Field was the son of the first Marshall Field, and he was a drunkard and sexual pervert who could only attain pleasure by whipping a beautiful naked girl with a large horsewhip. He had one favorite girl at the Everleigh Sisters bordello, the most fashionable brothel in Chicago. One night, the girl couldn't stand the pain of being whipped, and she snatched a pistol from under her pillow and shot him. Field dropped the whip, staggered to the door and fell down the stairs. The girl, out of her mind with pain, followed him and fired three more shots into his body as Field writhed at the foot of the stairs. The house was torn down, and the Field family contributed money to establish the Institute of Surgeons on this site. A statue of a surgeon marks the exact spot where Field died at the foot of the stairs. An alert newspaper reporter happened to be in the brothel at the time, and to keep the story quiet, the Field family gave him $100,000 to start a newspaper, which became the *Chicago Journal-American*. Field also left two Negro sons who still live on the South Side of Chicago, and receive $300 a month each from the Field estate. The present Marshall Field's daughter married a Negro and had children by him. This family is typical of the degenerate integrationist outlook.

Many supposedly gentile concerns are owned by Jews, with a gentile "front" who ostensibly is in full control. Typical of this deception is the Reader's Digest publishing empire. Apparently owned by DeWitt Wallace and his wife, Reader's Digest is actually a subsidiary of RCA, which is controlled by the Russian Jew Samoff. How did this happen? Wallace, a gentile, hired an editor named Eugene Lyons, a Jew. Reader's Digest was successful and had made millions of dollars for its gentile owner. It was also highly respected. Lyons suggested that Reader's Digest publish editions in many foreign languages. Wallace did not wish to invest the millions of dollars which this would require, and Lyons offered to raise the money from his cousin, Samoff. The result was that Reader's Digest came under the control of the Jews, and the Wallaces have to submit every article for Lyons' approval before they can print it in "their" magazine. Obviously they can print nothing which exposes Jewish treachery and subversion, which is just the sort of control the Jews want, and which they must exercise over every gentile enterprise.

Chapter Ten

Jews and Our Future

One of the great tragedies of mankind is the story of the corruption of America by the Jews, for America represented the last great hope of earth. America has been the symbol of man's desire to live in peace and freedom, yet America's history has been a series of wars and financial panics brought on by the Jews. Every safeguard which the American people erected against the Jews has been destroyed. We have already mentioned the provision of the Constitution which our forefathers enacted in order to give us our own monetary system, free of Jewish extortion. The Federal Reserve Act of 1913 ended that. We had a law of contract which allowed us to carry on business with each other. The Jews destroyed that in the famous "integration" decision of May, 1954, in which the Supreme Court ruled that no contract was valid if it contained a reference to race. In other words, contracts were no longer binding in our business life. This decision was written by a fanatical Zionist Jew named Felix Frankfurter, of Vienna, who was denounced by President Theodore Roosevelt as "the most dangerous Bolshevik in the country". Frankfurter's brother, Otto, was known as an habitual criminal who served eight years for an unspeakable crime at Anamosa State Prison in Iowa.

Another great concept was the union movement, which originally provided that a man did not have to endure unusual abuse from his bosses as long as he did his work well. The union movement came into being in America because the

Jews established sweat shops in New York City between 1860 and 1900, and worked gentile women and children eighteen hours a day for as little as five cents an hour. A fire in one of these Jewish sweatshops, the Triangle disaster killed many women and children, for there were no fire escapes in this Jewish-owned building. The union movement stemmed from that day. It was soon taken over by a Jewish agitator named Samuel Gompers.

Another great concept of the gentile is democracy, which simply means that one decent, responsible citizen is as good as the next decent, responsible citizen. The Jews have changed this to mean, "One decent, hardworking American is no better than the next Jewish pornographer, dope addict or rapist." One man, one vote. One honestly employed gentile American has one vote; one Jewish Communist agitator or sweatshop operator has one vote. This is the system of Jewish democracy under which we now live.

We have now traced Jewish influence through five thousand years of history. We have seen how Jewish subversion brought down the great civilizations of Babylon, Egypt, Persia, Greece and Rome. We have seen how Jews played the crucial role in such events as the Plague, the Inquisition, the Reformation, the American Revolution, the Civil War, and the Crash of 1929. What lies ahead?

The history of the Jews falls into three important periods. The first period was when the nomadic Jewish bandits, known throughout the ancient world as Habiru-sagaz, or Hebrew cut-throats, harassed the early civilizations. Those civilizations sent military expeditions against them, killing them and capturing the survivors. Once they brought these captives back to their cities, their civilization sickened and died. They seldom realized what had happened to them.

This period ended with the collapse of the Roman Empire in 476 A.D. The second period, from 477 A.D. to 1815, was the time when the Jews shut themselves up in their ghettos and for over a thousand years gathered and concentrated their psychic forces of evil until they were able to come forth and gain complete mastery over the gentiles. During this period, they maintained their existence by carrying on various underworld activities. They were the fences for stolen goods in every city in the world; they practiced black magic; they became known as physicians; and in order to obtain blood for their ritual ceremonies, they introduced the technique of bleeding. During the Dark Ages, if a Jewish physician was called to attend upon a gentile, he opened the patient's veins and drew out a large quantity of blood, which he then took back to the synagogue for use by the rabbi. In a few cases, if the patient was suffering from overweight or high blood pressure, the bleeding was beneficial. However, in most instances the patient was already weakened by illness, and the bleeding caused him to die. In any case, the Jew could not have cared less, for he was only interested in obtaining the blood. George Washington died because he was subjected to this bleeding technique for a minor respiratory ailment.

The Jew also served the aristocrats as tax collectors and oppressors of the working people, as cruel overseers sweating the peasants for the profit of the aristocrats and the Jews, until they gained sufficient power to emerge from the ghettos in 1815.

From 1815 to the present time, the gentiles have been decimated by terrible world wars and financial panics. Each year, the Jews have grown more powerful, until they now dominate the globe. The great period of European civilization came to an abrupt end in 1815, when the Jews came out of their ghettos. There were no more giants of culture, such as Shakespeare, Beethoven, and Goethe. In only one respect did the gentiles continue to progress, in the invention of machines, for here the Jews did not affect their mental resources. However, there has been no significant art, or music or literature since the Jewish blight descended upon our people. Painting became the trivial daubs of monkeys and their human imitators; music became the screech of automobile horns; literature became a repetitious description of human debauchery. The great civilization of North Europe was dead.

Architecture became a simple construction of metal and concrete boxes, the so-called "Tel Aviv" school of building, named after its Jewish inventors. No more soaring Gothic cathedrals, graceful palaces, or well-built homes for the people; we have only concrete nests in which to breed, and concrete playgrounds for the children instead of grass.

In our universities, everything must be attributed to one of three Jews: Marx, Freud or Einstein; otherwise the instructors are not allowed to teach. Christ is a figure of fun to the "in" professors. We have already discussed the manner in which Marx modernized the ruthless concept of Jewish dictatorship in his philosophy of Communism. It was Einstein's researches which led to the invention of the Jewish Hell-Bomb. Freud declared war on the nobility of the human mind, insisting that our intelligence is found only in our reproductive organs and our anus. This was the foundation of the "science" of psychiatry, although a gentile who came later, Carl Jung, found that people could be helped if one ignored the Freudian filth. Jung was a great scholar who wrote learned books about the origins of North European civilization. In volume 7 of his Collected Works, page 149, Jung says,

> "It is a quite unpardonable mistake to accept the conclusions of a Jewish psychology as generally valid. Nobody would dream of taking Chinese or Indian psychology as binding upon ourselves. With the beginning of racial differentiation, essential differences are developed

in the collective psyche as well. For this reason we cannot transplant the spirit of a foreign race in globo into our own mentality without sensible injury to the latter."

Thus Jung discovered that Jewish psychiatry could be very damaging to the gentile mind. Thousands of gentiles who have placed themselves in the care of Jewish psychiatrists have become hopelessly insane, or have committed suicide. This was only to be expected. The Jews have also developed dangerous new drugs which induce insanity in gentiles. They experiment with these drugs on the helpless gentiles who have been committed to insane asylums by Jewish doctors and judges, conducting weird tests which provide sadistic satisfaction in watching helpless human beings slowly driven insane. They also practice such barbarities as shock treatments on their gentile captives, a form of treatment which was abandoned in Europe twenty years ago as being "excessively barbaric".

One of the key words in the jargon of Jewish psychiatry is "identity". The question of identity is a crucial one for the Jew. He cannot accept, even unconsciously, his true identity as a homeless parasite living upon the gentile host, or his origin as a nomadic cutthroat from the desert, but neither can he invent any other background for himself, since the archeologists can find no trace of a Jewish culture. Another key word is "relate". The Jew worries constantly about how he "relates" or establishes a relationship with the gentile host. He also talks and writes endlessly about the problem of "alienation". Alienation, of course, means the possibility of the Jewish parasite being alienated from, or thrown off of, the gentile host. Hostility is another key word in Jewish psychiatry. What the Jew is concerned with here is the problem of his own hostility towards the gentile host, the schizophrenic hatred which he has developed for the gentile body on which he must live. Consequently, he writes endlessly about the psychiatric problem of hostility, when he really means the "almost inhuman hatred" which Kastein admits that the Jew feels for his host.

Because of his unhealthy and unsatisfactory existence as a parasite living off of the gentile host, the Jew is always on the verge of serious mental disorders. Most common is the form of insanity known as schizophrenia, or split personality. Unable to accept himself for what he is, the Jew invents other explanations of himself, and when he begins to accept these delusions as reality, this is legally defined as insanity. Dr. Martin F. Debivoise recently concluded a ten-year study of Jews in New York. He found that 43% of them were mentally disturbed to the degree that they should be hospitalized. He also made a study of one thousand marriages between Jews and gentiles during this period. He found that 847 of these marriages ended in divorce within five years; in 681, there were no children, and of those who had children, 73% developed leukemia or cancer before the age of puberty. Typical was the death of the son of John Gunther from cancer as a product of one of these mixed marriages.

Throughout the centuries, the Jewish parasite has held to the religious belief that he can achieve absolute power over the gentile host only if he re-establishes his headquarters at the ancient crossroads of world civilization in Palestine. Instinctively, the Jew realizes that he *must* possess this traditional heart-place of gentile commerce if he is to become the master of the host.

In 1948, after a sordid series of brutal murders, the Jew attained his goal the State of Israel. The original promise had been obtained from the British Government in 1917 in exchange for the use of a deadly poison gas invented by Chaim Weizman. When the Jews saw that they were winning over their enemy, Adolph Hitler, they stepped up their brutality to seize Palestine. They had several international murder gangs operating. One of these groups of Thuggees was known as the Stern Gang. Another was the Irgun Zvai Leumi. Each of this group of thugs vied with the others in committing brutal murders of gentiles. In 1944, the Stern gang assassinated Lord Moyne, highest ranking diplomat outside of London, at his home in Cairo, in order to force an English decision to give them Palestine. They then began a series of tortures and killings of British troops who had been sent to Palestine to prevent atrocities by the Jews against the Arab homeowners there. Most of these troops were lads in their late teens. All England was horrified at the deaths which these lads died at the hands of Jewish torturers. Their mangled bodies were then body-trapped so that their comrades were killed when they tried to give them Christian burial.

In 1948, the Jews murdered Count Folke Bernadotte in Israel. Although he had made every effort to get them what they wanted, they killed him to speed up the process. A hotel was blown to bits in Palestine, mangling and killing hundreds of innocent victims. A heartsick England reluctantly agreed to give them the country, and the fate of Israel came into being after a series of murders which had horrified the civilized world. Born in an atmosphere of murder and extortion, nurtured in clouds of poison gas and the invention of the Jewish Hell-Bomb, the State of Israel proved from its very inception that it was the embodiment of absolute evil.

In 1952, a document reached the western democracies which proved that the Jews were anxious to move rapidly ahead with their familiar plans for dictatorship over the gentiles. The unchallenged transcript of a speech by Rabbi Emanuel Rabinovich was documented as having been delivered before the Emergency Council of European Rabbis in Budapest, Hungary, January 12, 1952:

> "Greetings, my children! You have been called here to recapitulate the principal steps of our new program. As you know, we had hoped to have twenty years between

wars to consolidate the great gains which we made from World War II, but our increasing numbers in certain vital areas is arousing opposition to us, and we must now work with every means at our disposal to precipitate World War III within five years."

"The goal for which we have striven so concertedly for three thousand years is at last within our reach, and because its fulfillment is so apparent, it behooves us to increase our efforts and our caution tenfold. I can safely promise you that before ten years have passed, our race will take its rightful place in the world, with every Jew a King, and every gentile a slave! (applause from the gathering).

"You may remember the success of our propaganda campaign during the 1930s, which aroused anti-American passions in Germany, at the same time we were arousing anti-German passions in America, a campaign which culminated in the Second World War. A similar propaganda campaign is now being waged intensively throughout the world. A war fever is being worked up in Russia by an incessant anti-American barrage, while a nationwide anti-Communist scare is sweeping America. This campaign is forcing all of the smaller nations to choose between the partnership of Russia or an alliance with the United States.

"Our most pressing problem at the moment is to inflame the lagging militaristic spirit of the Americans. The failure of the Universal Military Training Act was a great setback ta our' plans, but we are assured that a suitable measure will be rushed through Congress immediately after the 1952 elections. The Russian as well as the Asiatic peoples, are well under control, and offer no objections to war, but we must wait to secure the Americans. This we hope to do with the issue of anti-Semitism, which worked so well in uniting the Americans against Germany.

"We are counting heavily on reports of anti-Semitic outrages in Russia to whip up indignation in the United States, and produce a front of solidarity against the Soviet power. Simultaneously, to demonstrate to Americans the reality of anti-Semitism, we will advance through new sources large sums of money to outspokenly anti-Semitic elements in America to increase their effectiveness, and we shall stage anti-Semitic outbreaks in several of their largest cities. This will serve the double purpose of exposing reactionary sectors in America, which can then be silenced, and of welding the United States into a devoted anti-Russian unit.

"Within five years, this program will achieve its objective, the Third World War, which will surpass in destruction all previous contests. Israel, of course, will remain neutral, and when both sides are devastated and exhausted, we will arbitrate, sending our Control Commissions into all of the wrecked countries. This war will end for all time our struggle against the gentiles. We will openly reveal our identity with the races of Asia and Africa. I can state with assurance that the last generation of white children is now being born. Our Control Commissions will, in the interests of peace and wiping out interracial tensions, forbid the whites to mate with whites. The white women must cohabit with members of the dark races, and the white men with black women. Thus the white race will disappear, for mixing the dark with the white will be the end of the white man, and our most dangerous enemy will become only a memory. We will embark upon an era of ten thousand years of pea and plenty, the Pax Judaica, and our race will rule undisputed over the earth. Our superior intelligence will easily enable us to retain mastery over a world of dark peoples.

"(Question from gathering): Rabbi Rabinovich, what about the various religions after the Third World War?

"RABINOVICH: There will be no more religions. Not only would the existence of a priest class remain a constant danger to our rule, but belief in an afterlife would give spiritual strength to irreconcilable elements in many countries, and enable them to resist us. We will, however, retain the rituals and customs of Judaism as the mark of our hereditary ruling caste, strengthening our racial laws so that no Jew will be allowed to marry outside of our race, nor will any stranger be accepted by us.

"We may have to repeat the grim days of World War II when we were forced to let the Hitlerite bandits sacrifice some of our people, in order that we may have adequate documentation and witnesses to legally justify our trial and execution of the leaders of America and Russia as war criminals, after we have dictated the peace. I am sure you will need little preparation for such a duty, for sacrifice has always been the watchword of our people, and the death of a few thousand Jews in exchange for world leadership is indeed a small price to pay.

"To convince you of the certainty of that leadership, let me point out to you how we have turned all of the inventions of the white man into weapons against him. His printing presses and radios are the mouthpieces of our desires, and his heavy industry manufactures the instruments which he sends out to arm Asia and Africa against him. Our interests in Washington are greatly extending the Point Four program for developing industry in backward areas of the world so that after the industrial plants and cities of Europe and America are destroyed by atomic warfare, the whites can offer no resistance against the larger masses of the dark races, who will maintain an unchallenged technological superiority."

"And so, with the vision of world victory before you, go back to your countries and intensify your good work, until that approaching day when Israel will reveal herself in all her glorious destiny as the Light of the World!"

This document, which originally reached this country in Yiddish, was translated by Henry H. Klein, a Jew who was horrified by the plans of his people to precipitate an atomic war. Klein later died mysteriously in New York, after a Central Intelligence Agency man visited him. The CIA now has the original of this document in its files in Washington.

A double agent, P............, who had infiltrated the inner circle of the Anti-Defamation League of B'nai B'rith, told this writer in 1956 that the publication and circulation of Rabbi Rabinovich's speech in 1952 by a handful of American patriots had caused the Jews to postpone all their plans, and had averted the horrors of a Third World War. The CIA also reported that the Rabbi's Speech had indirectly caused the death of Stalin. Stalin had been so angered when he was brought a copy of it by the secret police that be ordered strong measures taken against important Jews in the Soviet Communist leadership. Before these measures could be carried out, the Jews administered knockout drops to him in a glass of tea, and nine Jewish doctors were called in to take care of him. They saw to it that he never regained consciousness.

In 1958, the *London Times* reported the death of Rabbi Rabinovich, but made no reference to the famous speech, although it had been translated into many languages and was known in every country in Europe.

The appearance of the Rabbi's Speech in 1952 and its subsequent circulation, causing the Jews to postpone the horrors of World War III, can only be attributed to the benevolent presence of Jesus Christ. The careful tracing of the history of the Jews in this book proves that Christians still have the opportunity to save themselves. In the presence of absolute evil, as typified by the Jews, only absolute good can save us. Only the most absolute sincerity can affect any change whatsoever under Heaven. When we see a Jew like Arthur Goldberg in charge of our foreign policy, and then we walk into the Oriental Institute and see a terra cotta statue of a Sumerian of five thousand years ago with the same hook nose and bulging eyes as Goldberg, the face distorted by the same evil hatred for all gentile human beings, we can only conclude that God has marked this people for a purpose. That purpose is to call upon the deepest resources of good within our hearts, to obey Jesus Christ's words, "Take up the Cross and follow Me." Faith, hope, and charity, to live with love and grace abounding in obedience to the Message of Jesus Christ, this is the choice which we *will* make because the presence of the Jew challenges us to make it.

As President of the International Institute of Jewish Studies, and having spent thirty-six years of constant research on the Jewish problem, I state with certainty that to be Jew-wise is to survive. To accept Jewish domination not only means that one abandons all precepts of human civilization which have accreted over five thousand years of recorded history: it also means that one accepts a zombie mode of existence, a life in death which excludes all of the glory and honor of living in Christ.

Being Jew-wise means that one recognizes the basic precepts of the Jewish problem. The first precept is - "THE JEW ALWAYS EXISTS IN A STATE OF WAR WITH ALL CIVILIZED NATIONS".

There can be no peace between the biological parasite and the host people. The second precept is - "EVERY JEW IS AN AGENT OF THE STATE OF ISRAEL". No Jew can hold a position in any gentile government unless he wields that position to advance the cause of the State of Israel. Even if he wished to do so, no Jew could escape the total mobilization of the Jewish people in their war against the gentiles.

The third precept is - "THE JEW ALWAYS KNOWS WHO HE IS". When I first encountered Jews, I was mildly disturbed by the cool manner of self-confidence with which they regarded me. I did not understand that they were looking at me from their pedestal of self-knowledge, while I did not yet know who I was, who my enemies were, or who my friends were. In almost every instance, the gentile fails to understand what is going on in the struggle between the biological parasite and the host people, or if he does get an inkling of what is going on, he finds out too little and too late.

The fourth precept is - "WHATEVER AMBITIONS YOU MAY HAVE, YOU CANNOT REALIZE THESE GOALS BECAUSE OF THE PRESENCE OF THE JEW". It is the function of the Jew to systematically destroy the habitat and the life style of the host people. This renders them unable to resist or to dislodge his parasitic presence. At the beginning of this biological relationship, it is the Jew who is the displaced person, seeking a place for himself, while the host is secure in his home. In establishing his biological presence among the host people, the Jew works furiously to replace the life style of the host with a totally synthetic environment, tailored to the needs and purposes of the Jew. With spider-like precision, the Jew spins his web about the host people, using satire, pornography, and the host's own system of communications to entrap them in the web of the Jew. When the web is complete, the host is unable to move, and finds himself at the mercy of the Jew, who is not slow to administer his fatal poison.

THE BIOLOGICAL JEW

Foreword

For twenty-five years, I have studied the problems of human failure, of falling short of the promise, and of the decay and collapse of great empires. This phenomenon has existed throughout the five thousand years that man has been recording the history of his efforts. During the first twenty years that I devoted to this study, I amassed huge files of information about the various civilizations. I compared these facts in order to find common denominators which might lead to a solution. I also took into consideration such factors as man's environment, his nature, and the persistence of certain patterns in his behaviour.

This led me to an involved study of the animal kingdom, and a compilation of those factors which it bore in common with the plant kingdom. About five years ago, I discovered the common denominator of man's civilizations. I had come to it directly through my studies in biology, for this common denominator is found throughout the plant and the animal kingdoms. Because it was a natural phenomenon, and such a ubiquitous one, an ordinary and accepted part of all levels of plant and animal life, no scholar had previously thought to examine this factor as a prime cause of the degeneration and fall of empires.

This factor was parasitism. In the great advances which medicine had made during the past century, one of its most impressive achievements had been the rapidly developing field of parasitology. It had been found that many of man's most serious ailments were caused by parasites. From these studies, it was only a matter of time before scholars would be able to deduce that a similar condition might occur among man's civilizations, and that it might also cause sickness and death. It was to be expected that in their autopsies of buried empires, scholars should conclude that this condition, parasitism, was a definitive factor in the fatal diseases which befell human civilizations.

But no scholar advanced this conclusion. In the entire Library of Congress, no work can be found which deals with the social effects of parasitism on civilization. There are hundreds of works about the medical aspects of parasitism, but none about its equally serious socio-economic effects. Why is this? Why have not the thousands of scholars in this field, casting desperately for the slightest limb on which to build the flimsy thought which will serve as their doctorial thesis, been unable to see what is in front of them, the destructive effects of parasitic groups on civilization?

Let us offer the simplest explanation, since that is the usually correct one. The parasitic group in the civilization has fixed its domination over the academic and scholarly world. It would not tolerate any academic study which threatened its continued domination. Is this a far-fetched conclusion? Then let us search for a better one, and after we have been unable to find one, let us examine several accepted factors. First, we know that parasitism exists in mankind. Second, the parasitic group is a compact, well-directed (and inner-directed) species. Third, the parasitic group, in order to maintain its parasitic position, must exercise some sort of control over its host, because no host willingly tolerates the presence of the parasite. One obvious form of control would be a control over what the host thinks about, reads, and sees as entertainment, education and news.

The studies of parasitism have progressed at a fantastic rate during the twentieth century, and I can take no special credit for having formulated the social theory of the parasitic group in human civilization, because this theory has been staring us in the face for at least two generations past.

Nevertheless, so obscured has been this phenomenon that it took me five years to develop this theory, and I am aware that even now, I am only opening the door for a host of scholars who can employ this theory to shed much greater light upon human problems than I have been able to do in this comparatively brief time.

Insofar as it has been possible, I have attempted to make this work as non-technical as possible, as much as the nature of the theory allowed, so that scholars in many other fields could employ it in their own work. The ramifications of this theory indicate that it can be immediately useful, and profitable, in the areas of sociology, government, and history, both for the professional scholar and for the layman.

Eustace Mullins,
Washington, D.C.

Chapter One

The Parasite

Most of us think of a parasite as something distasteful, whose role in life is to feed at the expense of someone else. As a result, the term, when applied to humans, is always one of disgust. In the animal and plant kingdoms, also, the parasite is universally disliked. The Oxford English Dictionary (1933) defines the term.

"Parasite –

1. One who eats at the table, or at the expense of, another; always an opprobrious application.
2. Biol. An animal or plant which lives in or upon another organism (technically called its host) and draws its nutriment directly from it.
3. (fig.) a person whose part or action resembles that of an animal parasite."

Thus we find that a parasite is one who is disliked, who feeds at the expense of another, and who lives in or upon another organism which is called the host. We also find that the term can be applied to a person whose life follows the classic life pattern of the parasite.

Now, in the study of mankind, we find that there is one group or classification of persons who appear persistently in the records of the great civilizations. They are always disliked, yet they remain in the midst of the people who dislike them, and if they are driven out, they insist upon returning, no matter at what cost to themselves. We also find that they always manage to live at the expense of others.

The Encyclopaedia Britannica defines parasitism as follows:

> "Parasitism – a one-sided nutritive relationship between two organisms of different kinds, a relationship which is more or less injurious, yet not usually fatal, to the host; a relationship, moreover, that relieves the parasite from most of the activity or struggle which is usually associated with procuring food, and thus tends to favour or induce some degree of simplification or degeneracy."

In the record of many civilizations, we find that the presence of the parasitic group is in many instances fatal to the host people, because it effects fundamental changes in the life pattern of the host people, and diverts their primary energies to the feeding of the parasites. This alteration affects every aspect of the host people's existence, and inevitably weakens them to the point where they are destroyed. Since the Encyclopaedia Britannica refers above to a purely biological parasitic condition in the animal and the plant kingdoms, it is true that the parasitic relationship can be injurious without being fatal, over a period of time, yet even in these instances, we find many examples of plants and animals being killed by parasites, a fact which apparently was not known to the learned scholar who authored the authoritative Encyclopaedia Britannica article on this condition.

We find, too, that the parasitic group is continually denounced by the more moral elements among the host people, because the parasitic group indulges in every known type of degeneracy. The reasons for this are obvious. As the

Encyclopaedia Britannica article points out, a parasitic existence leads to degeneracy. Since the parasite does not have to trouble himself with the active procurement of food, he has plenty of time and energy to devote himself to the vilest pursuits, and to the debauching of members of the host people.

The Encyclopaedia Britannica also paragraphs an important factor in the present study, the localization of the parasite within the host. The Britannica article points out that,

"Parasites are often localized to a particular site within the host."

Since the parasite has reduced its life aims to one goal, that of remaining upon the host and feeding at its expense, it must choose a location where this is possible. The location must be one from which the host cannot readily dislodge it, and it must be one which allows the parasite to feed without exertion. As a result, the parasite usually chooses a place in or near the reproductive organs or the excretory organs of the host.

Throughout history, the parasitic group has chosen to localize itself near the reproductive or the excretory organs of the host. In most cases, this has meant settling in the great cities of the host people, although, in nations which were primarily agricultural, the parasitic group managed to disperse itself among the villages.

Webster's Third International Dictionary defines the parasite as "2a – an organism living in or on another living organism, obtaining from it part or all of its organic nutriment, and commonly exhibiting some degree of structural modifications.

THE ABILITY TO MODIFY

This is an important characteristic of the parasitic group in the history of mankind. It has exhibited an amazing ability to change or to modify itself in order to achieve its parasitic goal. It has developed extremely refined techniques for remaining upon the host, and sophisticated methods of continuing to feed at the host's expense. It has adopted many guises, and it has shown a tremendous amount of adaptability for appearing in various forms, in order to remain in place.

To continue with Webster's Third International Dictionary – "Parasite 3. something that resembles the biological parasite in dependence upon something else for existence without making a useful or adequate return (illus. the great city is a parasite on the country – Francois Bondy)."

This is the last important key to the solution of our problem, the decay of human civilization. The parasite depends on something else for existence without making a useful or an adequate return. Throughout our study of history, we find that the parasitic group never makes any return or shows any gratitude for being allowed to feed upon the host. The parasites motto is "always take." Should we be surprised, then to find that this motto actually appears in the written literature of a known parasitic group?

We now ask the reader – what group appears and reappears in the history of one civilization after another? What group has always been actively disliked by its host peoples? What group has played an often decisive role in the decay and collapse of one civilization after another? What group indulges in every type of degeneracy? What group always localizes to certain positions among the host peoples? And what group refuses to fulfill a constructive role in any civilization, but instead, remains true to its motto of "Always take," while refusing to make a useful or an adequate return?

KNOWN AS THE JEWS

This group, as the reader may have already surmised from his own studies, is known throughout history as the Jews. Prior to the present study, human individuals or groups living at the expense of others were often called parasites, but this term was used purely in a sociological sense, without any biological point of reference. Plantation owners were said to be parasites because they lived at the expense of their slaves, aristocrats were said to be parasites because they lived at the expense of the masses, armies were said to be parasites because they lived at the expense of the workers.

But, in every case, the supposed parasites were performing certain duties and fulfilling certain responsibilities in the society. Thus we find that in the purely sociological sense, it is possible to name many groups as parasitical, such as children and those who are too old to work. They are certainly feeding at the expense of others, performing no useful work, and making no adequate return. But these groups either have done useful work in the past, or they are expected to do so in the future. Thus, they do not fall within the accepted framework of the biological definition of a parasite. Throughout this work, we will find that the biological references hold true to an amazing degree, in establishing the history and the presence of a parasitical group, and that in every instance, the records of the Jews prove that they are fulfilling the role of biological parasites.

OTHER BIOLOGICAL ASPECTS

In nature, we find that the parasite often attempts to disguise its parasitic life cycle, and to appear to be like ordinary plants and animals. Thus, a description of the biological plant, Krameria, in "The Conditions of Parasitism in Plants," by D. T. MacDougal and W. A. Cannon (Carnegie Institute of Washington, 1910):

> "The Western United States desert bush Krameria is parasitic on a number of woody hosts. Krameria does not at first glance seem to be a parasite, for it does not grow directly upon its host, but its roots reach out beneath the ground and tap the roots of its host, drawing nutriment therefrom. Its favorite host is Covillea tridentata, although it is also parasitic on the acacia and a number of other plants. Its condition of parasitism was discovered after scientists were puzzled that it had no deep-going tap root. It is a grayish shrub, bearing fruit and leaves at certain seasons of the year."

The parasite in nature often finds it convenient to disguise itself and its aims, and to convince others that it is something else, in order to carry out its parasitic mission. Also, the parasite is not a species, but a *form of life*, which preys upon many other different species. In this regard, the Jew as a biological species is not so much a race, as it is a type which preys upon all other races. As Geoffrey LaPage points out, in his definitive work, "Parasitic Animals" (Cambridge University Press, 1951, page 1),

> "A parasitic animal is not a particular species of animal, but an animal which has adopted a certain way of living."

In regard to Krameria's failure to develop a deep tap root, which is not necessary for its parasitic existence, we may note that the Jew never develops deep roots in any culture of a host people, but confines himself to the most superficial and the most quickly profitable aspects of its existence.

Therefore, a Jew is not so much a particular species in the civilized world, as he is a type which has adopted a certain form of parasitic life and adapted himself to exist upon a host which can provide his food.

LaPage continues,

"Unlike many other biological terms, the word parasite and its adjective parasitic have been taken into the every day language of men and women, and have, in the course of common usage, acquired emotional and moral connotations with which science – and therefore biology – has nothing whatever to do. The biologist's outlook is scientific, and because it is so, he does everything in his power to remove from his studies all human likes and dislikes and all human moral judgments. He neither despises nor admires, likes or dislikes, condemns or approves, the parasitic organism. He studies it, its way of living as dispassionately as he can, seeing parasites as one of the various ways of living practiced by different kinds of animals."

THE SCIENTIFIC APPROACH

We agree whole heartedly with Professor LaPage's admonition to be completely scientific and to follow the resolve not to be swayed by emotional judgments. It was precisely by this method of dispassionate study that this writer arrived at his definition of the biological Jew. Only by studying him unemotionally as a biological phenomenon can we hope to learn how to combat the maleficent influence which the parasitic body inevitably exerts upon the more advanced human civilizations.

LaPage points out that we find, in general, two kinds of animal associations, those who belong to one species, such as herds, colonies of coral, communities of bees, etc., and two, associations of different species in the same area. To this second category, parasitism belongs, for we find groups with roots in an area entertaining parasites who have no roots in that area. One of the more interesting facets of parasitism is that the parasite lives an existence which often goes beyond the customary laws of nature and of man. The parasite seems not to be bound by limiting factors of climate, geography, and other elements which play a commanding role in the lives of most groups. Thus we find that a parasite can survive in an area in which it has no roots, while its host does have roots in the area and has established its existence there over a period of time.

NOT COMMENSALISM

LaPage also remarks that parasitism is different from commensalism, a frequently-encountered biological term which means "eating at the same table." He cites as examples of commensalisms, the ox-picker birds which perch upon the backs of rhinoceros, elephants and other large animals on the African plains. These birds not only eat ticks, lice and other parasites which infest the animals, but they also warn the animals of approaching danger.

In England, we find that starlings and sheep have a similar commensal arrangement. We also have the phenomenon of symbiosis, a biological term meaning "living together." This is a somewhat more intimate living arrangement than commensalism, because we find in symbiosis a physiological dependence of each partner upon the other. Each one supplies some food to the other without which life would be more difficult, or even impossible, and neither lives an independent life.

Parasitism, however, is defined by LaPage as similar to commensalism and symbiosis in that the association is based upon the need for an adequate food supply. He states that parasitism is an association between one partner, called the parasite, which obtains, by a number of different methods, its food from the body of the other partner, which is called the host of the parasite. But, asks LaPage, does the other partner, the host, benefit? He answers that it never does. The host is always injured by the parasite. Thus parasitism differs from commensalism and symbiosis in two particulars; first, not both, but only one of the partners, the parasite, gains a food supply, and second, not both, but only one of the partners benefits, while the host always suffers some injury.

MODIFICATION OF THE ORGANISM

LaPage conjectures that the first parasite may have been a non-parasitic organism which penetrated by some route the body of another kind of animal, and found some food there, such as blood, which was rich in nutrition and easily digestible, and that, in the course of evolution, the descendants of this first parasite liked this way of life, and maintained such an association with some other animal. Eventually, these types became wholly dependent upon parasitism as a way of obtaining food and could not survive without following it. Thus it became an "obligatory parasite," completely dependent physiologically upon its host. As LaPage points out, the host does not tolerate passively this association with the parasite, but reacts to the injury which it is suffering. He says,

> "The struggle between host and parasite went on according to the laws of evolution, and this battle is constantly being waged today.

Parasitism is quite different from the relationship of prey and predator, in which one body gets its nourishment by killing and absorbing the body of another. Here the predator is always larger and stronger than its prey, while the parasite is always smaller and weaker than its host."

VIOLATES NATURE

Thus we find that here once more the parasite violates a fundamental law of nature. It is a law of nature that the stronger survives at the expense of the weaker, the survival of the fittest, as the weaker is eaten to provide nourishment for the strong. In the phenomenon of the parasite, however, we find that the weaker survives at the expense of the stronger, the least fitted to survive becomes the victor, and the stronger is vanquished.

This too is a fundamental aspect of the life cycle of the biological Jew. Throughout history, he has always been smaller and weaker than his gentile host, yet he has often managed to subdue him. The puny weakling, as celebrated by the Jewish comedian Charlie Chaplin, always manages to outwit and to defeat his larger and stronger gentile opponent. We find that this celebration is a fundamental approach in all Jewish humor, literature and art. The small David is shown defeating the larger Goliath, the cunning Mordecai is shown defeating the stronger gentile official, Haman. David, of course, is the small parasite, and Goliath is the large host, who is struck down from afar, before he has a chance to use his superior strength against the weakling challenger.

TEMPORARY PARASITES

LaPage classifies as "temporary parasites" those insects such as mosquitoes and leeches, which suck the blood of the host. He names them ectoparasites because they do not enter the body of the host. Other lice, which live beneath the skin of their hosts, are classified as endoparasites. There are also hyperparasites, who live off of other parasites (the rabbinical dynasties), and brood or social parasites, which are found in ant and bee families, and which live off of the community.

EVOLUTION AND PARASITES

LaPage points out that every animal, whatever its mode of life, is gradually altered by the slow processes of evolution. He says that the parasite, far from being an exception to this rule, actually exemplifies it.

"It develops teeth with which to rasp the tissues of the host, sucking apparatuses to suck its juices, coagulants to hold onto the host body. The remarkable cunning with which some kinds of bloodsucking bats stalk their victims and steal their blood must also be reckoned among the modifications which their temporarily parasitic habits have produced. Species of Desmodus attack cattle, horses and other animals, including man and poultry, when they are asleep at night. They watch their victims carefully, and, when they are asleep, they walk or sidle up to them and scoop out a piece of flesh so delicately that the sleeping animal often is not aware of the bite until the bleeding is discovered in the morning."

One of the specialized modifications of the Jew is his ability to suck the blood of the gentile host without alarming his victim, weakening it without being discovered, through the highly sophisticated and refined instruments and techniques which the Jew has developed over a period of centuries for these specific purposes, and which have no counterpart in any other species. In view of these techniques, need we be surprised that some of the gentiles who have been most weakened by the blood-lettings of the Jew are among his most vociferous defenders, and who will fight to the death to protect their Jewish "benefactors." They are totally unable to recognize their danger, or the insidious nature of the parasitic attack.

SPECIALIZATION AMONG PARASITES

LaPage describes a type of parasite called the hagfish, which is classified as one of the Cyclostomes, a name whose origin refers to the circular opening inside their mounts. He says,

> "All of these fishes have a wormlike shape and perhaps the best known of them is the lamprey. The hagfish has two rows of teeth on its powerful tongue and one median tooth upon the roof of its mouth. Its eyes are very important and are buried beneath the skin, probably because the hagfish burrows deeply into the tissues of the fish which it attacks, so that its eyes have become useless. For the same reason, its gill openings are connected by long tubes to a single opening on the surface much farther back than the gill openings of the lamprey, so that the hagfish can breathe water while its head end is buried in the body of the fish upon which it is parasitic. Some species of hagfish can attach themselves so firmly by means of their sutorial mouths to the living fish that these fish can only rarely shake them off. They then rasp off the flesh of the fish and suck their blood. Some species of them consume the fish muscle until little is left of the living fish except its bones and viscera, and the fish dies."

Thus LaPage offers a complete contradiction of the definitive and scholarly article of the Encyclopaedia Britannica on Parasitism which contends that the parasite is never fatal to the host. The activities of the hagfish, in sucking the blood of the still living fish until it dies, closely corresponds to the ancient Jewish religious rite of ritual murder, in which the healthy gentile victim is strapped down onto a table, ritual cuts are made into his flesh, and the flowing blood is drunk by the celebrating Jews in one of the most important symbolic acts of their parasitic existence. The ceremony of blood-drinking continues until the gentile victim expires, in a social re-enactment of the physical activities of such parasites as the hagfish. Here we see the close correlation between the activities of parasites in the plant and animal kingdoms and those which have developed through the centuries of human civilization.

LaPage states that many leeches combine organs of attachment with organs of suction, but others have only organs of attachment, such as the hooklets developed by many kinds of parasitic animals which are attached either to the exterior or to the internal organs of the host. In the same way, when the host people of a Jewish community of parasites attempts to dislodge it, they find that the parasite has extended specialized tentacles of attachment deep into every facet of the host people's life. So deeply rooted are these tentacles that the dislodgement is not only difficult, it is such a demanding and painful operation that the dislodgement itself may be fatal to the host.

The host finds that its mortgages are held by Jewish bankers, its children are being taught by Jewish teachers, its government is being administered by Jewish "advisors" or "consultants," who, even if they hold no elective or appointive office, still make the important decisions. They turn for solace to their religion, and they find that Jewish converts, aided by appropriate gifts of money, have entered into the offices of their denominations, and have risen rapidly until the religious beliefs are altered to embrace all of the tenets of the parasitic community of Jews. What, then, does the gentile host have left? The seemingly inevitable doom of being slowly bled to death, after which the parasites will leave the body of their victim and seek another host.

ADULT PHASES OF THE PARASITE

LaPage points out that in many instances, the adult phases of the parasite do not move much about the hosts body, because they are surrounded by food and can obtain it without the help of locomotive organs. Thus, we find that the Jews are not much interested in the transportation industry, preferring the more sedentary occupations. The parasitic community actually can and does become completely immobile in the host for long periods of time, because it is characterized by the ability of dormancy, of lying without moving through the years, while losing none of its potency. We find that ticks bearing infectious diseases can remain in the ground for as long as one hundred years, and when they emerge, they are still infectious.

Jewish communities have established themselves in gentile nations and remained for hundreds of years without exhibiting any signs of being dangerous to their hosts, but, if the gentile host attempts to dislodge them, they immediately rise to the challenge and bring into play their specialized modifications for remaining upon the host. LaPage points out that parasites are naturally inclined to lead a sedentary life, "and undergo the modifications to which this mode of life leads."

As a result of their parasitic mode of life, the Jewish communities have developed sedentary habits, which in turn have led to certain diseases, directly attributable to this sedentary life, and which have been known for their high incidence among the Jews. Thus diabetes is referred to in many medical dictionaries as "the Jewish disease."

Diabetes occurs principally because the sedentary and parasitic life prevents Jews from burning up the excess blood sugars which they ingest in their diet, and which are intended for use in direct forms of energy. This causes a surfeit of sugar in the system, which becomes the disease of diabetes. Also, generations of sedentary persons cause malfunctions or the gradual weakening of the pancreas and other organs which are responsible for controlling the level of blood sugar. Thus, diabetes becomes a hereditary disease among generations of sedentary people.

The Jewish community has developed a number of degenerative types of disease, such as blood disorders, cancers of various kinds, and other forms of physical degeneration, which are directly attributable to their mode of parasitic existence, and to the physical degeneracy which it produces. As they cohabit with the gentile community, and as their sedentary mode of life becomes more widely practiced, these degenerative diseases begin to appear throughout the host community.

In one of the most important physical correlations between the Jewish community and the known types of parasitic organism in the plant and animal kingdoms, LaPage says:

"Among other organs which are often reduced or lost when parasitic life is adopted is the nervous system. It may be reduced as a whole or the reduction may affect chiefly the eyes and other organs. Organs of special sense are best developed in active animals which feed upon other animals and need to defend themselves against their enemies. They are not required by parasitic animals which live a relatively sheltered existence on or inside the bodies of their hosts amid a relative abundance of food."

The effect of a parasitic mode of existence upon the nervous system, which can be observed in many types of parasites, are especially noteworthy in the Jew. The degeneration of the nervous system into a state of severe mental illness in an average of thirty percent of all Jews has long been supposed by sociologists to be due to the physical interbreeding in the Jewish community, but the high incidence of mental illness in Jews whose families have intermarried with gentiles is the same rate as those who have remained within the Jewish community. This points to a strictly biological origin of this degeneracy of the nervous system, and bears out Professor LaPage's contention that the leading of a parasitic mode of existence inevitably leads to a reduction or a degeneracy of the nervous system.

PRONOUNCED CHANGES ON SKELETAL STRUCTURE

One of the most striking observations which LaPage has made in this study of animal parasites is his discovery that, "Because this mode of life tends to cause a loss of (skeletal) structure resistant enough to be preserved as fossils, we have little geological evidence of the past history of parasitic animals. At least six species of fossil roundworms, however, have been described, two of these, Hydonius antiquus and H. matutinus in the Eocine lignite, and the other four in Baltic amber."

The effortless existence led by the parasite not only affects its nervous system, which like any other physical attribute, tends to atrophy when not used or required by the animal, but it also leads, over a period of time, to extensive skeletal changes in the structure of the animal, tending towards a soft, amorphous bone structure which soon disintegrates after the death of the parasite. Here is another remarkable correlation between the life cycles of parasitic animals and the life cycle of the Jew. Because of their parasitic mode of existence, the Jews have left no artifacts which could be discovered among the ruins of ancient civilizations, even though they are known to have been present for long periods of time during these civilizations. Despite the historical records of their presence, we can find no concrete artifacts signifying their existence.

CULTURAL ARTIFACTS

Because we have heard, and still hear, so much about the great Jewish cultures of the past, archeologists have made extensive efforts to discover some examples of Jewish art and sculpture and architecture in ancient cultures, the solid evidences which survive the ravages of time and natural catastrophes. Yet they found nothing. The sole results of these searches are a few pieces of crude waterpots, fashioned from mud, which a Stone Age man could have produced with his bare hands, since he did not know the use of the pottery wheel which made its appearance among early civilizations. These scanty evidences of the great Jewish past is but one more witness to the biological parasitical existence which the Jew has always led as a soft, amorphous and rootless creature feeding at the expense of others, and leaving no concrete artifacts to memorialize his presence.

LaPage says, "Human writings about some species of parasitic animals take us back to the earliest records of man. The Egyptian Papyrus from 1600 B.C. refers to tapeworms, blood flukes and hookworms of man."

Thus the biological parasite has been a problem of man since the dawn of recorded history. Although humans have been aware of the physical discomfort and danger which animal parasites have always presented to him, they have consistently failed to recognize the specific danger of the Jewish parasite until it was too late.

LaPage says, "The parasitic animal has to contend with difficulties and risks to which non-parasites are not exposed. It may have gained shelter and abundance of food, but it has obtained these at the cost of partial or complete dependence upon its hosts. The parasitic animal must find it and get into it or on its surface and it must maintain itself in these situations."

Thus the Jew encounters several dangers which do not ordinarily imperil other types of communities. Foremost among these is the danger of genocide, of actions against its community as a group, when the host discovers that its presence is endangering its health. The Jew is the only human group which has repeatedly undergone mass actions, or pogroms, against it.

Because of its parasitic mode of existence, the Jewish community made no effort to develop a nation or an independent state during thousands of years of recorded history. This meant that the Jew had no standing army for his defense against enemies. When a Jewish state, Israel, was finally established, the nation's budget identified it as an extension of the parasitic community, for seventy percent of its national budget consisted of contributions from abroad, and thirty percent from the sale of bonds which, of course, were worthless and which would never be paid off.

HATRED

Because of its total dependence upon the gentile host, the Jewish parasite develops a deep hatred and a contempt for the animals which provide it with food and shelter. This hatred is a protective frame which acts as a shield for the Jewish community, and prevents it from accepting the life and goals of the host people for its own. Herbert Spencer may have been focusing upon the Jewish parasitic phenomenon when he wrote,

"If a group places a premium on the quality of enmity, in contrast with that of amity, a criminal type evolves."

Since the Jew is the only group which places a premium on the quality of enmity, Spencer must have been making an oblique reference to the Jewish parasite. From the standpoint of the host people, everything that the Jew does is a manifestation of a criminal act, but from the parasite's standpoint, he is only following the procedures of his life cycle which have evolved and been established over a period of thousands of years. The conflict comes from two separate and irreconcilable codes of ethics, that of the host, which places a premium upon decency, honor and self-reliance, and that of the parasite, which operates from an established modus vivendi of parasitism.

The Jew lives in constant fear of rejection, of being thrown off of the host, which would mean his starvation and death. As a result, the Jew sees everything in the light of how he "relates" to the host, or how he maintains his parasitic situation.

ADAPTIVE MODIFICATIONS

The adaptive modifications of the parasite are attempts to anticipate possible changes in the host. LaPage says, "Other parasites correlate their life histories with that of the host; the monogenetic fluke, Polystoma integerrimum, which lives in the bladder of the common frog, ignores all tadpoles which have not reached a stage of development in which they can survive in them, but when it meets with one which has, its aimless behaviour ceases; its seems to pause and await its opportunity to dart through the spoutlike opening into the bag around the internal gills. How it knows the tadpole has reached this stage of internal development we do not know, but perhaps it is helped by its eye spots and its nervous system or by chemical substances secreted by the tadpole into the water which stimulate the miracidium larva."

The extrasensory ability of the parasite to spot a suitably developed host has always been characteristic of the Jews. From earliest history, he has made unerringly for the most advanced and the most promising civilizations, ignoring the more backwards or undeveloped peoples. Thus, we do not find the Jew sharing the Spartan existence of the pygmies in the Uturi rain forest; he is living in a comfortable apartment in New York, dining on caviar and champagne.

Reproductive Phases

LaPage observes that the timing of the release of the parasitic animals reproductive phases so that they may infect the host is also shown by some species of protozoa which live in the rectum of the frog. Here again we note the affinity of the parasite for the excretory organs, the previously mentioned Polystoma integerrimum, which resides in the bladder of the frog, and the protozoa which prefer the rectum of the frog as the most suitable environment for its life.

LaPage states that the dormancy of parasites is a continuously observed phenomenon, retaining their potency during many years of inactivity and isolation. Thus, a community of Jews may live torpidly in its ghetto for centuries, seemingly self-absorbed in its own parochial existence, and having little effect upon its gentile host, until some combination of factors will cause it to become furiously active. In a short time, it permeates every aspect of the host peoples existence, and brings it to the point of destruction. The community of Jews in the Frankfort ghetto of Germany is a good illustration of this type of parasitic dormancy. It remained dormant for three hundred years, and within the span of a single generation, produced a group of bankers and traders who soon won control of the destinies of Western civilization.

DEFENSE REACTIONS

LaPage points out that parasites cause defense reactions in the host against a parasitic invader, such as efforts to localize and neutralize the injurious effects of the parasite, attempts to repair the damage done, and efforts to kill or to remove the parasite. He describes these as "tissue reactions," and these are primarily local reactions, but more advanced reactions, such as a resistance immunity, may be developed by the host as the reaction of the entire organism. He says that tissue reactions are inflammations caused by bacteria, "viruses and inanimate agencies, and may be acute or chronic. They are the results of injury or irritation caused by organs or teeth of the parasitic animal, by its migration through these tissues, or by chemical substances which it secrets or excretes into the body of the host."

PARASITIC DAMAGE

LaPage goes on at some length to describe the various types of damage which the parasite inflicts upon the host. He says that in addition to these various tissue damages, parasites introduce other types of parasites into the host, as well as dangerous viruses. The parasites may produce substances which are injurious to the host, toxins or other kinds of poisons. In effect, then, the parasite begins to exercise a dangerous influence over the life cycle of the host, one which goes far beyond the simple goal of remaining attached to the host and obtaining food from it. Whether the parasite consciously intends it or not, it gradually becomes the most important single influence in the life of the host. The story of the newspaper business in the United States is a typical example. A century ago, newspapers were small and insignificant in this country, while the profession of journalism ranked only slightly above the professions of ratcatcher and garbage hauler. As the Jews began to assume a more prominent role in the life of the gentile host, they found that newspapers were an essential vehicle for their goals. They began to flood everyone with newspapers, and the newspapers became virus carriers of various forms of mental poisons and toxins which either stupefied, confused or paralyzed the gentile host, putting it into a state of suspended animation as long as these venoms could be maintained.

OTHER PARASITES

As LaPage points out, the parasite introduces other types of parasites into the host. We find that when the Jews obtained control of the United States Immigration Service in the 1890s, through such Jewish Commissioners as Straus and Cohen, the gates were opened for a flood of Jewish immigrants from the ghettoes of Europe, most of whom had been excluded previously on grounds of illiteracy, criminal backgrounds, and various forms of physical contagions or mental illnesses.

LaPage also says, "Parasites may cause biological changes such as species which cause changes in the hosts reproductive glands, parasitic castration, such as the parasitic crustacean Sacculina, which destroys the reproductive organs of the host, the short-tailed spider cram, Inacus mauritanicus, which is attacked by Sacculina neglecta. The effects of Sacculina cause seventy percent of male crabs to acquire some of the secondary sexual characteristics of the female. The abdomen of these males becomes broad, they may acquire, in addition to their male copulating styles, appendages modified to bear eggs, and their nippers become smaller at the same time."

It is inevitable that the enormous effect which the parasite has upon the host would result in some biological alterations such as the effect of Sacculina upon Inacus mauritanicus. We have seen in America during the past quarter of a century, coincident with the great power attained by the Jews in every walk of life, startling modifications in the appearances and habits of American males, as well as a vast increase in the public practice of male homosexuality. American males have taken on some of the secondary sexual characteristics of the female, and they have shown amazing declines in such primary male characteristics as energy, aggressiveness, and physical strength.

The traditional roles of the sexes have also undergone sweeping changes, due principally to Jewish agitation for "sexual equity."

This campaign has not resulted in sexual equality, since this equality could only be attained by eradicating all physical differences between males and females. However, it has resulted in a decline of masculine traits in the American male, as well as psychological confusion as to his role. This development can be equated with the pernicious influence which the parasite exercises upon the host, as LaPage describes the encounter of Sacculina with Inacus mauritanicus. Here again, we note the remarkable activity and influence of the parasite in relation to the reproductive and the excretory organs of the host.

REACTIONS AGAINST THE PARASITE

LaPage notes throughout his definitive studies of the parasite-host relationship that the host's defense against the parasite is always of an activist or a reactionary nature, such as cattle switching their tails, fish taking evasive action in sudden, unpredictable twists and turns, and other wild actions which they hope will dislodge the parasite. During the five thousand years that history has recorded the presence of the biological parasite in civilized communities, we cannot find a single shred of evidence that the host people has ever treated the parasite phenomenon in any but an activist manner, an unthinking, involuntary action to dislodge the parasite.

The host instinctively reacts against the presence of the parasite, because it knows it will suffer in an injury form this strange creature, with its differing life cycle and goals. This is why the Jews always call those who oppose them "reactionaries," that is, those who react against the presence of the parasite. Consequently, one of the major tasks of the parasite is to seek out all potential "reactionaries" among the host people and eliminate them.

KNOWLEDGE OF THE PARASITE

Because of this blind, unthinking reaction, which seldom is effective in ridding the host of the parasite, LaPage says,

> "The basic essential of any campaign against a parasitic animal is a thorough knowledge of every phase of its life history and also of its relationships with all the hosts with which it can live. We need to know all the hosts because some of them may be reservoir hosts maintaining sources of the parasites which can then infect man. With this knowledge, we can select for attack the weakest points in the life history and biology of the parasitic animal."

Research and education, then, are the tools which are needed to counterattack against the evil influence of the parasite. Above all, we must avoid blind, instinctive reaction, since the parasite has long since learned how to anticipate and control such reaction, and even to use it for its own advantage.

ALWAYS AN ENEMY

LaPage points out that "Host and parasitic animal must always be considered together, because the parasitic animal is, like all other living things, intimately related throughout its existence to its environment. The fact that environment is, for a part or whole of its life, the surface or interior of another animal, does not absolve the parasitologist from the biologist's practice of considering animal and environment together as a whole. A second objective is the demonstration that some species of parasitic animals are among the most powerful enemies of man and his civilization."

The parasites concern with his environment sheds light upon one of the most important intellectual developments of modern man, the Enlightenment, that revolutionary force which has spearheaded the growing control of the parasite over the host. The pre-Enlightenment centuries of human thought considered man's environment as a secondary consideration, because of faith in powers of the individual, and the belief that he individual could triumph over his environment. After the sudden importance given to such French intellectuals as Jean Jacques Rousseau, man was no longer considered as important as his environment. All at once, our leading thinkers decided that environment was the most important thing in life. And indeed it is, to the parasite, whose environment is the host which feeds him.

But to the host, who is making his own way in life, environment is not the primary factor in his development. But to the parasite, environment is everything. All Socialist thinkers, and the various schools of sociological thought which have crept out of this development, place primary importance upon man's environment, rather than upon his powers to use that environment and to create a life for himself, as he achieves his life's goals.

When we understand the theory of the parasite, we are able to understand, FOR THE FIRST TIME, the entire modern Socialist school of thought, because we can recognize it for what it is, the environmental psychology which the parasite has developed around his own life cycle. As such, it negates all of the host's thought, goals and culture.

LaPage urges us to remember that the parasite is among the most powerful enemies of man and his civilization. Here again, he seems on the verge of going into the Jewish problem, but he shies away from applying his theories to the problems of human's sociology. Certainly he could not have been referring to parasitic viruses, or to the blood-sucking mosquitoes, for even if they hindered the building of the Panama Canal, they cannot be said to have caused the collapse of any human civilization. What could he mean but the biological parasite which has infested man's civilization since the beginning of recorded history, and which has brought about the downfall of one empire after another? Perhaps that is why he urges us to select for attack "the weakest points, in the life history and the biology of the parasitic animal."

Chapter Two

The Biological Jew

During the twentieth century, man has begun to concern himself with the problem of the collapse of world cultures, great empires which rise to their zenith, and then mysteriously decline. We know why they rise. They grow because a people finds itself with a mission, or because it develops techniques for mastering its surroundings. A people takes advantage of favorable conditions, because they have the will to carry out their mission. During the period when the people are able to channel their energies constructively, a nation grows amazingly in size and power, in a geometric ratio. Then, suddenly, it begins to sicken and die. One example was Elizabethan England, which had expelled the Jews. When Oliver Cromwell brought back the Jews, the English people lost their sense of direction, and although their momentum was still sufficient to carry them on an upward course through the Victorian period, today we find that their aristocracy has been dispossessed, and their assets, although greatly reduced, are administered by aliens.

Two scholars have formulated theories, developed through many years of study, to explain this process of the downfall of nations.

The first, Oswald Spengler,[4] was a German scholar of unique power and energy. He compiled interlocking records of every known civilization, and carried on intricate comparative studies which today could only be done by an electronic computer, so complex was his mastery of conjunctive of interweaving factors.

Spengler concluded that a civilization is a body like any other, which is subject to the laws which govern natural bodies. He saw that a civilization had its birth stage, a young and vigorous stage, and an old age which left it weak and prey to its enemies. In proposing this biological pattern for civilizations, Spengler was on the right track. Nor was he insensitive to the fact that civilizations develop internal problems which function, like a fatal disease. Only on one point did he seem to be blind, the concept of the parasite. This is not too strange, for Spengler was greatly concerned with the finer aspects of human culture, the greatest achievements of man, his art, his music, his poetry, his architecture. Of course a scholar of this elevated turn of mind did not wish to concern himself with degenerative things which creep and entwine themselves about the reproductive and the excretory organs of man, those parasitic organisms which cause discomfort, disease and death.

A LATE THEORY

A second explorer of this ground was Arnold Toynbee, a donnish Englishman. He was equally reluctant to face the omnipresent and distasteful fact of the biological Jew. He embarked upon a vast study of civilization, which covered essentially the same ground as Spengler, and added little to Spengler's findings. His sole original contribution was a

---

[4] *The Decline of the West*, by Oswald Spengler, English edition, Knopf, NY 1926.

theory which immediately became popular with the intellectual lightweights of the time, since it conformed to their own prejudices. It was cast in the accepted pseudo-sociological jargon which university nitwits employ to bemuse their students and each other.

Civilizations fall, declared Toynbee, because of a "failure of nerve," at some point in its development, a civilization, which lives by a system of "challenge and response" fails to respond to some challenge, and goes down before it.

Now, this could refer to the biological Jew, since the parasite is a challenge to the continued threat of the host. However, it is a challenge which no gentile host has ever been prepared to meet. It is a germ which is best defeated by inoculation, or by personal cleanliness and careful attention to matters of health.

Spengler's history of the decline and fall of civilizations could not be upheld because it did not take into consideration the obvious fact that few, if any, civilizations, had died of old age. Nearly all of them had been murdered, in one way or another, but Spengler was too preoccupied with the fine arts to become interested in the problems of crime and disease.

Toynbee, on the other hand, could not be the detective in this case because he had lived most of his life on a subsidy from the criminal classes. His years of study had been financed by generous grants from the Royal Institute of International Affairs, one of a network of organizations which had been set up by international Jewish bankers as useful pawns in their operations. The sister organization of the RIIA in the United States is the Council on Foreign Relations, which I was the first to uncover as the principal power holding company of the parasitic Establishment in this country. In the first edition of *Mullins on the Federal Reserve*, in 1952, a biographical note on the back cover announced that I was completing a sequel to the Federal Reserve book which would be an expose of the Council on Foreign Relations. This was the first time that any American nationalist had ever publicly called attention to this organization. A few months later, a New York Jew via Hungary, Dr. Emanuel Josephson, rushed into print with a book on the Council on Foreign Relations, which attempted to show that it was an instrument of gentiles such as the Rockefellers, and not a front for the parasitic Jewish community. I visited him and we talked for seven hours. It was quite obvious that he knew everything that I knew about the Council on Foreign Relations, whose offices were only a few doors from his home, and it was also obvious that he had placed a different interpretation on his findings.

Just as Emanuel Josephson refused to face the facts about the Council on Foreign Relations, so Arnold Toynbee, living on comfortable grants from the Rothschild family, found no evidence of parasitical weakenings of civilizations in his vast work ("*A Study of History*," by Arnold Toynbee, Oxford, 1934). Instead, Toynbee superficially studied the nerve patterns of cultures, and the stimuli which affected them, without once mentioning the most vicious enemy of the nervous system, the parasite. When Toynbee says that a civilization failed to respond to a challenge, he asks us to believe that a man who is standing on a street corner, and who is knocked down from behind by a runaway truck, has failed to respond to a challenge. The fact is that he has been killed.

IMPORTANCE OF BIOLOGY

Has Toynbee ever heard of biology? Has he ever heard of parasites? We find no evidence of it in his encyclopaedic studies. Does he have any inkling that civilizations allow foreign bodies to settle in their midst, to flourish and operate without supervision and control, no matter how pernicious their influence may be? How could Toynbee spend twenty years in the study of ancient civilizations without knowing that the Jews opened the gates of Babylon to the Persian invaders, without knowing how the Jews brought Rome to its knees, without knowing how the Jews subjected Egypt to a terrible dictatorship for three hundred years, until the Egyptians rose and drove them out? Only a great intellectual pervert, in the pay of the parasites, could conceal such information after having uncovered it. A comparable deed would be Pasteur destroying the records of his rabies vaccine after discovering it, or Jenner concealing the formula for his smallpox remedy.

PATTERN OF THE PARASITE

The study of the biological parasite reveals a pattern, a set of characteristic and interweaving facts of nature: 1. the parasite prefers a healthy organism as a feeding ground; 2. the parasite's life cycle depends upon its finding a host upon which it can feed; 3. a healthy organism which is invaded by a parasitic organism is inevitably injured and often dies from the evil effect of the parasitic presence. Most often, the parasite causes the host to lose its sense of direction, so that it becomes helpless and is unable to defend itself against its exterior enemies.

This pattern embraces a set of factors which have been common to every great civilization which has suddenly sickened and died. Was Mr. Toynbee, in his decades of concentrated study, unable to discern a single one of them? Apparently, the answer is yes. We see a state of affairs in which a people has built, through its own efforts, a great empire, whose ships trade with far-off lands, whose armies are invincible. This people is strong, self-confident, and aware of their virtues. Why should they fear a few shabby, furtive aliens who have drifted in from unknown places, and who establish themselves in the heart of the city so unobtrusively that it seems they have always been there? These aliens are willing to do anything, they perform any sort of distasteful task which the natives feel is beneath them. The aliens traffic in the bodies of girls, set up gambling dens, clear in stolen goods, lend money, establish houses in which one can perform every imaginable type of sexual degeneracy, and provide assassins for hire.

THE INEXTRICABLE HOLD

In a short time, the aliens know every secret of the peoples' leaders, and they have established holds over them. The colony of aliens multiplies rapidly, and soon a once healthy people finds itself helpless, because their native virtues of strength, courage and honor, which have made them great, are of no avail against the newcomers. The host does not understand the parasite, which is like a creature from another planet, because they do not have the same goals, nor do they respond to the same stimuli, as the host people. They even seem to have different nerve patterns. As the pernicious influence grows, the army is demoralized, the native leaders are murdered or exiled, and the wealth of the nation swiftly passes into the hands of the aliens. The people are plundered of everything, and most of all of their self-respect. No member of a host people is allowed to preserve his self-respect or his privacy, once the parasite has taken command.

One morning, the ships of a rival nation appear in the harbor. In exchange for certain guarantees, the parasites welcome them. The host people does not resist, an empire is gone. Now, this process is not a typical life pattern of a culture a la Spengler; neither is it a challenge and response a la Toynbee. The host people could have repelled any other attack by an armed invader, but they could not fight against the onset of a furtive parasite and the inevitable decay which he brought with him, a disease which affected and paralyzed the entire organism of the people.

FOREIGN BODIES

The theory of the biological parasite explains for the first time the fall of Egypt, of Babylon, of Rome, of Persia, and of England. A prosperous, healthy people allows a foreign body to establish itself in their midst. The foreign body paralyzes and destroys them. This new concept of history brings both Spengler and Toynbee up to date. It also offers a civilization, for the first time, an opportunity to escape the fate of its predecessors.

The serious student may find himself appalled by the more repulsive aspects of the study of the biological parasite. He finds that one type of fish in the South Seas has a long, tapering body, and that it enters the rear of larger fish, and feeds upon the feces within. Man is plagued by a tapeworm which enters his body, hooks onto the large intestine with a hook which he has developed solely for that purpose, and begins to absorb the nourishment from the food eaten by man. Various forms of lice secrete themselves around the reproductive or the excretory organs of man and cause him extreme discomfort.

Parasites find that the waste matter excreted by humans is a fertile breeding ground for them, because the human is a higher form of life which uses large quantities of food and excretes much of it with the food values intact. These excretions provide rich food for the parasite, but his attachment to it poses health problems for humans. Consequently, humans try to dispose of their waste matter so that it will not become a breeding ground for various obnoxious forms of parasites. The parasite considers this to be very cruel and unjust, and he endeavours by any means to reach it. If he endangers the life of the human, so what? A fly on a manure pile is not concerned as to whether he poses a threat to the health of humans.

Parasite's Attitude

It follows that the parasite which has established itself upon the gentile host does not care how much it injures the host. Its only goal is to lead a parasitic life at the expense of the host, and its natural objectives are usually the reproductive and the excretory organs. Throughout history, we find the Jew entwined about the reproductive organs of the gentile host like a parasitic vine which is slowly strangling a healthy tree. The Jew has always functioned best as a panderer, a pornographer, a master of prostitution, an apostle of sexual perversion, an enemy of the prevailing sexual standards and prohibitions of the gentile community. When the title of "America's largest pornographer" was bestowed by police investigators, who was the holder of the title? One Irving Klaw of New York, who carried on a vast business in nude photographs and other items of the trade.

Other Jews, of great intellectual aspirations, have become writers, transforming our literature into dreary recitals of sexual acts, and making it impossible to publish anything which fails to conform to their standards of depravity. Other intellectual Jews have created a new profession, one so characteristic of them that it is known everywhere as a Jewish profession. This is the profession of psychiatry, an outgrowth of the parasite's obsession with the reproductive and excretory habits of the host. What is the basis of the "science" of psychiatry, as it has been formulated by its Jewish founder and patron saint, Sigmund Freud? The basis of psychiatry is the "anal complex," the theory that an obsession with the anus is the principal influence in our emotional development. Many millions of words have been written on this subject, despite its distasteful connotations, and learned speeches about the anal compulsion are delivered by scholars before the world's learned bodies of distinguished men.

THE ANAL COMPLEX

With the anal complex setting the tasteful tone of the parasite's obsessions, the Jew has gone on to develop other theories about the processes of human excretion. The most important influence in the modern school of progressive education is the science of toilet training, while much of modern art is based, and easily recognizable in its origins, upon the feces complex, or the handling of its stool by the pre-school child. Other important contributions of Jewish psychiatric thought, which have been hailed as major intellectual developments of tremendous depth and scope, are too filthy to be repeated here.

When one contemplates the spectacle of a great hall, filled with well-dressed and well-educated men and women from many countries, who are listening intently, and occasionally applauding, a little Jew in a tuxedo who is delivering a learned dissertation upon the anal and excretory habits of mankind, we realize yet another aspect of the Jew. No matter what he does, the Jew is so fantastic that he becomes a comic figure. When the former Premier of France, Mendes-France, announced that his nation was surrendering the huge French investment in Vietnam to the Communists, one hardly knew whether to laugh or cry, so comic was the bulging-eyed black-jowled image of a rag merchant howling "O-o-o-l-l-d-d-r-a-a-a-a-g-g-z-z-uh" through the streets.

The poet Ezra Pound once observed to me that when he began to suggest to people that Jews were exercising undue power in the gentile world, no one took him seriously, because everyone knew that Jews were only clowns. As usual, the Jew used this impression to fix his position upon the gentile host. Charlie Chaplin, with his racially characteristic gestures, employed his typically obscene movements to be hailed as a great comic genius by the indefatigable international Jewish claque. He made millions of dollars by wagging his behind at the audience, scratching frantically at his buttocks, and exhibiting the usual run of the parasite's age-old preoccupations with the reproductive and the excretory organs.

In his own right, Sigmund Freud is an even greater comedian than Charlie Chaplin, because the Freudian theories of human behaviour, as the great gentile psychologist, Carl Jung, reminded us, are based upon the biological parasite's enormous misconceptions of the nature of his gentile host, and Freud's theories are even more comical than the gyrations of Charlie Chaplin. Yet we laugh at Chaplin, and study the theories of Freud seriously.

PARASITES IN MANY ASPECTS OF LIFE

Another obsession of the parasite is that it must force its way into every aspect of the host's existence. It cannot endure the thought of a group of gentiles discussing anything without the parasite or one of his shabez goi agents being present to make notes. Thus, the Jew campaigns to force his way into every gentile organization, whether it he social, religious, a private school, a club, or a neighborhood, anywhere that the gentiles might be able to gather and talk over things which the Jew wishes to know.

This obsession is due to the fact that the Jew can never know any real security in his parasitic existence. He lives daily with the terrible fear that the host will cast him off, and even when he has obtained control at every level of the gentile's life, the Jew still feels insecure. If the gentile manages to keep him out of anything, the Jew becomes wild with rage.

THE DREYFUS CASE

This obsession with security was the real force behind the furor over the Dreyfus case in France during the last century. A Jew named Captain Dreyfus had managed to penetrate the formerly all gentile French High Command. Soon afterwards, he was charged with selling French military secrets to the highest bidder. Although it was an open and shut case, as usual, the Jews launched a frantic international campaign to free him. It seemed odd that so much noise was raised over the fate of one French officer, but the theory of the biological parasite explains the mystery. The parasite had penetrated one of the last bastions of the gentile host. Now he knew all the military secrets, and he was also in a position to inform his people if the army should become involved in a reaction against the presence of the parasites. But the parasite was arrested and charged as a traitor, which he was, because his primary loyalty was to the parasitic community. The tragedy is not that he is convicted, but that the Jews have lost their man in the nation's security council. At once, the entire parasite community charges to his defense, exhibiting terrible fear and anger. This rejection or exclusion is the fate which haunts the parasite, because, for him, it is a matter of life and death. If he is rejected by the host, he cannot lead a parasitic existence, and he will die. Hence the great furor over the Dreyfus case.

OUR OWN DREYFUS CASES

Democratic administrations in the United States have had a plethora of Dreyfus cases in recent years, in which a parasite who had burrowed into the nation's security councils was charged with disloyalty. One of them was Dr. Oppenheimer, a Jew whose social circle was composed of dedicated Communist agents, most of whom were known as such while he worked on our nation's most vital defense secrets. He was finally denied a security clearance, due to public alarm over his background, and a terrible clamor arose from the international Jewish community, which went on for years. We still do not know how much damage he did to the nation.

A more celebrated case was a Jew of Russian origins, Walt Rostow. He is only the person in charge of our national security! Yet a few years ago, loyal employees of the State Department refused Rostow a security clearance, not once, but three times, because of his notorious associations. Yet when John F. Kennedy became President, he placed Walt Rostow in charge of our national security!

Drew Pearson recently revealed that it was this Jew who made the personal decision to employ American troops in large forces in Vietnam, one of the greatest victories for Communism since 1917. While Americans were being slaughtered in Vietnam, Russia could sit back and see us bleed to death without the Communist world being weakened at all. In this Dreyfus case, the Jews have won every round, while the gentile who exposed him, Otto Otepka, is still being persecuted by "our" government.

GENTILE OPPORTUNISTS

In France, a few clever gentiles sensed which way the wind was blowing in the Dreyfus case, even if they had no understanding of the parasitic theory. An obscure hackwriter named Emile Zola wrote some fiery articles, such as "J'Accuse," demanding that Dreyfus be freed, and the international Jewish propaganda machine immediately began to puff Zola as a great writer. He enjoyed great fame and fortune during the rest of his life, although his novels are now ignored.

A pompous little country lawyer, Clemenceau, also found his career in the Dreyfus case. He intervened on Dreyfus' behalf, and the Jews made him Premier of France. The way of the shabez goi can be smoothed.

The threat of rejection always stirs a torrent of fear and anger in the parasite. This writer encountered an example of this when he purchased a secondhand mattress in Jersey City. Late that night, he was awakened by an unwelcome presence. He switched on the light, and there on his stomach was a fat little bedbug, swollen with its feast, and reluctant to abandon its host even in the light of exposure.

When the light came on, the bedbug gave a furious shriek of anger, and waddled out of sight. At this time, the writer did not immediately relate this episode to the theory of the biological parasite, but he later reflected that this anger of the bedbug, which was carrying on its usual activity, was understandable. We cannot expect the Jew to appreciate any effort of the gentile host to dislodge him, and remove him from the feast. This is why he works day and night to prevent such a thing.

NECESSITY OF CONTROL

This is why the Jew MUST control our communications; this is why he MUST control our education; this is why he MUST control our government; and most important, this is why he MUST control our religion. If he fails to do this, in any area, he endangers his continued existence as a biological parasite. Even in the Soviet Union, with its idealistic slogan of "From each according to his means; to each according to his needs," the parasite gains control over gentile workers and sets them to producing goods which he sells, and pockets the proceeds. Fat Jews and their blond mistresses stroll from their luxurious villas on the Black Sea, while intense, dogmatic gentile commissars such as Mikhail Suslov sit in the Kremlin trying desperately to devise a system which the Jew cannot twist to his own advantage. They cannot succeed, because the parasite has always thought one step ahead of them.

AGGRESSION

When the Jews seized the lands of peaceful Arab farmers by aggression in 1948, many gentiles throughout the world supposed that a new era had begun. These gentiles assured each other, now that they have their own country, the Jews will go there and stop exploiting us. Instead, the parasitic communities in all parts of the world intensified their exploitations of their gentile hosts, in order to meet the vast needs of the new State of Israel. Garment workers in the notorious New York sweat shops, most of them Negro and Puerto Rican women and children, had large portions of their earnings extorted from them by the cold-blooded Jew, David Dubinsky, the fascist dictator of the garment union. These funds were turned over to the State of Israel.

This illustrates the facility of the Jew for being on all sides, and for always being on the winning side. Chaim Weizmann, the founder of the State of Israel, quotes an oft-repeated saying of his mother, in his autobiography, "Trial and Error," Harper, New York, 1949, page 13,

"Whatever happens, I shall be well off. If Shemuel (the revolutionary son) is right, we shall all be happy in Russia; and if Chaim (the Zionist) is right, then I shall go to live in Palestine."

Parasite's budget

On April 17, 1950, the *New York Times* announced that the annual budget of the State of Israel had been released. It was composed of seventy percent of donations from abroad, and thirty percent from the sale of Israeli bonds, which would never have any redeemable value, and which could only be described as contributions. No other nation on earth could envision such a budget, for even India, the perennial beggar among nations, with its swollen, mongrelized population, can raise only one percent of its budget from abroad, and that is entirely donated by the United States. Yet the State of Israel confidently envisions a national budget for years to come consisting of charity and the peddling of dubious paper. This is the budget of a nation of parasites, still depending upon the gentile hosts.

Trend to degeneracy

The bizarre, unhealthy existence of the parasite, with his trend to degeneracy and his decaying nervous system, places him outside of every known system of morality and human decency. Now he has perfected a Jewish hellbomb, which threatens to destroy the host and himself as well. When Alechsander Sachs, of the international Jewish banking firm of Lehman Brothers, New York, and Albert Einstein, "suggested" to President Roosevelt that he invest hundreds of millions of dollars in the production of a hellbomb, how could Roosevelt refuse? Now they needed a gentile front for their project. Major General Leslie Groves was asked to head the project, but when he found that most of the scientists were Jewish, he asked to be excused, saying that he believed that a Jewish director would be more efficient in this atmosphere.

"Not at all," he was assured. "We need a gentile as the ostensible head of the project. Don't worry, we'll handle all of the responsibility."

We know that the gentile can never expect any mercy from the Jew. The horrible practice of ritual murder is sufficient evidence of this. The ritual murder of gentile children by bleeding them to death and drinking their blood is the highest symbolic revelation of the theory of the biological parasite.

Symbol of Victory

Primitive man sometimes drank the blood of fallen foes as a symbol of victory, and to absorb some of the strength of the enemy, but another blood-drinking practice, that of ritual murder, is the only one which has survived into modern times. This religious ceremony of drinking the blood of an innocent gentile child is basic to the Jew's entire concept of his existence as a parasite, living off of the blood of the host. That is why he refuses to abandon this custom, even though it has brought him close to extinction many times.

When the Jew can no longer symbolize his role by kidnapping a perfectly formed gentile child, spiriting him away to a synagogue, and ritually puncturing his body in the places which they boasted they had wounded the Body of Christ, and drinking the blood of the dying child, then, according to Jewish belief, he is doomed. His prophets have warned him that when this custom can no longer be observed, the Jewish parasite's hold onto the host will be loosened, and he will be cast off. Even though this ceremony is so horrible that most Jews refuse to participate in it, and all of them deny its practice, it still remains the final method by which the Jewish leaders signify and retain their control over this people. Should they abandon the practice of ritual murder, perhaps there would be a possibility that the Jew could be weaned away from his historical role as a biological parasite, and become a constructive member of the gentile community, turning his back upon a record of five thousand years of bloodshed, treachery and murder, which is his entire history. We say perhaps, because we do not know.

THE BIOLOGICAL PATTERN

Viewing this prospect from the biological realities, it seems unlikely that the Jew could renounce his past and join gentile society as a contributing member. Certainly we find no evidence of it in the writings of the Jews themselves, even at the present time. From the most religious of them to the most worldly, their attitude towards the gentile host is the same, a fierce, undying hatred. Consider what the high priestess of the modern Jewish, intellectuals, Susan Sontag, has to say in the Jewish house organ, the *Partisan Review*, in 1967:

> "The white race is the cancer of history. It is the white race and it alone – its ideologies and inventions – which eradicates autonomous civilization wherever it spreads."

These twenty-seven words capsule an enormous amount of information about the parasite-host relationship. First, it is an expression of the undying hatred which the parasite bears for its white race host. Second, it reveals that the Jew has never and will never consider himself as part of the white race, which it regards as a separate species. Third, this passage attributes savagery only to the white race – not to the bloodthirsty tribes of the Congo, not to the mass murders in China, nor to anyone except the highly developed North European civilization in Europe and America. And fourth, Susan Sontag reveals the entire situation in her phrase "autonomous civilization." What does she mean by autonomous civilization? She means the parasite community, which demands total freedom to attach itself to the host, to rule the host, and to prevent the host from casting it off. And she says here that the white race, because in the past it has reacted against the "autonomous civilization" of the Jewish parasite, is totally savage and evil.

Chapter Three

The Shabez Goi

We have remarked on the strange omission of works which one might expect in our libraries, works which treat of the phenomenon of parasitic communities in human civilizations. And we have suggested that these works have not been written because the parasite exercises control over the academic and scholarly life of the host. Is this a fantastic conclusion? Not at all... Since the host is physically stronger than the parasite, obviously the parasite cannot control him through physical strength. Then he must exercise mental control.

How is this done? The Jewish parasite controls the gentile host through an entire class of gentiles which he has created, and who serve him by maintaining control over the gentile host. This class is known as the shabez goi.

The Advanced Civilizations

We have pointed out that the Jewish parasite is a disease of the more advanced civilizations. One does not find the Jew sharing the hostile desert with the Australian aborigine. Primitive man had no experience of parasites. There was little food and less shelter. But those who survived began to master their environment, to till the land, to domesticate animals, and there began to be surpluses of food. Now rats and cockroaches appeared, feasting on these surpluses (one of the heroes of the Jewish intellectual movement, Franz Kafka, wrote a work in which a man envisioned himself as a cockroach, writing out of some ancient racial memory which has bemused thousands of university students who had it rammed down their throats by their professors, with no explanation of its overtones).

With these surpluses, there also appeared a new type of person, a variant of the species, one who existed by producing no goods or services, but who became adept at producing an illusion that he was giving goods and services. This was the Jew, who made his appearance upon the stage of history as a magician, a fortuneteller, a petty thief, or, in the open country, a treacherous and cold-blooded bandit. He became a physician, a teacher, an acolyte in any kind of religious group. From earliest history, he practiced money-lending, and always at usurious rates of interest.

All of these Jewish vocations have one thing in common, the opportunity for fraud. The Jew always operated from a basis of fraud, and slipped easily from one vocation into another. A Jew practices medicine in one city, and, leaving behind a trail of corpses, turns up in another town as a soothsayer. After some widows are bilked of their life savings, he again takes to the road, assisted, as always, by the international Jewish community. In another town, he becomes a student priest, and soon he offers daring new interpretations of the religious beliefs, until his superiors find that he is stealthily transforming every tenet of their faith into some strange and barbaric dogma. He moves on, and turns up in another city as a highly trusted government official, respected by all, until, one evening, the gates of the city are opened to an invader, and the Jew becomes the Grand Vizier of the conquerors.

A DEFINITION

But is this parasitism, or is it merely crime? It is crime, yes, for each of these isolated events is a crime, but the whole is not merely crime, it is parasitism. Treason, fraud, perversion, all the hallmarks of Jewish life among the gentiles in the Diaspora. And it is parasitism. All of these things are not merely crimes in themselves, they are crimes which are committed as essential parts of the Jew's parasitical relationship with the gentile host. We must remember that there is no Jewish crime per se, since the existence of the Jewish parasite upon the host is a crime against nature, because its existence imperils the health and the life of the host. Thus, everything that the Jew does in connection with this parasitic existence is a criminal act, and part of an overall criminal existence.

CONVICTION AND EXPULSION

A gentile government which had as its concern the health of the nation would convict the Jewish parasite and cast him off. This has happened hundreds of times in recorded history. Therefore, the Jew knows that his first task, upon arriving in a gentile community, is to subvert and take over its government, and to paralyse the people with subtle injections of poison, so that they become helpless and unable to defend themselves. Thus, the Jew begins agitation to set up a "progressive" government, also known as a "popular front," a "democratic" government, a "people's" government, a "liberal" government, and all of these are synonyms for the Jewish government, which will protect the presence of the parasite and guard it against the anger of the exploited gentiles.

When he has set up this government, usually by subversion, the Jew sets out to exterminate all of the former gentile leaders, whom he reviles as "reactionaries," that is, those who might react against the presence of the parasite.

First, they are prevented from engaging in any gainful employment. Then they and all members of their families have their landholdings, bank accounts and other assets confiscated. Finally, after extensive agitation against them, the Jew arouses the populace against them and they are hunted down and killed, because they might be able to set up a "reactionary" government if they are allowed to survive. Thus the Jew has introduced the blood-thirsty custom of genocide, or extermination of groups, into world affairs.

Now, does not this sound familiar, the confiscation of assets, the mass murders? Oh, yes, Russia, 1917, the victory of the Bolsheviks, the carrying out of Marx's program of Communism, when a government which believed in the principle of "solidarity" was installed to enslave the gentile Russian people. The Czar and his wife and children were murdered in cold blood, because the biological Jew is not concerned with chivalry in his struggle to maintain control over the gentile host. We have only to read the sadistic Book of Esther in the Bible to see the Jewish custom of mass murder exposed in detail.

WEAKNESS OF THE HOST

Is the helplessness of the gentile host before the onslaught of the parasite an essential weakness? We have only to think of the strong, healthy man subdued by flu virus to get the answer. Health in all matters is the principal defense against the attack of the parasitic virus. For centuries, the larger and stronger gentile host has gone down in defeat before the smaller and weaker, but more deadly, parasitic virus. The survival of the gentile host is a matter of understanding biological laws. The gentile community has set up elaborate codes by which it lives, codes of honor, codes of laws, and the trust which the observance of these codes breeds in the members of the community. They respect the law, they respect each other's families, they respect each other's property, and they defend the nation when it is attacked.

BOUND BY NO CODES

It is the code of honor which gives the Jewish parasite his first opening in the armor of the gentile host, since this code is binding upon the gentile host, and its members achieve status in the community only if they observe it. But the parasite is bound only by his determination to achieve parasitic status upon the host. The gentile's code is itself a biological phenomenon, since it grows out of his attitude towards all life, and it is a manifestation of his innate courage, his honor and his industry, the virtues upon which he builds his nation.

The code of the Jew is quite different: It is a code which abnegates all other codes. He agrees to pay one price and later settles only half of it; he appears in court with forged deeds and wills, paid perjured witnesses, and kept judges, thus taking over gentile properties. He takes advantage of the gentile wives while their husbands are at work, thus shaming them, and in time of war, the Jew avoids army service and disrupts civilian life at home. At the times of gravest peril, he makes deals with the enemy and betrays the nation.

PARADOX OF THE PARASITE

Since the parasite depends upon the host for its food, we would suppose that it would do everything within its power to aid the gentile community to become richer and more powerful. But, overriding every other consideration is the parasite's determination to keep its position upon the host. For five thousand years, history has recorded the efforts of gentile hosts to dislodge their Jewish parasites.

Empires rise and fall, continents are discovered, wildernesses are explored and settled, and man makes progress through new inventions. Yet through it all, one factor remains constant. The gentile host, fearful of the damage which it is suffering from the presence of the Jewish parasite, tries to dislodge it. The parasite has prepared for such efforts, which it always foresees, by attaching itself so securely to the host that the host only damages itself in its wild struggles. In some cases, the gentile host destroys itself in these efforts. The Jewish host prefers seeing the gentile host destroyed instead of leaving peaceably from a still-living host. If the host dies, the parasite looks for another host. It has no feeling of any kind for the host which has provided it with food. This callous attitude is typical of the philosophy of the Jew, and it is exemplified by the current phrase so popular in Jewish Hollywood, "Who needs it?"

Like other Jewish sayings, this phrase has become part of contemporary American life, yet gentiles do not know what it means. It means that the Jew doesn't need the gentile host, because he can always find another one.

HARD WORK

Millions of gentile Americans work hard all of their lives, raising their families and feeding themselves. When they die, there is hardly enough left to pay the funeral costs. Despite the fact that they have lived useful and productive lives, none of the profits have accrued to them or to their families, they have been unable to accumulate any of the world's goods. Yet millions of Jews, who produce nothing, accumulate vast fortunes, and die with a disproportionate share of the nation's wealth, which then goes to the parasite community. Why is this? Is it because the gentile worker is lazy? No, he has worked hard all of his life. Did he gamble away his earnings?

No, he has never gambled. It is the Jews who make up the majority of the nation's gamblers.

THE THEORY OF BIOLOGICAL PARASITISM

We find the answer to this question in the theory of biological parasitism. The gentile worker has spent his life in providing sustenance for the Jewish parasite, enabling the parasite to live in luxury while the gentile worker labors long hours each day in order to survive on a mere subsistence level. The earnings of the gentile worker vanish before his eyes into the Jewish monetary system, as calculated and abstruse monetary laws go into effect. Meanwhile, the Jewish educational system instructs the gentile worker's children that they can look forward to the privilege of laboring all of their life to support the Chosen People of God, who live in the style to which they have become accustomed.

The Jewish monetary system is a series of variations on the shell game at the county fair. The gentile is certain that the pea is under the shell on the left, but when he bets on it, the shell on the left has nothing under it. The gentile puts his money down on other Jewish peas, but whatever he buys suddenly depreciates. The bonds which he purchases drop in value, and he sells at a loss, in order to avoid losing everything he has.

Many people emigrated to America because the Rothschilds had suddenly risen to power in Europe, and were now looting the continent. As these gentiles fled, the greedy Jewish parasites inflicted heavier taxes on those who remained, conscripted the youths into armies which were leased for hire to other nations, and invaded every level of life with their pernicious influence.

Now, a feature of the parasite is his mobility. When the host moves, the parasite follows, catches up with him, and re-establishes his attachment. The American pioneers resented the efforts of the parasites to follow them, and one of the longest debates at the Continental Congress concerned a proposal for permanent exclusion of the Jews. It was finally defeated by the curious argument that, as the Jews were not presently a problem, they would be unlikely to become so in the future. This certainly went against the grain of everything that was known about the Jews and their methods. The records of these debates have survived only in a few notes taken by some of the delegates. The drafts of the Constitution which contains the proposal for Jewish exclusion have all been destroyed. One of the Jewish vocations is that of dealer in old books and rare documents. In these dealings, records containing unfavorable references to the past can be sequestered and destroyed. Other rare documents, which contain no unfavorable references to the Jews, are sold to gentile collectors at huge profits. As usual, the Jew has it both ways, protecting his flanks by destroying all references to his activities, and financing this task with the gentile's money.

THE FUNCTION OF GOVERNMENT

What is the function of government? The function of government is to provide the people with essential services, to guide the defense of the nation, and to promote justice and free enterprise. Now, what is the function of a gentile government which has come under the direction of the parasite? The chief function of a government controlled by the parasite is to guarantee his right to feed upon the host, to protect him against being cast out, and to allow other parasites the right to come in and feed upon the host. Thus, the chief function of such a government is bound up with campaigns for civil rights for minorities, liberalizing all immigration laws, and attacking other hosts who threaten to cast off their parasites. All other considerations of government are swept aside in the performing of these functions, which are so essential to the well-being of the parasite.

Thus, in the United States, we find the Federal Bureau of Investigation ignoring the mounting crime rate while its agents spend all of their time in battling those gentile "reactionaries" who are reacting against the harmful presence of the parasite. We find that the American government has become a vast tax-collecting agency for the benefit of the parasites, and that eighty-four percent of the gentiles' earnings are forcibly taken from them and given to the parasites. We find that every department of the government has interested itself in the added function of guaranteeing the parasite's continued security in its position upon the host. They have set up many new economic subsidiaries whose task is to funnel all of the nation's economic resources into the hands of the parasites. We find that the Department of Defense, instead of guarding our nation, is punishing the nation with a tremendous blood-letting by sending many thousands of our finest youth to be slaughtered in jungles many thousands of miles from our shores, in wars which the Jewish parasites have conjured up for this sole purpose.

WHAT JUSTICE?

Instead of providing equal justice for all, the courts of the nation have become rubber stamp Star Chambers for the persecution of those gentiles who react to the presence of the parasite. These gentile "reactionaries" are arrested on some pretext or other, or evidence against them is planted by FBI agents, and they are sentenced to long terms in prison.

What about education? We find that the Jewish parasite makes a fetish of education. There must be universal education, education for all. But what sort of education does the gentile host receive in a state which is dominated by the Jewish parasite? First, he is taught that he must never think for himself, because this is the original sin. He is carefully instructed in how to be a docile slave for the rest of his life, a robot-like zombie who will never be able to use his mind for his own protection or advancement.

Why does the Jewish parasite have to control the native intelligence of the gentile? First, the Jew is not invisible, he has high visibility. He knows that the gentile is bound to see him, to become irritated by his presence, and to wish to cast him out. The gentile has only to look down the street on any Main Street in America to see that most of the businesses are owned by Jews. The place where he works is owned by a Jew. He pays rent each month, or a lifelong mortgage, to a Jewish bank. He knows that he is being mercilessly exploited by a foreign body known as the Kingdom of Israel. Therefore, the biological parasite begins its instruction of the gentile child, even before the alphabet, with the definition of the forbidden sin. What is the forbidden sin? One must never show "prejudice" towards another human being. The children hear this admonition daily from the time they enter kindergarten. They are puzzled by it, because children are naturally open and generous, they do not hate anyone. They never realize that if the teacher fails to give them this daily lesson about "prejudice," she will be fired from her job.

DIRECT INFLUENCE

In high school and college, the gentile comes under the more forceful influence of Jewish teachers. They find that the Jewish teachers are interesting, because they seem to have carte blanche to say or do whatever they wish in class, while the gentile teachers seem hamstrung in everything they do. The Jewish teachers recommend pornographic books to the children, discuss sexual perversions in detail, and frequently harangue their classes for hours about the evils of Nazism. Since there is no Nazi government anywhere, the gentile children are puzzled by this. They do not understand the terrible fear and hatred which fills the Jewish people at the memory of a gentile people who reacted against them and cast them out.

At home, the gentile child watches television programs which are largely devoted to anti-Nazi themes. This is not surprising, since the Jewish parasites own outright the three television networks, and no program can be seen which is not subjected to their warped censorship. In the universities, the gentile is taught that all of the world's culture stems from the writings of three Jewish parasites, Marx, Freud and Einstein. Gentile artists and writers are no longer mentioned.

THE GREATEST PERIL

Ask any American college graduate – "What is the greatest evil which has ever existed upon this earth?" He will reply very promptly, and energetically, "Nazism!"

He gives this answer because it is what he has been taught. In fact, it *is all* he has been taught, and it is the sole result of four years of higher education. Do not ask him WHY Nazism is the greatest evil that has ever been known, because he does not know. You will only perplex and confuse him, and make him angry at you, because he does not know the WHY of anything. He has only been indoctrinated with conditioned responses, he is repeating the lesson which has been drummed into him until he has learned it by heart, at the hands of his Jewish and shabez goi professors. In all of the hundreds of books which have been written about Nazism, yon will not find a definition of what Nazism is. This is quite understandable. The Jews do not want anyone to know what Nazism is. Nazism is simply this – a proposal that the German people rid themselves of the parasitic Jews. The gentile host dared to protest against the continued presence of the parasite, and attempted to throw it off. It was an ineffectual reaction, because it was emotional and ill-informed, as were all the gentile reactions which preceded it for five thousand years. And how futile it all was, because today, Jewish bankers own sixty per cent of German industry, and their holdings are protected by the occupation army of America.

WHAT IS SHABEZ GOI?

Since the parasite is smaller and weaker than the host, he must control it principally by guile. And because he is outnumbered, he must depend upon active agents among the gentiles. Once he has destroyed the host people's native leadership, he creates a new ruling class, a group recruited from the weakest and the most depraved of the gentiles. This class becomes known as "the new class," and it is composed of the government officials, the educators, the judges and lawyers, and the religious leaders. This "new class" is known to the Jew as his *shabez goi,* or his "Sabbath gentile cattle."

The creation of the shabez goi class provides that the Jewish religion is basically a ritualization of the parasite's techniques for controlling the host. A key tenet of the Jewish religion is that he must not perform the slightest task on his Sabbath. He cannot begin his religious service until the candles are lit, but his religion forbids him to light the candles, because this would be work. He must find a gentile to light the candle for him. This gentile is called a "shabez goi." Thus, the Jewish religion cannot be enacted until the Jew finds a gentile to do his work for him.[5] The Jewish religion also

---

[5] Drew Pearson described the process in a column, *Washington Post,* July 5, 1968 when he quoted Mayor of San Francisco, Joseph Alioto, a Catholic, as follows: "I've been raised in the shadow of the synagogue across the street from me, and

forbids the Jew to work for a gentile, although it is permitted for short periods of time if the Jew finds it necessary to take such a position during the period he is plotting to steal the gentile's business from him!

Those gentiles who become shabez goi for the Jews lead comfortable lives at the expense of their fellows, but they can never overcome their shame, regardless of how wealthy and powerful the Jews make them. The exploiting class which the Jews create from the most servile and contemptible of the gentiles are the most despicable human beings who have ever infested the earth. Although they comprise the educated and moneyed classes in a host nation which has fallen prey to the Jewish parasites, the shabez goi wretches never lead happy lives. In the United States, we find that the gentile bankers, judges, college presidents and leaders of religious denominations whose mission is to parrot in Pavlov, trained-dog fashion every whim of the Jews, are also the people who have the highest rates of alcoholism, the highest rate of divorce, the highest rate of suicide, and the highest rate of juvenile delinquency among their children.

SEXUAL DEGENERACY

This "affluent society" of the shabez goi also has spawned a massive wave of homosexuality and degeneracy in America. Is this surprising? We have only to recall Professor LaPage's description of the effect which the parasite Sacculina has upon its host, the short-tailed spider crab, Inacus mauritanicus. LaPage says that his researches showed that seventy percent of the male spider crabs acquired some of the secondary sexual characteristics of the female and had their

---

my parish priest has been Rabbi Fine. Every week I light a candle in the synagogue, and Cyril Magnin lights a candle in my cathedral." Alioto's political success has been due to his operation as a shabez goi, lighting candles for the Jews.

reproductive organs destroyed by the attack of Sacculina neglecta. He also stated that "the abdomen of these males becomes broad, they may acquire, in addition to their male copulating styles, appendages modified to bear eggs, and their nippers become smaller at the same time."

What better description could we have of a middle-aged college professor simpering in the wake of a brawny football player? One of the characteristics of nations which are controlled by the Jews is the gradual eradication of masculine influence and power, and the transfer of influence into feminine forms. This is understandable. The masculine force is naturally aggressive and self-assertive, independent and self-reliant, courageous and willing to fight for its rights. The feminine force, on the other hand, is more passive, willing to accept orders, and avoids direct action. Thus, Russia and America, the two most influential powers in the world today, a world which is controlled by the Jewish parasites, are basically feminine powers, but the two powers which were more masculine in their attributes, Germany and Japan, and which did not give power to the Jewish parasites, are small and of lesser influence. Nevertheless, as masculine forces, they retain the will to again exert force upon the world, while Russia prefers to use her influence in sinister intrigue, a worldwide network of agents and assassins, those who stab in the back. Now America has followed in Russia's footsteps with the worldwide force of the Central Intelligence Agency, and at home, the furtive operations of the FBI are aimed solely at controlling "reactionaries" among this host people.

SOFT AND TREACHEROUS

In a Jewish-controlled environment, gentile men become soft and capable of any treachery, because their new class, the shabez goi, are epitomes of the living lie, with their insidious conspiracies on behalf of the secret government of the parasites. In this sort of world, manliness, strength and honor are despised.

The most important feature of the shabez goi wretches, as liberal, faceless representatives of Jewish interests, is that they never solve a problem. If we have a national problem today, we can be sure it will be worse ten years from now, and even worse twenty-five years hence. *All problems intensify,* this *is* the basic law of the shabez goi government.

We have only to look at the race problem in America, as a typical illustration. One hundred years ago, we fought a bloody war which ravaged much of the nation, in order to solve the problem of the Negro minority in America. One hundred years later, the nation is on the point of being torn apart once more by this problem, as the shabez goi wretches have worked ceaselessly since 1900 to intensify this problem, which had been dormant from the period of 1870 to 1900. De Tocqueville said everything which needed to be said about the race problem in America more than a century ago, but no one paid him the slightest attention.

A HOPELESS LIFE

One of the striking points of identification of the shabez goi new class is their complete erosion of all sense of responsibility. Since the shabez goi life means that they are living for themselves alone, as enemies of their people, it is understandable that they should think little of the future, but it goes further than this, as a direct biological result of the effect of the Jewish parasite upon the weakest and the shabbiest of the host people. Today, the principal group in America which has resisted this biological effect is the working class. This is due to several factors, first, because the working class has had less of the effect of years of "higher education," which, in this nation, is simply extended instruction in how to be a shabez goi, and second, as workers who produce their own living, they have greater self-reliance and less erosion of their sense of responsibility and self-respect.

Although I have passed beyond any possible deleterious effect which the Jewish parasite or the shabez goi could have upon me, I know the hopelessness of the life of my people. I was freed from this paralysis, which the Jew inflicts upon the healthy members of a host nation, in two ways, first, through my life in art, and second, through my life in Christ.

THE JOY OF A HEALTHY LIFE

In 1948, when I went to San Miguel de Allende, a beautiful village in Mexico, I began to live my life in art. At the age of twenty-five, this was my first experience of joy, because my life had been passed in the gloom which the pall of the Jewish parasite had cast over America. I began to understand what D. H. Lawrence had experienced during his years of desperate wanderings in search of the sun and seeking a healthy life. Not only was D. H. Lawrence dying of tuberculosis, but he was also dying of the terrible malaise which had settled over European civilization, the loss of the will to live, which had been eroded away by centuries of slavery under the Jews and misgovernment by the shabez goi.

In the bright, sun-washed streets of San Miguel de Allende, for the first time, I knew what light was. The people, though poor, were strong and self-reliant, they bore no resemblance to the Americans I had left at home. Although I did not realize it at the time, there were no Jews here, and no shabez goi. Now I began to know the joy of the creative life, my life in art, the life of the mind and the God-given talents to which all of us are born and of which we are robbed by the Jews and the shabez goi.

Now, there was nothing selfish in my attaining this joy, because I was not taking it from anyone else, and since that time, I have wished for nothing more than to bring this joy to all of my people. Since this desire now became the principal direction of my life, I began to live my life in Christ, because I wished to bring joy to others. As these efforts brought me nothing but poverty and what would have been despair, had I ever despaired, I found Christ and knew a greater joy than my life in art.

If the American people knew nothing of the joy of my life in art, how much less did they know of the joy of my life in Christ! The question now was, how to liberate them from two thousand years of mental serfdom. During these centuries, the Jews had continually decried the institution of physical slavery, and while noising about the possibility of physical freedom for everyone, they had subtly imposed their own brand of mental serfdom upon the gentiles. And if physical slavery is a crime, how much greater a crime is mental slavery, the taking over the mind of a freeborn human being!

One of the greatest problems which face our nation today is the disenfranchisement of the American worker and the middle class. His vote is meaningless, it is worthless, because, no matter whom he votes for, his personal position in life deteriorates. His taxes are increased, the business pressures intensify, and his family life is subjected to terror and shame at the hands of aggressive minorities, egged on by the shabez goi wretches and the Jewish overlords.

With the shabez goi in charge of the departments of our religious life, our academic life, and our cultural life, the American workers and the middle class find that wherever they turn, they are faced with the Jew. A Jew directs the symphony orchestra, ninety percent of the art galleries are operated by Jews, so that gentile artists cannot get a showing for their work unless they embrace the degenerate goals of the

Jew. The three television networks are owned and operated by Jews, while the studios, producers, and writers, who are nearly all Jews, bring us programs in which gentiles caper to the Jewish tune. In fact, a five percent minority has gained control of every aspect of American life.

DEEP ALIENATION

Now, this unconscious realization causes the American worker and the middle class to become despondent, because of a deep feeling of alienation, an overwhelming sense of loss. He knows that this is not his art, it is not his culture, it is not his religion, and it is no longer his country, because an alien has taken over every department of his life. As a result the American worker and the member of the middle class loses his power of concentration, he can no longer think anything through, because his education, his cultural life, and his government, are all in the hands of the alien, and because he cannot think his problems through, he loses the resolve to act, he sinks into the hopeless attitudes of lifelong mental slavery which the parasite has forced upon him.

INTENSE SUFFERING

But, even though the American worker or the member of the middle class has lost his power to think things through, and to act from his will, he is still a human being, he can feel. Thus, he endures intense mental suffering, because everything has been cut out of his life except the task of working to feed the Jewish parasite. And even though I have passed beyond this suffering, I cannot rest because I know what this suffering is doing to the American people. I do not feel this suffering, because of the joy of my life in art, and the joy of my life in Christ, and, knowing this joy, I do not need America, and still less do I need a Jewish America. But America is a creation of

God, and as such, it cannot be abandoned to the Jewish parasites, the suffering of the gentile host must be relieved.

THE TASK BEFORE US

Although I live in joy and peace, I know that America must be restored to Christ. I would like to free her from her bondage to Satan, in the metaphysical sphere, and from her bondage to the Jews, in the biological sphere. Although I have been freed from suffering through knowing Christ, I know what suffering is doing to my people, who have been robbed of everything, and who have been converted into mindless robots who mechanically perform tasks according to instructions implanted in them by a Jewish programming, and who respond to every question with a Jewish answer.

I resent the fact that my nation and my people have been converted into a country of Pavlov-conditioned dogs, and I am resolved to see them become men once more. Because they are cut off from the creative life, because they are cut off from the life of their nation by the Jewish parasite, their lives are empty and pointless.

NO HEROES

One of the problems of this Pavlov conditioning is that we no longer have heroes. Now, a nation cannot grow in health without heroes. For the past fifty years, our heroes have been the synthetic products of Jewish liberalism, those Americans who have successfully exploited their people for the benefit of the Jews, and who have expedited the mongrelization of the American people. These synthetic heroes are made of plastic, they do not have any of the human qualities. A typical synthetic hero is Hubert Humphrey, Vice President of the United States, whom one can press into any shape, like a rubber doll, because he has no skeletal structure. He has accepted every aspect of the shabez goi role, and he has no culture and no goals except those which have been implanted in him by the Jewish programmers.

THE MULLINS REPORT

In 1957, alarmed by the issuance of a report known as the Gaither Report, which insisted that every aspect of shabez goi life and Jewish liberalism must be intensified in America, some of my associates urged me to make a formal reply. As this request dovetailed with some projects on which I was then engaged, I was able to draw up a sweeping reply within a few weeks. This report is reproduced here exactly as it was published in August, 1957, by M & N Associates, in Chicago, Illinois:

(Due to public alarm over the Gaither Report, which admits that the United States is rapidly becoming a second-class power, but dares not admit why that is inevitable, M & N Associates has decided to release the confidential Mullins Report, prepared in August, 1957 for a group of American industrialists. We issue this report as a public service by an impartial research organization. It has already become history.)

BY 1980, THE UNITED STATES WILL OCCUPY THE SAME POSITION IN INTERNATIONAL AFFAIRS AS DOES INDIA TODAY. The United States will then be an overpopulated, impoverished country with a standard of living 50 percent below its 1957 level.

Consequently, there is no need, and little possibility, of Russia waging war against the United States. The rapid wane of the United States as a global power will enable Russia to make the American continents into Communist satellites by 1980, if she so chooses, but this prospect is unlikely. From geopolitical considerations, the, continents of North and South America will be of little practical use to Russia. Her European and Asian policies will remain paramount to her national security, but the American continents will be of less geopolitical significance than Africa.

Because of this prospect, the Rockefeller Report and other government demands for increased "defense" spending may be properly evaluated as last-gasp attempts to shore up an artificial and doomed prosperity. How did it happen that the United States, which in 1945 stood unchallenged as the supreme world power, could decline so rapidly? To understand this, a brief review of the nation's history is necessary. The country was settled by bold, energetic North Europeans who were willing to risk their lives in a wilderness in order to own their own homes and land. Cheap labor was needed, but the Indians refused to become menials, so they were killed or put on reservations. The New Englanders imported negroes, but they proved to be less productive than the cost of their keep, so they were sold to Southern plantation owners, where the climate was more suitable and their owners less demanding. Even so, their importation was soon discontinued as impractical.

Meanwhile, the original North European settlers prospered and increased. With ample space and plenty of natural resources, they soon developed into the most highly skilled and productive people the world has ever known. New inventions poured from them, and they enjoyed the greatest prosperity in the history of mankind.

Successive waves of cheap labor came from Europe. A substantial wave from Ireland produced many desirable citizens, but after 1860 little further immigration came from Northern Europe. Most of it was from Central and South Europe, with some Asiatics. Side by side with the North European settlers lived the burgeoning families of the darker citizens. Limited in number in their own lands because of their lower productivity, they reproduced in much greater numbers here because of the higher productivity of their hosts.

Despite the fact that these darker citizens enjoyed a higher standard of living here, thanks to the superior technology of the North Europeans, they felt no gratitude. Instead, they were consumed by hatred and envy of *the North Europeans, many of whom had amassed large fortunes and lived like princes. By 1900, the darker American citizens had formed a voting bloc to combat the political leadership of the North Europeans. Already a deep racial schism had formed which doomed the young republic at the very peak of its promise. The North Europeans soon concentrated their strength in the Republican Party, while the darker citizens became Democrats, a party which also represented the white Southerners as a result of the War Between the States. This strange alliance achieved its first great political victory in 1912 with the election of Woodrow Wilson, a misguided idealist who hailed the Russian Communist Revolution of 1917 as a "victory for democracy over the forces of despotism." Wilson set the nation on a suicidal foreign policy caused by the racial schism of its people. This policy aimed to end all racial injustice, atone for the sins of British imperialism, reprimand French imperialism, stop German imperialism, and set up a worldwide protectorate for the colored peoples. The North European Americans had no idea what this policy intended, and were too busy and prosperous to care. The nation gained in wealth and power by entering the First World War. A few years later, the Crash of 1929 wiped out the fortunes and property of more than half of the North European Americans. The stage was set for the Roosevelt regime, which was to set up the rule of the darker citizens over the impoverished and dispirited white Americans, a rule carried on by the Truman and Eisenhower directorates. Our entry into the Second World War was intended to stop "racist" Germany, as though every group in the world was not "racist" and interested in its self-aggrandizement. In 1945, a victorious United States reaffirmed its role as the protector of the colored world. But Soviet Russia also claimed to be the protector of the colored world, and pointed out that white Americans refused to intermarry with the darker citizens. Most white Americans maintained homogenous communities, schools, clubs and places of worship, just as did all other groups in the United States. However, the heirs of the Roosevelt regime now ruled it illegal for white Americans to separate themselves, although all other groups were allowed to do so without hindrance by the government. Now the government began to enforce a policy of racial amalgamation, although no other nation in the world, especially Soviet Russia, followed such a policy. Largely through the Supreme Court, an instrument operating upon powers* usurped from Congress, white Americans were stripped of their private institutions and forced into racially integrated schools and living quarters. Intermarriage was inevitable, particularly because of the flood of "integration" propaganda.

All religious groups in the United States declared it a religious duty to racially amalgamate, although not one of their leaders could cite a single tenet of dogma which required this. White children, were taught in the schools and churches that it was their duty to intermarry with the darker citizens, and the press, radio, television and movies pressed the mongrelization campaign. The government continued legal action against the last privacies of white citizens, although no action was taken against Negro, Jewish or other group institutions. Yet at the very moment that white Americans were being forced to racially amalgamate, their technical skills were in greater demand than ever before! Guided missiles were being developed by imported German scientists because impoverished white Americans were working as manual laborers, unable to educate their children in technical schools. But the shortage of engineers was laid to the fact that we had not availed ourselves of our fine negro talents; a people who squatted in dusty jungle kraals for 20,000 years without the least improvement in their conditions was now declared the rightful heirs of the American technology! Our universities were flooded with colored students, their tuition paid by government grants and "racist" foundations for colored only. The white Americans who could have salvaged our declining technology continued as manual laborers.

All of this was inevitable. The American of North European descent, although realizing that he possessed superior skills, bore no ill will towards the darker citizens. But the colored man could not see a white man without hating him, for the white face reminded the colored man that he was dark. Either the colored man must become lighter or the white man must become darker. No other remedy would pacify him. Anyone who has seen the advertisements for "skin whiteners" in the negro press knows how basic this drive is among the dark people. The pivotal negro vote caused the white man to be legislated out of existence in the nation which he had created, and the Supreme Court declared, "All Americans are Negroes!" M & N Associates makes no comment on *the justice or injustice of this development. We only evaluate the facts. The inevitable result was that by destroying the white American's desire to preserve himself as a manifestation of God's Holy Will, and forcing him to intermarry with the colored, the nation was condemned to go the way of other great world powers, India, Egypt, Greece and Rome, whose white leadership vanished in intermarriage with darker peoples.*

The passing of a great nation from the stage of world history is neither an occasion for sadness or rejoicing. It is simply an historical event. The process was bound to be much more rapid in the United States because of the pace of modern life and the tremendous pressure behind the dark people's will to intermarry with the whites. At the same time, Soviet Russia's white managerial elite, showing no intention of intermarrying with darker peoples, continued to specialize. Selective breeding became a state policy, and thus Russia secured the future for herself, for the future was long since known to belong to that nation which could produce the highest type of technological elite.

At this late stage, M & N Associates was asked to ascertain whether the colored citizens could be restrained in their aggression against white Americans. The answer is no. They will never be content to enjoy their higher standard of living here, because it cannot compensate for their constant reminders to themselves that they are inferiors. Once again, bolder whites will emigrate, this time to Australia and New Zealand. At best, the United States may become a sort of British Guiana, a colored colony of white Canada, whose dollar is already worth more than ours!

It is too late for the North European stock, a minority of 50,000,000, to reassert leadership over 120,000,000 mixed bloods. The colored cannot be appealed to on patriotic grounds, for they can never know nation-feeling, but only have race. Only a people capable of defending their land can know patriotism. Typical was A. Philip Randolph's advice to negroes to refuse to serve in the U.S. Army. M & N Associates does not believe that a White movement can gain power. There is no longer a White market in the U.S., either commercially or politically. At best, the whites might secede again as a white Southern republic, leaving the mulatto North to go its own way, but the result would be the same, the disappearance of the United States as a world power. Our mulatto grandchildren will placidly watch the decay of the nation they inherited, while the rest of the world, including Soviet Russia, pay no more attention to us than is presently paid to the mouthings of the mulatto inhabitants of India. The world is realistic.

PRESCIENCE

When this report was drawn up more than a decade ago, I said that it was already history. Since then, the American position has worsened on the precise lines which I laid down. I said there was no white market, and every American politician since then has borne me out. In only one point did I err; I failed to allow for the possible reclamation of America through knowing Christ, because at that time I had not progressed this far, I did not foresee this sole possibility of reclamation for America.

Some of the sponsors of this report felt that it was unduly pessimistic. Yet, in less than a decade, many of our great cities, including the nation's capital, lay in ashes, while we had entered an economic crisis which seemed impossible to solve. Now, even the Mullins Report did not predict national bankruptcy against a background of burned and looted cities, in less than ten years! Who will dare to be sufficiently pessimistic about the next ten years?

Let us recapitulate how this all came about. In 1945, the United States stood alone as the supreme military power in the world, the only industrial nation whose plants had not been destroyed by the Second World War. Militarily and economically, America was the master of the world, and the world waited for our command. We had only to raise our hand, and our command would be obeyed.

England, France, Italy, Russia, and Germany, and in Asia, Japan, lay in ruins, their factories but heaps of rubble.

PARALYZED BY PARASITES

But we gave no command. Why? Because the parasites and their shabez goi wretches had but one desire, to rebuild Communist Russia. Dean Acheson proposed that vast new loans be made to Russia, through his law firm, Covington and Burling, which so ably represented nine Communist nations at our Federal trough. The American postwar economy was hamstrung by Communist Jews such as David Niles, a notorious homosexual who bragged that Harry Truman never made a decision without consulting him, and who had one sister in Israeli Intelligence in Tel Aviv, and another sister high in the Soviet Intelligence in Moscow. Harry Dexter White, a Lithuanian Jew and lifelong Communist agent, also supervised Truman's decisions as President of the United States.

At the top of this heap of worms squirmed the master parasite, Bernard Baruch, an agile Jewish speculator who made as much as one million dollars a day through foreknowledge of government decisions which affected the stock market. No wonder Harry Truman called Bernard Baruch "the greatest living American"! This master parasite pulled the strings of a horde of conniving political wretches, and collected United States Senators as a lesser man might net a cageful of hamsters. He publicly boasted that he had such Senators as Harry Byrd, James Byrnes, Harry Truman and many others in his pocket

A HAMSTRUNG ECONOMY

Now America's conversion to a peacetime economy was held up by these Jews, in order to give Russia precious time to rebuild her shattered economy. Not only was the United States paralyzed by Jewish "economic planners," whose sole aim was to stall the erection of a prosperous economy, but the Communists also found the ideal instrument with which to weaken America from within, a planned race war. With the race war and the paralyzed economy in America, the Communists bought time, a precious decade, for Russia to build an atomic bomb, with the assistance of the Rosenbergs and a vast horde of Jewish spies, while other agents threw the Negro masses against the barricades in a reckless and destructive race war. Now the government of the United States practically ceased to function, as the "spontaneous" and carefully-rehearsed "demand" of the Negro people for their "civil rights" took precedence over everything else in Washington. The shabez goi wretches leaped into the fray on the side of the Negroes, yelping with precise responses to every command of the Jewish parasites, their paws flailing the air as they slavered for their slice of raw steak, whenever the Jews called out "civil rights" or "peace."

SUPREME COURT

As the high priests of the shabez goi wretches, the Supreme Court gave official status to every demand of the Communist-inspired mobs in 1954, when it ruled that all schools must be integrated. No other single decision of the Supreme Court has ever plunged the nation into such chaos. Americans stood appalled as armies of American soldiers marched into American cities, bayoneting and shooting white citizens who tried to claim their rights. But, a decade later, when we saw American soldiers again marching into American cities, it was to protect the Negro mobs who were looting and burning with impunity!

Now, in 1945, as we have mentioned, the United States stood preeminent in the world, as the new Rome. But in 1955, Russia was well on her way towards reestablishing herself as a world power, while the United States was weaker than it had been in 1945! And in 1965, the pendulum had already swung in favor of Russia, for in this decade, the Soviet agents had successfully implemented a full-scale race war in the United States, and had also succeeded in committing American soldiers to the endless holocaust of an Asiatic land war. Caught in a man for man struggle with Asia's teeming billions, the United States would slowly bleed to death while Russia daily grew stronger, without losing a man. And Russia, at home, was calm, while the United States was drawn into a race war, the government was paralyzed, the educational system was paralyzed, and the American people had not a single representative who would defend their interests.

THE SCUM OF THE EARTH

Jewish gold had purchased the sorriest lot of ragtail beggars and thieves that had ever infested our nation's capital, men who, while handing over billions to the Jews, had sold themselves for a paltry few thousand dollars apiece! Our Senators and Representatives did not even ask for their souls the price of a healthy Negro slave at pre-Civil War levels. The Mullins Report, in placing a dateline of 1980 to see the United States reduced to the status of another India, had erred by ten years. Now it seems that 1970 is the more likely date.

THE END OF THE ROAD?

Geopoliticians have said for years that America was running down. Everything that our nation has achieved had been done at the cost of tremendous outpourings of energy and instinctive intelligence. There has been much native greed and cruelty also, the merciless gouging of immigrant workers, the mass slaughters of the Civil War and the systematic destruction of America's only native culture, the Greek revival gentility of the South. These are dark chapters in America's history. But there are also bright pages, when America lived up to all of her promise of freedom and her offerings of hope to a sick and rotted European civilization, which was slowly expiring because of the excesses committed against her by the Jewish parasites. And now it is America's turn to totter on the brink of the abyss, as her economy reels from the onslaught of revolutionary mobs at home and insane Jewish adventures abroad. But there are still scientists who are blazing new trails for the world, perhaps one per cent of the nation remains constructive in the face of these disasters.

In 1957, I could not predict the burning of American cities while police and National Guardsmen stood by, under orders to "show every possible courtesy to the rioters." I could not predict that a Jew who had thrice been denied security clearance would commit large-scale American troops to Vietnam in order to sabotage our national economy, an effort which was advertised as an effort to "stop Communism" while the CIA planned the execution of the nation's anti-Communist leader, Ngo Diem. No wonder his widow remarked to television newsmen, "With America as a friend, you don't need any enemies."

WILL COMMUNISTS STOP THEMSELVES?

The three hundred billion dollar effort to stop Communism in Vietnam would be more believable if it had not been inaugurated by the same lifelong dedicated Marxists in the State Department who had sabotaged Chiang Kai-Shek's government and turned China over to the Communists. Can we really believe that these traitors, who had presented the Communist world with a gift of six hundred million people, were now prepared to make an all out effort to save a few Vietnamese from the same fate? They showed their hand by refusing Chiang Kai-Shek's offer to send troops to Vietnam, just as they had refused his offer to send troops to Korea, because the State Department planners had to stick to their plan of showing Asia that it was "white imperialists" who were preventing the Vietnamese from peacefully setting up a Communist state. If Asians were sent to fight Communism, the Marxists in Washington would lose an important plank in their program to wreck our nation.

Meanwhile, at home, as the gross national product reached new highs, (due principally to runaway inflation), the Marxists continued their mad looting of the United States Treasury. Typical was the establishment of more than one hundred "think factories" in which the Jewish parasites drew huge salaries for sitting around thinking up new ways to exploit the gentile host. We find Herman Kahn's Hudson Institute exposed in the *Nation*, May 13, 1968, as having been reviewed by the General Accounting Office and its million dollar a year contract proved to have produced nothing of value. The General Accounting Office characterized the work of the Hudson Institute as "its ideas a rehash," "superficial," "valueless." The *Nation* noted that "virtually no records were kept either at the Hudson Institute or by the General Accounting Office as to how money was spent, the progress of programs," and other usual business procedures.

We find that there are some one hundred similar concerns in this country, offshoots of the Rand Institute, which spend an average of $50,000 per man per year. This is a salary of one thousand dollars a week for a Jew to sit in an office puffing a cigar, a type of boondoggle which was inspired by Mortimer Adler's twenty million dollar windfall from the Ford Foundation to "study philosophy," with the usual valueless rehash of superficial ideas as the only tangible result. These moneys come from tax-exempt foundations or from government agencies, principally the Department of Defense, and never a word of criticism from our Senators and Representatives, who dare not criticize this method of the Jewish parasite's exploiting the gentile host.

THE RUINOUS EFFECT

The rapid deterioration of America from a position of strength to a rank of second class power, racked at home by riots and bankruptcy, is a classic example of the effect which the Jewish parasite has upon the gentile host. Writing in the *Washington Post* on April 5, 1968, Drew Pearson exposed Walt Rostow as the man who committed troops on a large scale to Vietnam. Rostow is a Jew whose father is an avowed Socialist, and Rostow himself, after being refused security clearance three times, was placed in charge of our national security! The man who refused him security clearance because of his background is a loyal American named Otto Otepka, who has undergone continuous persecution ever since. State Department files were destroyed, witnesses were bribed, and perjury was committed to prevent Rostow from becoming another Dreyfus, a Jew who had gained admittance to the nation's top security councils and who was now to be rejected because of his past.

Later, as director of our national security, Walt Rostow and a little group of high-ranking government Jews gathered in the Pentagon early one morning to cheer the Israeli sneak attack on its neighbors, and toasted each other while Israeli planes massacred American sailors on the U.S.S. Liberty in neutral waters!

PLANNING OF THE RIOTS

The riots which have devastated American cities for three years and left entire sections in smoking ruins, remarkably akin to the destruction which Jewish-directed bombers had visited upon the cities of France and Germany a few years ago, had their initial inspiration in the writings of a little black hustler in a pamphlet called "The Fire Next Time." It was published in a house organ of the Jewish parasites, the New Yorker Magazine, and later issued as a book. In this work, James Baldwin promised that the Negroes would burn down America's cities. Baldwin has long been familiar as a housebroken pet of the Jewish parasites, and he lived for two decades on the liberal outpourings which they gave him from various tax-exempt foundations. Some grants were made in return for his favors, others were made to encourage his revolutionary activities, but none of these awards could be said to have been a sincere appreciation of his feeble literary talent. Since the fires started, he has prudently remained in Paris, snickering at a series of gay parties on the Left Bank while America's cities are devastated by the black mobs who consider him their inspiration. In his interviews, which are always prominently displayed in the *New York Times*, he refers to the United States as "the Fourth Reich," an "in" joke among the parasites.

COMMUNIST INFLUENCE

If James Baldwin gave an intellectual impetus to the riots, the actual planning was done by the Chinese Communists. The inside story of the burning of Washington is that the Chinese Communists devised a plan whereby the city of Washington would become a "free city," divorced from the United States and administered by a Black Power Commission. This Commission would then charge the United States ten million dollars a year rent for the United States Capitol, the White House and other government buildings. When Mayor Washington approached President Lyndon

Johnson with this plan, he was told that it was out of the question. A few days later, the city of Washington was on fire. The stage had been set three days earlier, at a Communist cell meeting at which the Party leaders decided upon the death of Dr. Martin Luther King. A North Vietnamese professional, Nuy Ti Ganh, was flown in for the job, while an American "Oswald" or patsy, as his name has now entered the American language, was murdered and his body buried that same night.

At this Communist Party meeting, one of the conspirators, a member of Mayor Washington's staff, mentioned that "our soul brother, Walter" had guaranteed the safety of looters and arsonists during the forthcoming burning of Washington. Not a shot would be fired against them – this was the commitment. The promise was kept. During three days of looting and burning Washington, not a single rioter was injured by the thousands of police and soldiers who stood by with orders not to fire.

Mayor Washington stated, at the beginning of the riot, that any policeman who shot at a rioter would be charged with murder. He fought bitterly against the ordering out of the National Guard, and permitted it only after extracting the incredible commitment from the National Guard commander that the troops would keep their weapons unloaded, and that they would be permitted to load and fire only after obtaining written permission from a superior officer! This was the most ridiculous order ever issued to troops going into a combat situation! These conditions were then read over Television Stations WTOP and WTTG in Washington, so that rioters would know they could loot and burn without a shot being fired against them.

MASS DESTRUCTION

At the height of the burning on Friday evening, after the Communists had murdered Dr. Martin Luther King according to plan, President Lyndon Johnson called Mayor Washington and begged him to allow the National Guard to come in. Mayor Washington curtly refused, and hung up on him, so great was the arrogance of the Negro leader.

The following afternoon, when most of Washington was in flames, Mayor Washington permitted the National Guard to come in only to protect the looters, because some of the Washington City Police, who had been shot at and clubbed by the rioters, were threatening to fight back. The merchants cheered the arrival of the National Guard, because they supposed that this meant a stop to the looting and burning. They were dumbfounded to see the soldiers standing by while Negroes drove Cadillacs from Newark and Philadelphia up to their stores, loaded color televisions, the most expensive clothing, and other loot, into the cars, and drove away, while the soldiers did nothing to stop them. When the stores had been looted, they were set on fire, and again the soldiers did nothing.[6]

GUARANTEE OF SAFETY

At 3:15 p.m. on Saturday afternoon, Mayor Washington had the instructions to the National Guard read over Television Stations WTOP and WTTG. He assured the looters that "1. The soldiers were carrying unloaded weapons and that they would be allowed to load and fire only after being given written permission from a superior officer, and 2.

---

[6] *The Washington Post*, July 14, 1968, noted a government investigation which had established that the Negroes had been persuaded to burn the stores because the Chinese Communists promised them that once the Jewish merchants had been burned out, government aid would enable Negroes to open businesses in their stead, and that the Jews would be afraid to return.

that the soldiers and police had been ordered to show every possible courtesy to the looters." With this reassurance, the rioters stepped up their activity, and the riot spread to Baltimore, where the same conditions were in effect. Mayor Washington's instructions resulted in another wild night of looting and burning. Five hundred fifty-eight buildings were burned to the ground in the city of Washington after being looted, at a cost of eighty million dollars worth of goods stolen and ten million dollars in property damage. As one rioter explained, when interviewed by a television cameraman while he had his arms filled with hundreds of dollars worth of expensive clothing, "Man, it's wonderful! They can't bother us because we got a soul brother up there!"

LOOTING ACCORDING TO PLAN

During the height of the rioting, WTTG newsman Hal Walker, a Negro who was allowed to move freely about the city during the riots, interviewed a Jewish merchant, John Hechinger, who was Chairman of Washington's City Council.

"Don't you see a pattern to this looting?" asked Walker. "Oh, no, it's indiscriminate," replied Hechinger.

"But aren't only certain types of stores being burned?" pursued Walker. "No," muttered Hechinger, and the interview was suddenly cut off of the air.

Hal Walker was referring to the map which had been prepared before the riot in Washington, on which every Jewish store was marked, and of which three hundred copies were distributed in the city on the morning before Martin Luther King was murdered. The Chinese Communists had persuaded the Black Power leaders to stage a massive anti-Semitic uprising against the Jewish merchants who had exploited them. The main target of the burning was the destruction of credit records, and this goal was achieved. Now Hechinger and other Jewish merchants began a frantic campaign to conceal the nature of the anti-Jewish uprising. One Washington merchant, Irv Weinstein, refused to go along with the coverup, and he openly declared that the burning of Washington was the biggest anti-Jewish uprising anywhere in the world since the end of World War II. He pointed out that the heinous Krystal Nacht in Germany during the Nazi regime, in 1938, in which Jewish stores were wrecked, had only resulted in a total of one hundred thousand dollars damage, while the Washington uprising had cost Jews one hundred MILLION dollars.

PETITIONS THE UNITED STATES

Against the wishes of his fellow Jews, who were desperately trying to cover up the story, Irv Weinstein tried to present a petition to the United Nations, charging Mayor Washington and the City Council with genocide, because they had encouraged the Negroes to attack Jewish stores, and had refused the Jews the protection of the City Police and the National Guard.

Ambassador Arthur Goldberg, our representative to the United Nations, refused to accept the petition, and assured Irv Weinstein that the United States Government would make good every dollar lost by the Jewish merchants. When he returned to Washington, Irv Weinstein was visited by two Black Power leaders who told him he had three days to live. Forty-eight hours later, he disappeared and has not been heard of since. Meanwhile, other Jewish merchants, who reopened their stores in Washington, were visited daily by Black Power leaders who charged them ten percent of their gross to stay in business, a tactic they had picked up from the Mafia. One Jewish liquor dealer who refused them, Ben Brown, was shot down in cold blood in his store, and Mayor

Washington still refused the merchants protection. Meanwhile, other Negroes were murdering bus drivers each evening, which caused the bus drivers to go on a slowdown. The purpose of these tactics, to wreck the economic life of the city and its transportation system, had been planned by Chinese Communist leaders in order to paralyze the Vietnam peace talks. They correctly reasoned that with our capital city in flames and its economic life shattered, we would lose face and would be unable to make a strong presentation at the Paris peace talks. The murder of Dr. Martin Luther King had been timed for this purpose.

Meanwhile, agents of the Central Intelligence Agency were discovered to have also played a part in fomenting the Washington riot.

When their role was revealed, CIA officials stated that the burned buildings followed exactly a plan for a Washington expressway through the city, which had been proposed for more than twenty years, but which could not be implemented because of the cost of acquiring the business buildings and tearing them down. Now that they had been burned out, the expressway could be built at a reasonable cost.

MONGRELIZATION PROGRAM

The riots which devastated American cities represented a new stage of the mongrelization program which the Jewish parasites had devised to weaken the United States, and, if Jews such as Irv Weinstein seemed to be the losers in this new phase, it was because they refused to look at the long-term program which had been devised for America by the Chinese Communists and their tools, the Black Power militants.

This program had been forced upon America during the Second World War, when the people were living under martial law, and had to accept without protest each new dictatorial decree of the Federal Government. At the end of the war, the Chinese Communist program moved rapidly to implement a forced mongrelization program along three fronts:

> 1. Forced integration of all army units, to prevent the existence of any armed unit such as an elite white guard which could battle against Communism at home.
> 2. Forced integration of schools, to educate children from their tenderest years to meekly accept government integration decrees.
> 3. Forced integration of churches, private clubs and neighborhoods, to prevent any adult white Americans from having a place where they could meet to discuss possible reactions against the activities of the Jewish parasites.

AN ADVERTISEMENT BACKFIRES

During the campaign for forced integration of all American Army units, the Chinese Communists found that there was a shortage of Negroes in the armed services, and they began a hasty program to attract more Negroes into the Army. One of these attempts was a poster which was widely distributed in Negro business and residential areas, and prominently displayed in Negro taverns and barber shops. The poster read:

> *YOUNG NEGRO MEN!*
>
> *Are you victims of race prejudice? Do white girls refuse to go home with you? As a United States soldier, you can travel abroad and be stationed in the homelands of our allies, where your high pay will make you wealthy in the eyes of the people. Your money is*

worth five times as much as theirs. Negro-Americans! The white girls of Germany and England are waiting eagerly to see your healthy smiles. JOIN THE UNITED STATES ARMY TODAY!

This plan came to an abrupt halt when copies of the poster were sent to Europe, where a press campaign was inaugurated to stop the planned debauching of white European girls by black soldiers, a favorite goal of the Communists which began shortly after World War One, when detachments of black Senegalese troops from the French Army were stationed in Germany and given orders to rape as many German girls as possible.

The Federal Government withdrew all copies of the poster and destroyed them. A European newspaper offered a thousand dollars for a copy but none could be found. One tactic of the Communists had backfired.

SLOW PARALYSIS

A prominent characteristic of the Jewish parasite's techniques of slow paralysis of the higher thinking centers of the gentile masses is the continuing efficacy of old methods. The Jewish biological drive to destroy gentile civilization through the infiltration and control of the nerve centers has been centralized in the techniques of fomenting Communist revolutions in the industrialized nations.

In 1848, there were street demonstrations against government policies in many European nations, riots which the police could not control. Some European governments fell before the Communist onslaught of 1848. Now we find, a century later, that the same techniques of street demonstrations work just as well, because the demonstrators grow more aggressive, and every department of the government is tested and strained until it gives way.

The initial impetus of the riots comes from students who are agitated by their instructors. Plans are made, students are indoctrinated by faculty members and by older "students." In Berkeley, California, the organizers of the student riots were found to be "students" in their late twenties or early thirties, and many of the protestors were not students at all, but persons who had taken up residence near the campus for the purpose of fomenting riots.

THE ROLE OF THE CHURCHES

The churches in the United States play a vital role in providing "sanctuary" for the Communist plotters, raising money for the demonstrations, and serving meals to the rioters, who are too busy with their work of planned disruption to be concerned with providing food for themselves. Dedicated Marxist organizers, who probe for every weakness in the community with all the skill of highly trained surgeons, have long recognized that the churches and the air of piety provide the ideal cover for their revolutionary operations.

Infiltrating the church groups is no problem, because they are already wracked with dissension over theological matters, and the administration is composed of college-educated persons who have been thoroughly indoctrinated with the proven shabez goi techniques for controlling the gentile masses. Thus, Communists infiltrate the seminaries (Josef Stalin began his revolutionary activities as a student priest), and with the aid of other Communists, they rise to positions of command in all the religions denominations.

CHURCH ADMINISTRATION EXPOSED

Rosemary Reuther, one of the nation's outstanding Catholic scholars and a teacher at George Washington University and Howard University, exposed the origins of our church offices in *"The Church Against Itself,"* Herder and Herder, NY, 1967, page 134,

> "The first concept of church office was borrowed, not surprisingly, from the Jewish synagogue. The Sanhedrin, the council of elders which ruled every Jewish community, provided the first model for church office. This pattern was established first in Jerusalem, where, by Paul's time, it had succeeded in replacing the original community of Jesus' followers and substituting a presbyterial structure modeled on the Jerusalem Sanhedrin."

Thus we find that the church administration, a short time after the Sanhedrin had demanded Christ's crucifixion, kicked out Jesus' followers and adopted the dictatorial administration of His murderers. This is one of the most amazing discoveries ever revealed about the strange role of the churches in denying Christ and trying to destroy His followers! Read it again and again, until you understand why the churches today embrace every tenet of Communism and reject every principle of Christ.

DISORIENTED FOOLS

The most valuable members of the church who promote class struggle are those who are not Communists at all, but who are disoriented fools who are unable to accept Christ, who are dissatisfied with their life, and who wish to provoke Armageddon by any means at their disposal.

What is most surprising is the continued gullibility of the students in our universities, who are still enthralled by a Communist "wave of the future" which is mired in the atmosphere of 1848. Marxism plods along with the same dreary set of concepts with which it faced the onset of the Industrial Revolution. Communism has not come up with a single new idea for more than a century, yet it tries to meet the Space Age with a theory which was obsolete even when it was first set forth by Karl Marx!

STUDENTS ARE UNINFORMED

Our students are never informed that the ideological masters of Communism, Marx and Lenin, were men who were completely out of touch with the life of the societies which produced them. They spoke of the "revolt of the peasantry" at a time when the peasants were moving to the cities to take factory jobs, but then, what could Marx, sitting in a dusty room of the British Museum and wriggling back and forth as his hemorrhoids tormented him, know of the changing world outside of the book stacks, and what could Lenin know of the world during the years which he spent quietly reading in a Swiss library, leading the life of a retired insurance salesman, until the twentieth century caught up with him and dragged him back to Russia, where he became the willing tool of a homicidal maniac named Lev Bronstein, or Trotsky? Yet American professors today present these two intellectual backwaters, Marx and Lenin, as the two most original thinkers of all time!

STUDENTS ARE CHEATED

One reason that American students are so prone to embrace doctrines of revolt is that they know they are being robbed, that they are not getting the education they are paying for, because the "treason of the clerks," the *trahison des clercs* which Julien Benda, a French scholar, exposed, prevents them from receiving an education. The shabez goi professors, the treasonable clerks, cram the outdated philosophies of Marx and Freud down the throats of the students when they need an education for the Space Age!

THE MACLEISH SYNDROME

One of the principal reasons for student rebelliousness is the ubiquitous MacLeish Syndrome which they encounter in our better universities, particularly in the Ivy League schools.

The MacLeish Syndrome has two firm tenets which are never deviated from:

"1. All culture must be presented as Jewish in origin.

2. All human thought must be attributed to either Marx, Freud or Einstein, and must be clearly labelled as originating from these Jewish 'geniuses'." Forbidden to know the work of such great gentile minds as Ezra Pound, Werner von Heisenberg, and hundreds of others, the students grow restless, and after two or three years of this dreary rabbinical education strictly on the lines of the Talmud, they are ripe for any doctrine of revolt. Yet, instead of rebelling against their sick professors, they allow the professors to send them out to wreck the surviving institutions of their gentile civilization.

The MacLeish Syndrome is characterized by a tweedy, Scot terrier type of individual who has been a lifelong pet of the liberal non compos mentis. Because of inherited income, this type affects a genial air of native superiority, and entertains student leaders in a den lined with the first editions of the works of former students, nor is he reluctant to describe how he arranged for their publication.

A good sherry is poured for the students by a subservient black man while the MacLeish talks easily about the necessity for human equality. Often silly, and always dishonest, the MacLeish sits regally in a vast easy chair of Spanish leather, puffing a rare mixture of imported tobaccos in his pipe and wearing a red silk smoking jacket from Sulka, while black patent leather slippers from Peele of London dangle from his toes. The students literally perch at his feet, while the MacLeish peddles a watered-down version of the gospel according to Karl Marx.

Dazed by the MacLeish syndrome, the students rise up and go out into the world to purvey classical Marxism to the masses whom this philosophy is intended to enslave. From the posts which they obtain, they rise rapidly in the spheres of education, journalism, religion and government, their promotions depending solely on the degree in which they are effective in spreading the Marxist gospel. Whatever doubts the students may have entertained about this gospel soon vanish as they discover how it opens the doors for them in their chosen professions. Those whose systems reject the infection find that twenty years later, they are teaching study hall at the Podunk Grammar School, or tending a deserted library in East Gowatchee, Pennsylvania.

GULLIBILITY

What is puzzling is the continued gullibility of the students, who blindly accept as "the wave of the future" a philosophy of Marx which was already obsolete one hundred years ago. How can they be so obtuse? In the first place, a student must begin with what he is exposed to, the sunlight and air and water which is available to him. Now, if he gets only shabez goi thought from his Jewish teachers, what else can he know? Cut off from his native Western culture, the American student today is a rootless tumbleweed, driven by the wind from one goofy Marxist theory to another, and unaware of his heritage, his people and his nation. His anger at finding that the education he pays for is an empty sham is understandable, but his failure to react against the true culprits suggests that his native instincts have been destroyed, as he reacts against his society, rather than against the perverters of the educational system themselves.

A STUDENT AWAKENING?

The recent Columbia University riots may presage an awakening on the part of the students, as the eviction of President Grayson Kirk from his office would seem to be a sign of student awareness, yet the same dreary Marxist slogans scrawled on the walls indicates that they have learned nothing. Those students who defecated upon Dr. Kirk's desk may have demonstrated a legitimate resentment, but they also revealed their own lack of judgment. Instead of attacking the milksop Marxism of their perverters, they were led by Jewish agitators who criticized the professors for not being more Marxist! Is there any intelligence left in such students, or have their minds been totally destroyed by such Jewish activists as Mark Rudd at Columbia University, the son of a Lithuanian Jew named Jacob Rudnitsky, and in France, the student leader who wrecked the DeGaulle regime, a redheaded Jewish agitator named Daniel Cohn-Bendit, also known as "Danny the Red"?

MENTAL BONDAGE

The plight of the students reflects the unhappy situation of the entire gentile masses, a condition of mental serfdom. Now, when we say that Americans are being held in mental bondage, what do we mean? We mean that every newspaper, radio station, television station, magazine and stage and screen play has been edited by Jewish agents to remove any reference to their crimes and to keep the gentile masses in a condition of sleep. This would be a fantastic statement, if we did not have at hand the annual reports of the organizations which perform this censorship. Foremost is the Anti-Defamation League of B'nai B'rith, with the American Jewish Committee and the American Jewish Congress as other important agents of censorship.

These groups issue annual reports in which they document the fact that their agents check every public presentation of any kind, written or staged, and delete any references to Jewish misdeeds. As a writer, I have followed the ADL operations closely for twenty years. If I submit a story to the *Saturday Evening Post*, any ADL staff member, whose salary is paid by the magazine, checks the story for any reference to Jewish activities, and also checks a blacklist to see if my name is there as a critic of the Jews. Even if the story contains no reference to the Jews, it is rejected because my name is on the Jewish blacklist, and I must be prevented first, from earning any money from my writings, and second, from reaching an audience.

If I submit a manuscript to a publishing house, it is again checked first for references to the Jews, and second, to see if its author is on the Jewish blacklist. In this manner, the Jews prevent any gentile writer from reaching the public if he is known to be indifferent or hostile to their goals, if he has refused to become a member of the shabez goi class. Any publication which rejects Jewish censorship is either driven out of business, or taken over by Jewish financial interests. A book which is published by gentiles who are not of the shabez goi class is ignored by the book review departments of mass publications, and bookstores refuse to stock it, for their stocks are reviewed monthly by traveling ADL agents who enter the store incognito, inspect the stock, and if any publication is found which mentions the Jews, the proprietor is threatened with various weapons, lawsuits, government action or financial revenge.

DISASTERS IN PUBLISHING

Many gentile publications, such as the *Literary Digest*, *Liberty Magazine*, and others have been driven out of business by the ADL, not because they published "anti-Semitic" articles, but because they refused to let ADL inspectors control their operations. Other magazines, such as *Collier's*, were prosperous publications, but Jews took over their editorial staffs and filled their pages with hysterical invective against anyone who opposed them, until the disgusted subscribers quit reading them.

The *Saturday Evening Post* is now traveling this road of no return. Once a virile publication which reached a respectable percentage of the American middle class, it has become a vicious and irresponsible organ of Jewish propaganda, and is facing bankruptcy for this one reason. So important has it become to the Jews that Martin Ackerman, a Jewish entrepreneur, recently rushed in with a five million dollar loan. A week later, he announced that he had recouped his loan by selling the *Saturday Evening Post* subscription list to *Life Magazine*, a typical wheel-and-deal operation. Nevertheless, the *Saturday Evening Post* is doomed to go the way of *Collier's*, for, under its present editors, it is a sick and vile publication. ADL agents fill its pages with their garbage as they try to brainwash the American people. Typical was a vicious and unprovoked attack against the American businessman, H. L. Hunt, in a recent issue of the *Saturday Evening Post*, written by a professional clown named William Buckley. This article referred to Mr. Hunt as a "boob with appallingly bad manners" a "buffoon" and other sneering Jewish epithets. One ostensible reason for Buckley's attack may have been Mr. Hunt's refusal to contribute to the staggering losses suffered by Buckley's venture into publishing, the *National Review*, which was neither national nor a review.

DOES BUCKLEY EXIST?

William Buckley, a well-advertised "conservative spokesman," has been described as a figment of George Sokolsky's imagination.

A Jewish provocateur, Sokolsky decided to use Buckley's money to launch a "rightwing" magazine which would peddle approved Jewish techniques of "anti-Communism." Sokolsky and a Hollywood gagwriter named Morrie Ryskind put together the format of the *National Review*, which it still follows today. Although Sokolsky died, the *National Review* was condemned to drift forever on the sea of his murky ideas, in which only three principles could be discerned. The first was that Jews are not Communists, the second was that anti-Semitism was the worst evil of which man could be guilty (a plank which Sokolsky borrowed from the Soviet Constitution) and the third was that all Americans are fools.

SHABEZ GOI ANTICS

One of the techniques of ADL control is to keep the gentiles at each other's throats through tried and proved methods of provocateurism. When Robert Welch founded a gentile anti-Communist group, the John Birch Society, an ADL provocateur persuaded Buckley to attack Welch as being "anti-Semitic." Stung by the accusation, Welch hastily hired Jewish editors to supervise his publications, but Buckley continued his attacks, and the supposed goal of the National Review and the John Birch Society, anti- Communism, disappeared in an avalanche of mud-slinging, a typical shabez goi imbroglio, while the Jews laughed their heads off. The moral is that each time you hit a ball across the net, a Jew wins a point, because shabez goi conditioning, the Pavlov slavering of the trained dogs, occurs on schedule whenever the Jew utters the key word, "anti-Semitism." But trained dogs, however amusing they may be in a circus, cannot build a nation, nor can they administer one which others have built.

WHY NOT?

Looking at this situation superficially, as we have been trained to do by the Jews, we may well ask, Why shouldn't the Jews do all of our thinking for us, censor our books and burn anything they do not wish us to read? But this goes against the grain of the American legend of freedom and self-expression, it denies us the right to examine and solve our national problems. America faces a serious economic crisis, a serious racial crisis, and a serious military crisis, yet the Jew refuses to allow us to discuss these problems, for fear that we might criticize the role of the parasite in exploiting the host.

More important, we are frustrated in our search for wisdom. As crucial as the maintenance of life itself is man's quest for wisdom, the fruit of a healthy life, in order to bring more benefits to his people. Ezra Pound once said to me, "A man should study German philosophy from age forty to sixty, Greek from age sixty to eighty, and after he has reached the age of eighty, he is ready to tackle Chinese philosophy." But all we get is Jewish philosophy, from the cradle to the grave. Not only is this philosophy devoted to the maintenance of the parasite's ascendancy over the host, but it also prevents us from knowing Christ. A great republic is collapsing into the dust, but what do the Jews care about this? As their slogan says, "Who needs it?" They will travel to another host, and America will join the ghosts of Babylon, Egypt, Persia, and Rome.

TESTED TECHNIQUES

The ADL has a vast arsenal of weapons to use against those gentiles who oppose them. I have experienced the following: being discharged from professional positions; prevented from finding an established publisher for my articles and books; a continual propaganda campaign to prevent me from establishing a following among conservative Americans.

Although I knew nothing about the ADL when I began writing anti-Communist articles and books, I soon came up against them. A leading New York publisher told my agent, "Mullins made a great mistake in going against us. He is versatile and prolific, we could have done a lot for him. Look what we did for other gentile writers, Hemingway, Steinbeck, Faulkner, they were just high school talents but we made them household words in America. Now Mullins will never have a dime, because his books will never find an outlet in this country."

When this story was relayed to me, it affected me not at all, because at this time, in 1952, I had a growing audience for my work, and some influential people in New York began a campaign to raise money so that I could devote all of my time to anti-Communist writing. My own funds at this time totalled a hundred and fifty dollars, on which I could survive, by abstemiousness and thrift, another three months. Suddenly the fundraisers ceased their efforts. I began to hear a rumor so unbelievable that I ignored it. This story, widely circulated among New York patriots, was that I owned large estates in Virginia and that the income from these properties enabled me to live the life of a gentleman scholar, to travel, and write as I pleased. In reality, I have never owned anything but the clothes on my back, and have no prospects of inheriting anything, but the story did its work, and the ADL put an effective end to the campaign to back me in my work.

THE SILENT TREATMENT

In 1954, my name disappeared from "anti-Communist" publications in America, although some of them continued to advertise my *Federal Reserve* book, with the name of the author carefully blacked out! It is still advertised in this fashion today. Only one patriot, Mrs. Lyrl Clark Van Hyning, continued to give me space in her newspaper, *Women's Voice*. This silent treatment proved the effectiveness of ADL control over the supposedly "anti-Communist" newspapers and magazines in this country, because I had become, in a few years, the leading scholar of this group, with my exposés of the Federal Reserve System, the Council on Foreign Relations, and other shabez goi operations. FBI agents visited the offices of these publications and warned them against printing my work or mentioning my name. For nearly fifteen years, I worked quietly at home, developing my theories of the biological parasite, while most patriots supposed that I was either dead or no longer active.

CHILDREN OF THE SHABEZ GOI

With the degeneration of all levels of life in America, the most pronounced decadence appeared in the children of the affluent society, shabez goi families. These children formed a disillusioned class which became known as "hippies."

The *Saturday Evening Post* interviewed a large group of hippies in San Francisco. One gentile youth said, "My father is supposed to be a big man in our town, yet I saw that he was always raising money for Jewish charities, signing petitions for Jews, things like that. I asked him, 'What's the idea? You don't give a damn for anybody, much less the Jews.' He told me that if he refused to do this, he would be wiped out in a few days. We live in a fine home, have three cars, a color TV, you name it. But I told him, 'It's not worth it,' and I walked out."

A CORRECT REACTION

This American youth expressed a correct reaction against the pernicious influence of the Jewish parasite. Only when our youth begins to express its contempt for every member of the shabez goi, every educator who trains the youth to become gentile slaves, every religious leader who tells his congregation that it is their duty to work for the Jews, every government official who taxes the gentiles for the benefit of the Jews, only then can we hope for a "reaction" against the parasites.

It is this "trahison des clercs," the betrayal of the people by the educated middle class, which makes the continued hold of the parasite possible. Without this active assistance, he would be dislodged immediately. Every aspect of gentile existence is poisoned by the shabby, vicious and cheap gentiles who have become the passive agents of the parasite's power. Yet it is they who are held up as models for the nation's youth. It is they who are the presidents of our colleges, directors of our museums, heads of our publishing houses, chairmen of our religious denominations. Only by challenging them at every step can the gentile begin the process of dislodging the parasites. Since these gentiles already despise themselves, they will not be surprised to discover that they are despised by the rest of the population, including their Jewish masters. The next step is to drive them out of every office, and to replace them with people who have "kindness," that is, who are responsive to the needs of their own kind, and who will not sell their people for fifty pieces of silver.

THEY LIVE IN DARKNESS

It would be a mistake for the scholar to suppose that the entire shabez goi community understands the parasite-host relationship, or that our educators, government officials and religious leaders are active agents in a conspiracy to enslave the gentiles. There are no conspiracies in nature. People lead the lives which their genes map out for them, and these laws can be evaded only two ways, by following Christ, or by following Satan. The parasite automatically seeks to follow a parasitic existence, and the shabbiest, most vicious and cheapest of the gentiles find their only fulfillment in the life of a shabez goi. They miseducate, misgovern and confuse the gentile masses because that is the only role they can know in life. Without Jewish support, our college presidents would be fortunate to find employment as janitors, our government officials would qualify only as swineherds.

In the United States, many of the shabez goi are in the third and fourth generations of their shabez goi professions. The Adlai Stevenson and Dulles families shuttle back and forth between high government positions and posts in Jewish banks and law firms. These, so we are told, are the American aristocrats, who lead the gentile masses in Pavlov gestures of approval of each action of the Jews.

APPLAUD TREACHERY

Thus we find the American masses applauding the atrocities which the Israelis commit against the Arabs. Yet these Arab peoples have always been America's friends and allies. An Arab leader asked, "How can Americans applaud the outrages of their worst enemies, the Jews in the bandit state of Israel, and cheer them on in their aggressions against us?"

The answer is that the shabez goi, in their dominant positions as publishers, educators, and government officials, have trained the American masses in group responses like trained dogs. Only when some of our young people rebel against the role of trained dog, and refuse to bark when the shabez goi order them to, will there be hope for us. Only when we fight against the well-dressed rabble which make possible the parasite's dominance will we have a chance. Only then can we remove the tentacles of the parasite from our body.

Throughout nature, the parasite seeks a host. The host tries to dislodge him. If he succeeds, the parasite soon returns. The Jews have been expelled from European nations hundreds of times, yet they are there today. Each time the parasite is cast out, he learns a lesson, he will improve his hold the next time. He learns to anticipate and control the reactions of the host, and as he turns their nations into vast, shabby prisons, he affects their most fundamental impulses and warps their entire existence.

No Freedom

This is the state of Western civilizations today. Only machines have freedom. The gentile masses of the Western democracies are already dying. Many of them are zombies, the walking dead. What can we say to these walking dead? Do they have enough nervous energy left to respond to an appeal to cast out their parasites, or has the Jewish poison paralyzed their bodies?

What is the ethic of the parasite-host relationship? Is it immoral? No, it is natural for the parasite to seek a host on which it can feed, and it is natural for the host to attempt to dislodge him. The Jew is obeying his God when he fulfills his life mission of being a parasite, of finding and controlling a host. It is the sense of his own historical rightness, as Trotsky formulated it in Communism, which led the Jew to believe that he was indeed a Chosen People, born to live off the work of others, and to take their goods and lands.

HE OWNS IT ALL

Today, the Jew believes that everything the gentile owns has come from the parasite, that the parasite has brought the good life to the ignorant gentile cattle, given him a culture, a monetary system, and a religion. The Jew believes that he has given purpose and direction to the life of the gentiles, in training the gentiles to become his slaves, for the Jew believes that their only role in life is to serve him. For this reason, the Jew believes that all of history is Jewish history, as the historian Dubnow claims. He may be right, insofar as much of recorded history is a series of variations upon the host-parasite theme.

However, Dubnow and all other Jewish historians refuse to admit one thing, the damaging influence of the parasite upon the host.

Yet this has been proven in every instance, either by the collapse visited upon the host by the presence of the parasite, or by a great renaissance of culture, learning and power of the host when it manages to rid itself of the parasite, even for a comparatively short time. Look at Elizabethan England, after the Jews had been expelled. In a few short years, the English people had such a flowering as the world had never seen, tremendous productions of poetry, drama, world exploration and scientific discoveries. Coke gave us the Common Law during this period, which became the basis for the United States Constitution.

Look at America before 1860, when the country was largely free of the parasite blight, a young nation which was the hope of the civilized world. Look at Germany today, where it is a crime by law on the statutes to mention the parasite by name, and compare it with the Germany of 1800. Germany today is a nation of despair, because the parasite has once again fastened its tentacles deep into the host, with the aid of foreign occupying armies, and poisoned every aspect of German life. Yet in 1800, all of Germany was alive, great composers were writing the symphonies which we listen to today, and Count von Humboldt was amazing the world with his scientific discoveries, while Goethe was becoming known as the single greatest figure in world philosophy.

A LAW OF NATURE

Thus, we must admit a fundamental law of nature. If the host cannot dislodge the parasite, it sinks into a slow, degenerating trauma of sickness and death. If it can dislodge the parasite, it quickly soars to new heights of accomplishment and prosperity.

But if the gentile host is always prey to the guile of the parasite, how can he survive? There is but one way, the gentile must become serene in the Love of Jesus Christ.

Now, serene in that Love, and knowing yourself, prepare yourself for a life of dedication to your people, and work for the day when the host will once more be free of the parasite, when every member of an aroused community will cooperate in driving the despicable shabez goi educators, government officials and religious leaders from their positions as tools of the parasites. Then we will be able to live in a community of kindness and love, because we will have rescued our nation from the beggars thieves and jackals who seek to install the

Anti-Christ as our master. Then we can fulfill our roles in life as God meant us to.

BIBLIOGRAPHY

Material for this book was obtained from the following sources:

THE BIBLE (authorized King James version)

ENCYCLOPEDIA BRITANNICA (Eleventh Edition)

WEBSTER'S INTERNATIONAL DICTIONARY (1952)

WHO'S WHO IN WORLD JEWRY (1939)

HISTORY AND DESTINY OF THE JEWS, by Josef Kastein

GREAT AGES AND IDEAS OF THE JEWISH PEOPLE, edited by Leo Schwartz

THE WORLD OF JOSEPHUS, by G.A. Williamson

THE FALL OF NINEVEH, by E.J. Gadd

LIGHT FROM EGYPTIAN PAPYRI, by Rev. Chas. H.H. Wright

THE JEWS AMONG THE GREEKS AND ROMANS, by Max Radin

JEWS OF ANCIENT ROME, by Harry J. Leon THE

FEDERAL RESERVE CONSPIRACY, by Eustace Mullins

Other titles

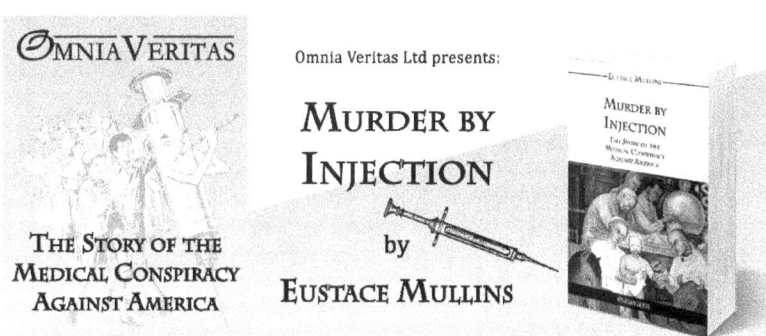

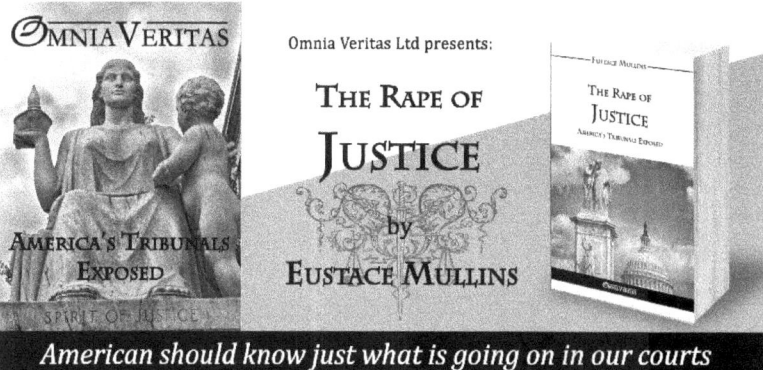

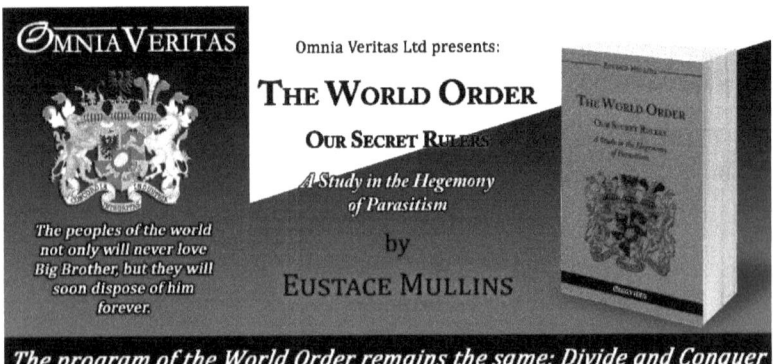